The Bible
Culturally Speaking

*Understanding the Role of Culture
in the Production, Presentation, and
Interpretation of God's Word*

Glenn Rogers

Published by

Mission And Ministry Resources

Visit Our Website At:

www.missionandministryresources.net

TABLE OF CONTENTS

Introduction 6

Part 1
The Role of Culture in the Production of the Bible

Chapter 1 The Divine-Human Communication Context.....................10
  Human Culture 12
    Understanding Culture 12
    Culture and Communication..16
  Human Language..16
    Defining Language..17
    Language and the Communication Process 19
  When the Divine Interacts with the Human
  in the Communication Process 26
    God and the Two-way Nature of the
    Communication Process 26
    God and Human Culture..27
    God and Human Language 28
    God and Meaning..30
  The Implications of God Communicating in the
  Human Cultural Context 31

Chapter 2 The Divine-Human Communication Process 32
  The Divine-Human Communication Process is
  Receptor-Oriented...32
    What is Receptor-Oriented Communication.........................32
    The Communication Needs of Receptors 33
      Worldview Assumptions 33
      Cultural Considerations..36
      Language Requirements 38
      Relevance Issues 39
  The Divine-Human Communication Process is
  Relational in Nature...41
    Relationship in the Communication Process 42
    The Divine-Human Communication Relationship.................42
      God Knowing His Receptors 42
      God Making Himself Known to His Receptors 43

Chapter 3 The Divine-Human Communication Collaboration 46
  The Divine Origin of the Message..46
  The Human Conveyance of the Message 48

Peter's Thoughts on the Divine-Human Collaboration 48
Paul's Thoughts on the Divine-Human Collaboration 50
Jeremiah and the Divine-Human Collaboration....................55
Culture and the Divine-Human Collaboration 57
Dictation Theology in Disguise 59
Recommunicating God's Message—Then and Now 61
Cultural Relativity...62
Summary 65

Part 2
The Role of Culture in the Presentation of the Bible

Chapter 4 The Bible's Ancient Multicultural Context 68
Ancient Near Eastern Literature 69
Major Ancient Cultures Represented in the Scriptures 70
Mesopotamia 70
Babylonia..76
Assyria..78
Egypt..80
Canaan...88
Persia...93
Greece 98
Rome..106
The Implications of the Bible's Multicultural Context..............112

Chapter 5 Israelite Culture 114
Stages of Worldview and Cultural Development......................114
A Canaanite Semi-nomadic Pastoral Culture.....................116
Adjusting to a New Way of Living 116
Ancient Worldviews..118
Abraham's Culture...119
An Egyptian Captivity Culture 120
Egyptian Culture..121
The Israelites as Slaves in Egypt................................122
A Desert Semi-nomadic Pastoral Culture...........................124
A Pre-monarchy Agrarian Culture......................................125
A Monarchy Agrarian Culture..132
A Captivity Culture...133
A Post-exilic Agrarian Culture 137
A Roman Subjugated Agrarian Culture...............................140
The Implications of Israelite Cultural Development
for Biblical Interpretation..144

Chapter 6 Conflicting Cultures Within the First Century
Community of Faith...148
    Walls of Separation...149
    Three Kinds of People in the World 151
    Culture Clash in Acts 10 152
    Culture Clash in Acts 15 156
    Jewish Churches and Gentile Churches 158
    The Implications of Ancient Christian Cultural
    Conflicts for the Church Today 161

Part 3
The Role of Culture in the Interpretation of God's Word

Chapter 7 Culture-related Issues in Interpretation 165
    Horizons, Spirals, and Responses 167
    Avoiding Extremist Reactions...171
        Simplistic Literalism..171
        Absolute Relativism...175
    Hermeneutical Assumptions...177
        The Nature of Scripture: Prescriptive, Descriptive, or Both 177
        The Nature of Interpretation: Objective or Subjective 182
    Finding the Interpretive Middle Ground 185
        The Cultural and the Supracultural 185
        Form and Meaning...190
    Implications..193

Chapter 8 Culture in Scripture and Interpretation: Two Examples....196
    Patriarchy 196
    Homosexuality...214
        Causes and Inclinations...215
        The Bible's condemnation of Homosexuality:
        Cultural or supracultural..222
    Summary..227

Chapter 9 Interpretation in Cross-cultural or Multiethnic Contexts...229
    Interpretation in Cross-cultural Contexts 231
    Interpretation in Multiethnic Contexts 246

Conclusion 254
    The Cultural Context of God's Communication
    to Human Beings 254
    The Need for Hermeneutical Humility.............................256
    Being Careful Not to Throw Out the Baby with

the Bath Water...257

Works Cited 260

Introduction

The Bible is God's inspired, authoritative communication to his human children. But what, exactly, does that mean? A biblical theology of inspiration is difficult to arrive at with any certainty because while the Bible claims to be inspired it does not explain precisely what was involved in the process of inspiration (that is, how the process worked) as the Bible was being produced. However, as difficult as the task may be, arriving at a biblical theology of inspiration, as best we can, is foundational to the larger task of seeking to understand the role of culture in the production, presentation and interpretation of the Scriptures. Therefore, Part 1 of this study will be rooted in issues related to the production of the Bible text.

The inspiration of the biblical text is not in question. The Bible is God's inspired, authoritative communication. However, being God's inspired communication to his human children does not mean that the Bible fell out of heaven in its finished form, void of human influences. The Bible is the result of a *divine-human collaboration*. The challenge is in determining how much of the collaboration was human. How was God's communication to his human children impacted by their humanness? How was human culture a factor in what God said and how he said it? To answer these questions it is necessary to think about how humans communicate. Is the communication process between God

6

and humans the same as the communication process between humans and humans? If so, what role does culture play in that process? What role, then, did culture play along with God and his people in the production of the biblical text?

Discussing the role of culture in the production of the biblical text leads into a consideration of the key cultures presented in the biblical text—cultures which impacted the production of the text. God's communication to his human children was not delivered in a cultural void. The people to whom and through whom God spoke were products of human culture. The cultures that impacted their lives impacted the communication they received from God. Those cultures also impacted the way those people communicated with others as they delivered a message from God or told stories about God and his interactions with people. It is essential, therefore, to understand as much as possible about those cultures. Part 2 will contain an overview of each of the major cultures present in Scripture, including the various stages of development through which Israelite culture passed from the days of the semi-nomadic patriarchs to first century Palestine under Roman rule. That cultural overview will also include the larger Greco-Roman culture of the Hellenistic world, which was the cultural context in which the letters of the New Testament were written.

Having examined, in Parts 1 and 2, the nature of the divine-human communication process and the cultural context in which it occurred, Part 3 will focus on concerns related to interpreting and applying Scripture in light of cultural considerations. There are extremes to be avoided as we seek an interpretive middle ground. Making everything culturally relevant is an extreme that must be avoided. Absolutes exist and we must discover and apply them appropriately. The opposite extreme, denying cultural considerations in the interpretation and application of Scripture, must also be avoided. Balance is crucial. We must discover an interpretive middle ground between these two extremes if we are to use God's Scriptures appropriately.

The relationship between form and meaning is a crucial part of the discussion, as we struggle with how to appropriately contextualize God's message in differing sociocultural settings. We must also discuss our hermeneutical assumptions, that is, our assumptions about how to interpret and apply the Scriptures. Everyone has hermeneutical assumptions. But do we understand what ours are? Have we identified and analyzed them? And are we capable of hermeneutical humility? Can we allow people to have an interpretive opinion different from our own? What are the implications of hermeneutical humility?

Using God's Word appropriately, as Paul encouraged Timothy to do, requires that we ask and at least attempt to answer questions such as these.

Note: To accomplish my purposes in this text it will be necessary to discuss *worldview*. I do not use the term in the popular sense of perspective, but in the technical anthropological sense of the term—one's underlying, deep-level, unconscious assumptions about the nature of reality. Readers are encouraged to consult another of my works: *The Role of Worldview in Missions and Multiethnic Ministry* (2002, Missions and Ministry Resources) for a detailed explanation of worldview from an anthropological, missiological point of view.

PART ONE

THE ROLE OF CULTURE IN THE PRODUCTION OF THE BIBLE

CHAPTER 1

THE DIVINE-HUMAN COMMUNICATION CONTEXT

Paul told Timothy that Scripture[1] was inspired by God. *Inspired* is from *theopneustos*, God breathed. What does it mean that Scripture is *God-breathed*? Is Paul describing process or origin? Peter's comments on the inspiration of Scripture may be helpful in answering that question. Peter said, *"Above all, you must understand that no prophecy in Scripture ever came from the prophets themselves or because they wanted to prophesy. It was the Holy Spirit who moved the prophets to speak from God"* (2 Peter 1:20-21). The Spirit "moved" the prophets. Or, as some translations have it, the Spirit "carried" the prophets. Again, is this process or origin? It is origin. The point is not how the Spirit conveyed a message from the mind of God to the mind of the prophet, but that the messages delivered by the prophets did not originate with them, but with God. That is Paul's point as well. The origin of the message is divine,

---

[1] Contextually Paul was referring to the Hebrew Scriptures, the Old Testament. The New Testament, as a collection of books and letters, did not yet exist. As the books and letters of the New Testament were gathered into a collection, it too was considered to be inspired.

not human. Neither Peter nor Paul explained how the process of inspiration worked. They asserted the fact of inspiration. The messages contained in Scripture originated with God not with human beings.

Peter's comment that the Spirit moved or carried the prophets cannot be construed as an explanation of a process. If I say Glenn carried the chair, the fact that Glenn carried the chair is clear, but not *how* he carried the chair. Perhaps he carried it by holding on to some part of its back. Perhaps he carried it by one of its legs. He may have carried it with his right hand or his left, or in both hands. He may have turned it upside down and carried it on his head or put it in his truck and "carried" it across town. The fact that Glenn somehow carried the chair does not explain *how* he carried it. Peter's statement that the Spirit moved or carried the prophets refers to the Spirit's activity in delivering to the prophets a message that originated with God, prompting them (moving them) to *recommunicate* the message to the intended audience. Peter's (and Paul's) goal was not to explain the *how* of inspiration but the *fact* of inspiration.

The Scriptures assert the fact of inspiration but do not explain how the process of inspiration occurred. If we want to have some idea of how the process might have occurred we must deduce a probable process from: 1) what we understand about the divine-human communication process, and 2) what we observe in Scripture—that is, the results of the process.

God spoke to Adam, Noah, Abraham, Moses, and everyone else he spoke to, in their native language. There is nothing in Scripture suggesting that God may have spoken some sort of heavenly language that then had to be translated into the language of the person to whom God spoke. God spoke to human beings in human languages, in the languages they spoke on a day-to-day basis. Human languages are part of human cultures. In utilizing human languages to convey his divine messages, God entered the human communication

11

context. This chapter has to do with 1) human culture, 2) human language, 3) how meaning happens in the human communication process, and 4) how meaning happens in the divine-human communication process.

Human Culture

Culture is all around us. But what is it and what does it do?

Understanding Culture

Paul Hiebert defines culture as "the integrated system of learned patterns of behavior, ideas, and products characteristic of a society" (1983:25). In the simplest terms, culture is everything about a group of people. Culture includes: 1) the worldview of a people, 2) the values, feelings and thinking of a people, and 3) the social structures and behaviors of those people.

Worldview is the deep-level, unconscious assumptions a people have about reality and the world as they perceive it[2]. The values, feelings and thinking of a people grow out of their worldview assumptions. The social structures and behaviors of a people grow out of their worldview and out of their values, feelings and thinking. Culture can be diagramed as a three-tiered phenomenon, as Figure 1 illustrates.

People learn their culture as they grow up. The process is called *enculturation*. As children grow, observing and absorbing everything that goes on around them, they develop their worldview. They accept the worldview of their society without even being aware of the process.

---

[2] For a fuller discussion of worldview from an anthropological perspective see Rogers 2002 *The Role of Worldview in Missions and Multiethnic Ministry.*

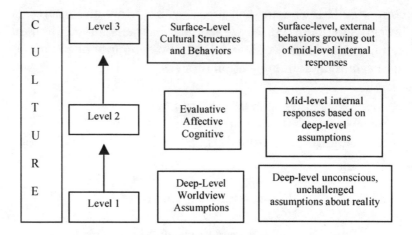

FIGURE 1 CULTURE AS A THREE-TIERED PHENOMENON

If the society's worldview is naturalistic, they learn to think in naturalistic ways and understand the world from a naturalistic perspective. If the worldview of their society is supernaturalistic, children learn to see the world from a supernaturalistic perspective. If the worldview of their society is individualistic, children learn to live life and relate to others as an individual. If the worldview of their society is rooted in a group orientation, they learn to think of themselves and to relate to others from a group perspective. Thinking and acting as an individual in a group-oriented cultural context would never even occur to them. They are part of a group. They have no frame of reference for how to think or function as an individual. All people, whether they realize it or not, think the way their worldview teaches them to think.

Worldview is made up of all of a people's assumptions about reality, assumptions about the nature of the world, about life in this world, about how to live, how to act and react as they encounter the realities of life, and how to interact with other people (Kearney 1984). This is level 1

13

in Figure 1. Because the deep-level assumptions of worldview are unconscious and go unchallenged as they are acquired, people are unaware of them. This does not mean, however, that worldview is unimportant. While people do not normally think about their worldview, they think *with* their worldview (Hiebert 1996:142). Worldview provides the framework for a society's values, and for how a people feel, think, and act.

A society's values grow out of their worldview. They determine what is highly valued or not so highly valued based on their worldview assumptions. A society may place a higher value on group relations than on individuality. They may place a greater value on peace and harmony within the community than they do on truth and justice. They may value traditions more than progress, relationships more than productivity, the quality of an event more than punctuality. The way people react emotionally grows out of their worldview. People feel sad or happy, anxious or calm, excitement, despair, joy, hopeless, or optimistic based on how their worldview prompts them to interpret events in their lives. People think as they think because of their worldview. They categorize, analyze, synthesize, surmise, hypothesize, and theorize all based on their worldview assumptions. These things represent level 2 in Figure 1.

The deep-level assumptions of worldview (level 1) and the mid-level responses of values, feelings, and thinking (level 2) lead to the third level of culture, the surface-level behaviors or cultural structures. These are the things a people do on a day-to-day basis, the way they live their lives. These cultural behaviors grow out of or reflect the unconscious assumptions and the values, feelings and thinking of a society. Level 3 surface-level structures include the language a people speak, the clothes they wear, the food they eat, the shape, size, construction and layout houses they live in, the way they sleep (on a mat or in a bed, the whole family in one room or in separate rooms), the way their structure their family relations, how property is passed on from one generation to another, birth customs, coming of age traditions, marriage traditions, customs related to death, their religious rituals and ceremonies, practices related to education, to politics, economy, technology, and so forth. Specific cultural practices and *cultural subsystems* (Kraft 1996:122-123) allow for the expression of values, feelings, and thinking that grow out of a people's deep-level worldview assumptions.

The process of enculturation teaches people how to think and how to live in their cultural context. Culture provides a framework for thinking and living. Culture does not determine in any kind of absolute sense how people live, for people have the ability to think beyond the limits of culture if they determine to do so. However, most people do not. Most people in any given society simply do that which they have been taught to do the way they have been taught to do it. Their culture seems right to them. It is logical, sensible. It is how they learned to live. Everyone around them lives according to those same ways of thinking and doing. Doing things differently just doesn't feel normal. This is why most societies resist changing their cultural patterns.

Most people who do not study culture for a living do not understand the impact of culture in a person's life. Most of us simply do not realize that virtually all of what we do (and the way we do it) is determined by our culture. It is essential, however, that we think more deeply about the impact of culture on our lives. It is imperative that we understand that all humans are shaped by the cultural context in which they grow up. We do what we do the way we do it, including thinking the way we think, and communicating the way we communicate, because our culture tells us to do it that way. We are cultural creatures, shaped more than we realize by our cultural context.

Culture and Communication

Cultural is a powerful force that shapes and drives our lives. Worldview, as the underlying, deep-level assumptions upon which cultural is built, determines how we understand our world and how we live our lives. There is no area of life that is not governed by worldview. What a group of people thinks and how they think is determined by their worldview. The way they use language to communicate with one another is determined by worldview (Rogers 2002:17-96). Worldview is so much a part of the communication process that people with very different worldviews have tremendous difficulties communicating with each other. In fact, the only way for a person from a culture rooted in (let us say) worldview "A" to successfully communicate with a person from a culture rooted in worldview "B" is for the person from worldview "A" to learn the culture of worldview "B" and communicate as if he or she was a worldview "B" person. The key to effective cross-cultural communication is learning the culture and worldview of the people with whom one wishes to communicate. Missionaries have known this for a long time. So have diplomats. Effective cross-cultural communication requires that the communicator understand his audience (the receptors) and, as much as possible, think and communicate like they do.

Culture is a crucial factor in the communication process. Culture is a factor each time one person wishes to communicate with another person. And *culture is a factor when God communicates with human beings.*

Human Language

We use language all the time, but seldom do we pause to analyze and understand what it is and how it works.

16

Defining Language

What is language? Language is a "system of arbitrary vocal symbols employed by members of a community in socially approved ways for purposes such as communication and expression" (Kraft 1991:89). First, language is systematic. It is structured according to agreed upon rules and all its various elements fit together to be used in a systematic way to accomplish a purpose—communication and expression.

Second, language is arbitrary. It is arbitrary in the sense that each group of people made up their system of language as they pleased (Littlejohn 1999:70). One sound follows another sound because the people who designed that language decided that was the way they wanted their language to work. There is no universal language rule book telling people how to structure their language. Each group of people decides how they want their language to work.

Third, language is vocal. Languages can be written, but spoken language always precedes written language.

Fourth, language is symbolic. Sounds are combined to created words. Those words are symbolic representations. For instance, the word "dog" doesn't mean anything by itself. That particular group of sounds, d/o/g, only has meaning as it represents the canine animal we think of (perhaps a beloved pet, or a non-specific, generic canine animal) when we hear the sounds of the letters that combine to create the word "dog". The word "dog" is a symbol which represents something else. All words are symbols that represent something else. Thus, language involves the use of vocal symbols.

Fifth, language is employed by members of a community. Often the community is an entire society of people. The people of Germany speak German. The people of France speak French. The people of Nigeria, however, do not speak Nigerian. Nigeria is a West African country where over 250 different tribal languages are spoken. Each of those languages represents of community of people, a tribe, a society.

Sixth, language is used in socially approved ways. The specific community to whom the language belongs determines how to use their language. Smaller communities notice less variation in usage while larger communities will notice more variation. In larger communities (such as America) there will be sub-communities that modify the rules to suit themselves. These modifications may take many forms: 1) accent, a slightly different way of pronouncing words, 2) rate, speaking very fast or more slowly, 3) vocabulary, such as forming unique contractions (for instance, in the south "y'all" instead of "you all"), or utilizing figures of speech (people in Maine may speak of having "weather" instead of saying that it is going to rain). Those variations, however, are usually minor and are agreed upon by a sub-group within the larger language group. Even the variations must be agreed upon or meaningful communication would be impossible.

Seventh, language makes communication and expression possible. All of the above elements combine to make a specific language a functioning reality, facilitating communication and individual expression within a community of people.

Without the complexities of human language, communication would be limited to the lower level of grunts and groans, whistles and chirps, growls and whines and roars common among animals. One of the things that separate humans from animals is the depth and complexity of our communication skills. Humans possess these advanced capabilities because humans are created in God's image.

18

Language and the Communication Process

Language is the basic tool of communication. Aside from the specific rules of a given language, how is language used to facilitate the communication process? Communication is a process that involves the encoding and decoding of linguistic symbols in the sending and receiving of messages between a communicator and a receptor. The communicator has an idea in his mind that he wants to share with the receptor. The communicator must encode that message in linguistic symbols (words) and send those symbols (by speaking) to the receptor. The receptor hears the incoming message that has been encoded in linguistic symbols and begins the process of decoding the message. As the message is decoded and interpreted by the receptor communication occurs. Language is the system of symbols used to send messages back and forth between communicators and receptors.

The role of language in the communication process can be discussed in brief overview fashion by examining six features.[3]

First, language is used in a communication context— a general cultural communication context (the remote context) and a specific event communication context (the immediate context). We exist within the context of our cultural environment, acting, reacting, and interacting within that context. Communication is part of our cultural interaction. For communication to be meaningful it must be contextually sensitive and appropriate. If you speak to someone about something that is beyond their cultural frame of reference, they will not understand. Effective communication will not occur. For instance, if a man of the Samo people of Papua, New Guinea spoke to the typical

---

[3] The original source of these six features can be traced to Stephen Tyler in his 1978 book, *The Said and the Unsaid, Mind, Meaning and Culture*.

19

American regarding the *kogooa* and the *oosau*, the American would not understand. If the Samo gentleman were to explain that the *kogooa* are beneficent ancestral departed spirits and the *oosau* are malevolent bush sorcery spirits the American would most likely still not understand what the Samo was referring to (Shaw 1990:1). The American may have some vague idea that the reference is to good and bad spirits, but would not understand in any meaningful way the significance of what was being discussed. Meaningful communication would not have occurred. Why not? Because the reference was beyond the cultural context of the American.

The communication context of a people includes not only the cultural concepts of that society, such as the *kogooa* and *oosau* of the Samo culture, but also the specific language a group of people speaks and their communication techniques or methodology. For instance, as noted earlier, there are over 250 tribal languages spoken throughout Nigeria. One of those languages is Efik. Efik is a tonal language. The precise meaning of words depends on how the word is pronounced. The letters *o/b/o/n* (*obon*) can represent one of five different words depending on the tonal inflections applied to the word. One of the ways of pronouncing *obon* means chief. Another way of pronouncing it means mosquito (Adams, Akaduh, and Abia-Bassey 1981). One must take care that he or she does not mispronounce the word and refer to the chief as a mosquito!

If communication is going to be meaningful it must be accomplished within the general cultural communication context, which includes aspects of culture such as the cultural concepts, language, and linguistic techniques described above. However, for communication to be meaningful it must also function within the context of a specific communication event. If I am ordering dinner at a restaurant and have ordered a baked potato, I am not confused when the waiter asks me if I want butter and sour cream. However, if I am at the bookstore buying a book and I am asked if I want butter and sour cream, it would leave me at something of a loss as to how to answer. Why? Because being asked if I want butter and sour cream makes no sense in the context of buying books at a bookstore. Meaningful communication can only occur if appropriate attention is paid to both the remote (cultural) and the immediate (event) communication context.

Second, language is used to convey an intended meaning. When a communicator speaks to a receptor the communicator has a specific message (meaning) he hopes will come through as the receptor hears and interprets what the communicator says. The receptor understands that the communicator is attempting to convey a specific message. For communication to occur, it is essential that the communicator be clear as he speaks, that is, he must word his message in a way that the receptor can understand. It is also essential that the receptor assume that the communicator has a specific point he is trying to make, an idea he is trying to communicate. Just as the communicator must attempt to be understood, the receptor must attempt to understand. If the receptor assumes that the communicator's intended meaning is irrelevant or attainable, the receptor may ignore the message or may attach whatever meaning he or she prefers to the communicator's message, guaranteeing a miscommunication. Miscommunication occurs quite often even when receptors are trying to understanding a communicator's intended meaning. The reason for such miscommunications will be addressed below. But when receptors do not even make an effort to understand the communicator's intended meaning the communication process is doomed to failure.

Third, language is used to convey ideas to which receptors can respond in a meaningful way. That is, for communication to be meaningful, the content of the messages must be understandable and/or feasible. For instance, if both communicator and receptor do not share common language skills, communication is not feasible. Or, if communicator and receptor share common language skills but the communicator presents the receptor with a concept the receptor cannot understand, or if the communication involves a request or requirement with which the receptor cannot comply, meaningful communication can be disrupted.

Fourth, language makes use of commonly shared background information. Without commonly shared background information communication becomes difficult and cumbersome. In Southeastern Nigeria many merchants carry on business by means of a traveling market, known as the Big Market. The merchants of a given geographic region travel between four established locations. Each day the market would be conducted at one of the four different locations, making each fourth day Big Market day at that location. Rather than being conducted on a set day of the week, Big Market day is every fourth day. If someone, for instance, said they would stop by for a visit on next Big Market day, you had to know that Big Market day was every four days. You also had to know when the last Big Market day was to be able to calculate when to expect a visit. Without this specific but commonly shared background knowledge about market days in that region of Nigeria, effective communication was unlikely to occur.

Different cultures have different kinds of commonly shared background knowledge that facilitate communication in that culture. For instance, most people in America who are under the age of fifty would understand the term "log on" as related to internet usage. Most Americans would understand the difference between an "air bag" and a "wind bag," while most Africans would not. Having a common pool of shared background knowledge aids communication; not having that pool of commonly shared background knowledge hinders communication.

Fifth, language is, by nature, inferential. Meaning is not in linguistic symbols. Meaning is in people (Berlo 1960:175). When a communicator *encodes* and sends a message to a receptor, that is, when a person has an idea, puts it into words and speaks the words, the receptor must interpret the message. He must decide (infer) what the communicator intended to convey (Beamer and Varner 2001:126-127). The communicator selected words (linguistic symbols) which he hoped would convey his intended meaning to the receptor. He sent (spoke) those words to the receptor who received (heard) the words and attached his (the receptor's) meanings to the linguistic symbols sent by the communicator. If the meanings attached by the receptor were similar to the meanings attached by the communicator, meaningful communication occurs. If the receptor's meanings are different from those of the communicator, miscommunication occurs.

Nearly everyone has had the experience of being "misunderstood." Our response when someone misunderstands us is to say, "That's not what I meant." Why do misunderstandings happen? Misunderstandings occur because the meaning the receptor attached to our words is different than the meaning we attached to our words. Since the receptor's meaning did not match up to ours, there was a misunderstanding. Such misunderstandings occur because communication is inferential. Meaning is inferred by individuals engaged in the communication process (Littlejohn 1999:130).

Accepting that meaning is inferred by receptors is crucial to understanding how the communication process works. It can be unsettling to think that the receptor has that much power in the process. Unsettling or not, it is the reality of the process. Ideas in my mind are expressed in a meaningful way by means of linguistic symbols. I *encode* my ideas by selecting symbols which, in my mind, convey meanings that corresponds to the ideas I want to express. As

I speak, using the linguistic symbols I have selected, I am sending a message to you. As you receive the incoming message you must *decode* it, attaching meanings that you believe correspond to those in my mind. If the meanings you attach to the words I spoke are similar to the meanings I attached to the words I spoke, we have communicated. The closer your meanings are to my meanings the better we are communicating. If, however, the meanings you attached to the words I spoke are not close to the meanings I attached, we miscommunicate.

The fact that we are often "misunderstood" and have to respond by saying, "That's not what I meant," is irrefutable evidence that meaning is not in linguistic symbols. It is in people—receptors who interpret messages as they are received. Understanding this is crucial to understanding how people communicate with one another *and how God communicates with human beings.*

People who share a common language agree on the basic meanings of words. These are the meanings we find in the dictionary. However, those generally agreed upon meanings do not take into consideration the complexity of the communication process. What a receptor may "understand" in any given communication event depends on the specific context of that event and on the way the communicator sends his or her message: rate, tone, volume, passion, complexity, technical level, and so forth. What the receptor understands also depends on his familiarity with what is being discussed, his education, previous experience, potential positive or negative emotional factors, preconceived notions, perceived relevance, and many other factors. Factors such as these work in combination to impact the way a generally agreed upon word is precisely understood as one linguistic symbol in a larger communication context.

Beyond the way individual words are understood by a receptor in a communication event is the way a complete message may be construed by a receptor. A communication event may involve the exchange of hundreds of individual words. In that kind of a communication event there is more at play than the meaning of individual words. The specific context of a communication event will impact the meaning of that event. Context, in fact, often has more to do with meaning than generally agreed upon definitions of individual words. So does tone of voice, facial expression, passion, and many other factors.

What all of this adds up to is the inferential nature of language. Meaning is inferred by receptors as they receive incoming message from communicators. Responsible receptors will make every attempt to understand the communicator's intended meaning, but the process is subjective and imprecise.

Sixth, effective communication is dependant on perceived relevance. Receptors will only listen and make a serious attempt to understand the communicator's intended meaning if they determine that an incoming message is relevant (Sperber and Wilson 1995:46). This means that communicators must find ways to encode and send their messages so that those messages seem relevant to the receptors. Receptors will then pay attention and spend the necessary time and energy to receive, decode and attach meaning to the incoming messages.

Human beings communicate with one another by means of human language within the context of individual human cultures. It is not an exact or precise exercise. If both communicators and receptors carry out their communication responsibilities well, communication can be a satisfying experience. If either communicator or receptor fail at their part of the two-way process, miscommunication and frustration are inevitable.

When the Divine Interacts With the Human in the Communication Process

God is the all-powerful, all-knowing, sovereign ruler of the universe. His ability to communicate is flawless. Ours, however, is not. What happens when the infinite and perfect God attempts to communicate with finite and imperfect human beings? He encounters our finite imperfections. God can communicate perfectly. We cannot. In the divine-human communication process God is limited by our inability to communicate perfectly. A number of factors become crucial in our understanding of the divine-human communication process.

God and the Two-way Nature of the Communication Process

The communication process is a two-way process. Both the communicator and the receptors play a crucial role in the successful completion of the process. The communicator can be flawless in the execution of his part of the process, but if the receptors do not execute their part of the process perfectly, miscommunication is the result. The fault in that case is not the communicator's, but the receptors'. When examining the nature of communication between God and human beings it is necessary to acknowledge the imprecise nature of the process, not because God is in any way less than perfect, but because humans are in every way less than perfect. *Because communication is a two-way process there is the potential for miscommunication—even when God is involved in the process.* God's involvement in the process does not mean it will be a flawless process. If only he was involved it would be a flawless process. But because humans are involved it is not flawless.

26

The two-way nature of the communication process is a significant factor in the divine-human communication process (Caird 1980:39-40). Another significant factor is the dynamics of God interacting in/with human culture in order to communicate with humans.

God and Human Culture

In his book, *Christianity in Culture*, Charles Kraft discusses various theological positions that have been put forward regarding God's view of and his relationship with human culture (1979:103-115). Much of his discussion involves interactions with Richard Niebuhr's classic work *Christ and Culture*. Kraft's position is that God exists above (outside) human culture, but that he chooses to engage and interact with his human children in the context of their human culture. That is, God uses human culture as a vehicle for interacting with humans. Obviously this is true. God interacted with Abraham, Israel, and the Prophets, with Jesus, with the apostles, and with everyone us (including you and me) not in some otherworldly or heavenly context, but in the context of this material world, a world of human culture.

Why does God use human culture as a vehicle for interacting with human beings? Because humans cannot relate meaningfully to that which is beyond their cultural perspective or experience. Our perception of the world and our ability to relate to it in a meaningful way grows out of our worldview, which is the foundation of our culture. If we encounter something that is beyond our cultural frame of reference (that is, beyond the realm of our experience), we do not know what to do with it. We do not know how to act or react. What this boils down to is quite simple, *if you want to engage in meaningful communication with a human being you must do so in a way that is consistent with that person's worldview and culture.* You cannot confront people with things that are beyond their frame of reference and expect a positive response. God uses human culture as a vehicle for interaction and communication with humans because human culture is the only context in which humans can communicate. This is not because God is limited. It is because humans are limited. Human culture is the only frame of reference humans have. If God wants to communicate with humans it must be within the framework of human culture.

God and Human Language

When God uses human culture as a vehicle for interaction and communication with human beings, human language comes into play. Communication that is culturally sensitive and appropriate is *language specific*. That is, culturally appropriate communication involves the specific language of a person or group of people. For instance, Abraham was from the city of Ur, part of the ancient Sumerian empire. When God first spoke to Abraham, he would have spoken to him in his native language—probably Akkadian, the Semitic language spoken throughout Sumer at that time (De Blois and Van Der Spek 1997:13). After leaving Ur, Abraham lived many years in Haran and may have learned to speak the Western Semitic language of that region. When he moved into Canaan, Abraham probably learned to speak the Northwest Semitic language of that region—the language which gave birth to the Hebrew language spoken by the Israelites (Schmitz 1992:Vol. 4, 204-206). Regardless of how many languages Abraham eventually learned to speak, God may have always spoken to him in Akkadian because that was Abraham's "heart" language, his first language and the language in which he thought best about those things in life which are most important: matters of family and faith. Hundreds of years later, the oral traditions about Abraham that had been handed down for dozens of generations were written down in the

28

Hebrew language. Why would God have spoken to Abraham in one language and spoken to his descendants generations later in another language? Because Hebrew was the language the people of Israel spoke at the time God communicated with them. God's communication to them, whether verbal or written, was in the language they spoke. We see the same principle at work in the Scriptures themselves. The Old Testament was written in Hebrew and the New Testament written in Greek. Why did God change languages? Because the linguistic context had changed and Greek was the language that would serve God's communication purpose. When the communication context changed the language changed. God adjusted his behavior to the human cultural context.

When God uses human language to communicate with human beings, he uses it in the same way humans use it when they communicate with each other. This is a crucial point. When God's communication with humans takes a verbal form it parallels normal human to human verbal communication. The process of verbal communication is not different because one of the parties in the process happens to be God. So, too, when God communicates with humans through written language, that written communication is subject to the same rules and processes as written communication that originates in human minds. The process of communication between author and reader is the same process whether the author is divine or human. In other words, when God uses human language, spoken or written, to communicate with humans, he engages in the process the same way humans do, following the same rules, experiencing the same limitations and frustrations, and getting the same mixed bag of results. Sometimes people understand what he is saying, sometimes they do not.

If you are not sure you are comfortable with this idea, read through the Old Testament again and notice how many times the Israelites missed entirely what God was trying to communicate to them.

God and Meaning

Why do people misunderstand what God is saying to them? They misunderstand God for the same reason they misunderstand a human communicator—because meaning is not in linguistic symbols, even when those linguistic symbols are used by God. Meaning is in people. When God communicates with humans, he encodes his message in human linguistic symbols and sends his message in spoken form, written form, or both. Human receptors receive the message (hearing it or reading it) and must then decode the message by attaching meaning to the linguistic symbols. If the meanings they attach are different than the meanings God had in mind when he encoded and sent the message, they will misunderstand God's intended message.

Unless God miraculously plants in the minds of receptors the meanings he attached to the linguistic symbols he selected (and there is nothing to even hint that he might have done that), he is subject to the same communication risk to which humans are subject—the risk of being misunderstood.

One does not have to be a biblical scholar to note how many times in his dealings with the Israelites God was misunderstood. Meanings must be attached to linguistic symbols by receptors, even when those linguistic symbols are used by God in the encoding process.

The communication process is inferential and, therefore, subjective. It is not so subjective, however, that effective communication is a hopeless impossibility. People in every culture communicate effectively every day. Effective communication is a complicated process, but it can be accomplished.

The Implications of God Communicating
in the Human Cultural Context

What are the implications of God communicating with humans from within the human cultural context? There are several:

First, while God exists above (outside) human culture, he is willing to enter human culture and work through it in order to engage in meaningful communication with humans. This is illustrated very clearly for us in the Scriptures.

Second, God understands that people cannot comprehend in any meaningful way things that are beyond their cultural frame of reference. It is not just that God is *willing* to enter and communicate through human culture; unless God is going to miraculously plant ideas and concepts in every person's minds, thus eliminating the possibility of misunderstanding, he *must* communicate with them through human culture.

Third, God understands that human language is a dynamic two-way process in which receptors must infer and attach meanings to the linguistic symbols he uses to send messages to them. God is fully aware of the limitations of the system.

Fourth, God understands the subjective nature of the human communication process and is prepared to accept the results associated with that subjectivity.

Fifth, however, God also knows that in spite of its subjective nature, human communication is precise enough for effective communication between humans to occur.

Therefore, effective, satisfying divine-human communication can also occur.

CHAPTER 2

THE DIVINE-HUMAN COMMUNICATION PROCESS

We have discussed the divine-human communication *context*. Part of that discussion necessarily involved discussing the communication *process*. It is necessary, however, to examine the process in more detail. This chapter will focus on the divine-human communication process as being *receptor-oriented* and *relational* in nature.

The Divine-Human Communication Process
is Receptor-Oriented

Communication is a process. For that process to be effective it must be *receptor-oriented*.

What is Receptor-Oriented Communication

What does it mean to say that the communication process must be receptor-oriented? If a communicator wants to get an idea that is in his mind into the mind of a receptor, he must anticipate how the receptor will interpret the linguistic symbols he intends to use to encode his idea. The fact that meaning is attached to messages by receptors as they receive the incoming linguistic symbols is crucial. Communicators must understand how the process works and encode their messages with their specific receptors in mind. The more the communicator knows about his receptors the more effectively he can encode his message so that they will be likely to interpret his message in a way that is consistent with his intended meaning (Hesselgrave 1991:44).

Communication is a two-way process. Each side of the process is important and each participant in the process is crucial. However, since receptors attach their own meanings to the incoming linguistic symbols of incoming messages, it is essential that communicators focus their attention on the communication needs of their receptors.

The Communication Needs of Receptors

All people have needs. Some of them are surface-level needs such as the need for food, shelter, sleep and so forth. Some needs are deep-level needs such as the need to be cared for, to be valued, trusted, to contribute, and so forth. All people have these kinds of general needs in life. Kraft discusses these kinds of needs in his book *Communication Theory for Christian Witness*. When I refer to the needs of receptors I am not referring to these kinds of general life needs, but the specific communicational needs of receptors as they participate in the communication process. What do receptors need from communicators to help them understand the communicator's intended meaning?

Worldview Assumptions

Receptors need a communicator who understands their worldview assumptions. This is especially crucial in a cross-cultural communication setting such as we have when God, who is not part of any human culture, speaks to

33

individuals who can only think and communicate from their own worldview and cultural perspective.

Worldview is like a data filter. Think of all of life's experiences as incoming data. Everything a person experiences, all incoming data, is filtered through that person's worldview. As data passes through the filter, extraneous is material is filtered out. Relevant data passes through the worldview filter and is, in that process, shaped so that it conforms to the individual's worldview, to his or her perception of life in this world. Nothing a human being can experience comes to him or her without passing through and being affected by his or her worldview.

Figure 2 illustrates how this process works.

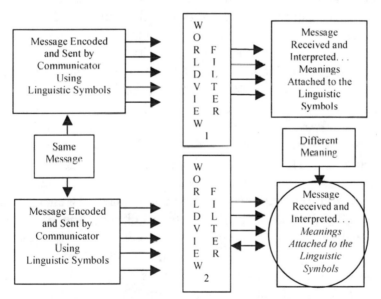

FIGURE 2 WORLDVIEW AS AN INTERPRETIVE FILTER

Messages sent from communicator to receptor pass through the receptor's worldview. The meanings receptors attach to messages are shaped by their worldview.

Communicators must take this into consideration as they encode their messages. God, as the one communicating with humans, had to be aware of the worldview of the people to whom the biblical messages were originally addressed. God had to take the worldview of his receptors into account as he encoded messages for them.

We will discuss the divine-human collaboration involved in producing the Scriptures in more detail in the next chapter. At present, the point is that God, as an effective communicator, takes the worldview of his receptors into consideration. Because God did this, when we read the biblical text we encounter the worldviews of the various people to whom the Scriptures were originally written— people with worldviews very different from our own.

An example of God doing this can be found in Exodus 20:2-5. God tells the Israelites not to worship any gods other than him. The actual reality is that there are no gods other than Yahweh. But the Israelites, at that time, did not understand that. According to their worldview at that time there were many gods. God (Yahweh) did not speak to them about realities that were beyond the scope of their worldview assumptions. He did not tell them there were no other gods. He said simply that they should not worship other gods. God communicated with the ancient Israelites from within the framework of their worldview. Generations later, after a good deal of growth and change, the Israelites realized that there were no other gods. They became a monotheistic people. But at the time God entered into the Sinaitic Covenant with them they were a polytheistic people, so God communicated with them from that perspective.

Good communicators, such as God, will always take the worldview of receptors into consideration as they encode and send messages.

35

Cultural Considerations

Just as communicators must take worldview assumptions into consideration in the communication process, they must also be aware of the importance of cultural considerations. Worldview assumptions are the deep-level, unconscious assumptions people have about reality. When I refer to *cultural considerations* I mean the surface-level behavioral aspects of culture. For instance, if a society's worldview assumptions regarding the respective roles of men and women in society result in patriarchal attitudes, their surface-level behaviors will reflect that thinking. Men will dominate women. Property will be owned and inherited by men. Women will have few rights. Their lot in life will be to submit and serve.

Cultural considerations include everything in the behavior of a people: the way they eat, dress, sleep, live, work, play, worship, and fight. Surface-level cultural structures include a people's traditions and habits regarding government, education, technology, society, religion, birth, death, sickness, wealth, poverty, conflict, harmony, and so forth. Everything that makes them who they are (behaviorally) comes under the heading of cultural considerations. Effective communication must occur within the context of a people's cultural reality.

Good communicators, such as God, take the cultural needs of receptors into consideration when encoding and sending messages. How does one do that? By sending messages that are connected to and rooted in the cultural practices of the receptors, by sending messages that make sense to receptors given their cultural context. The levirate law of the Mosaic Covenant provides an example of how communication and culture must be linked. In Deuteronomy. 5:5-10, God's law made provision for a marriage that could result in polygamy. If two grown brothers (which implies that they were married) were living near each other and one of them died childless, the surviving brother was to marry his dead brother's widow and have children with her. The first son born of that union would take the dead brother's name, thus carrying on his name in the family, inheriting his property. The requirement to marry his dead brother's wife did not hinge on whether the surviving brother was single or married. Even if he was already married he was still expected to marry his dead brother's wife. This requirement from God sounds strange to contemporary Western believers, for from our perspective no man, regardless of the reason, should be married to two women. However, polygamy was an accepted cultural practice in that part of the world at that time. And many cultures practiced levirate marriage. It was not a new concept that originated in the Law of Moses. God used a widespread cultural practice to see to it that inheritance and property rights were maintained among his people. The levirate law made sense to the Israelites because it was a common cultural practice with which they were familiar. This is an important concept to understand. Many of the things God required of his people (or things he accommodated) were not newly invented ideas, but long-established cultural practices that were familiar in many ancient Middle Eastern cultures.

Another example of cultural accommodation had to do with God's instructions regarding the tabernacle. At the time God entered into the Sinaitic Covenant with Israel they were a semi-nomadic pastoral people. They did not live in walled cities or utilize permanent structures of any kind. They lived in tents. Therefore, when God gave them instructions regarding a special structure specifically set aside for worship activities, he had them make a special worship tent called the tabernacle. His communication to them (and his expectations of them) was related to the unique nature of their culture. God did not tell a people who used no permanent structures to build a permanent structure.

Instead, when their culture changed after the conquest and they became a settled people who lived in walled cities and utilized permanent structures they (David) realized that a permanent structure would be appropriate and inquired of the Lord regarding such a structure, which his son Solomon built.

It is highly significant that God was sensitive to cultural considerations and communicated with his people from within the framework of their culture. These two examples could be multiplied dozens of times, but are sufficient to demonstrate that God follows the same basic rules of good communication that all effective communicators follow.

Language Requirements

The worldview and culture of a person or a group of people must be taken into consideration as communicators endeavor to get their intended meaning across. A third consideration in the process is the specific linguistic requirements of receptors. Messages must be delivered in a language the receptors can understand. On the surface this may appear to be overly simplistic. It is not. Regardless of how many languages people may speak, they will process matters related to the most important issues of life, especially matters related to family and faith, in their heart language, that is, in the language they learned as a child—the language through which they acquired their worldview.

Throughout the centuries, from the time of Noah and Abraham, to David, to Nehemiah, to Peter, and to Paul, God's people have spoken many different languages. God spoke to them, or had his representatives speak or write to them, in languages that accommodated their linguistic needs. The Hebrew Scriptures were produced at a time when God's people spoke Hebrew. When they no longer spoke Hebrew, priests, such as Ezra, had the Scriptures translated and

38

explained to them so they could understand God's
expectations for them (Neh. 8:1-8). When it was time to add
the New Testament literature to the canon of Scripture, the
common language was Greek. God spoke through writers
who wrote in the Greek language. Why? Because few
people would have been able to understand Hebrew. God
was accommodating the linguistic needs of the people. Even
though Jesus and his followers spoke Aramaic, the stories
about them, including dialog that originally would have been
spoken in Aramaic, was written in Greek in order to
accommodate the linguistic needs of the people.

One of the gifts the Holy Spirit gave believers in the
first century was the gift of tongues, that is, the ability to
speak in a language or languages they had never learned
through the natural process of language acquisition. The
purpose of the gift was to facilitate the communication of the
Good News about Jesus. The Holy Spirit would give
believers the ability to speak in a language they had never
learned so they could speak to people in their heart language
about spiritual matters. Greek was the common language
(the trade language) of the Roman Empire. Everyone could
communicate in Greek. But spiritual matters are part of
one's worldview. Those matters are best pursued in one's
heart language. God understood this. So the Holy Spirit
enabled some believers to speak the heart languages of the
people with whom they came in contact. In doing this God
was being sensitive to the language requirements of
receptors.

Relevance Issues

A fourth issue related to the communication needs of
receptors is relevance. A communicator must present his
message to receptors in a way that convinces receptors that
the message is indeed relevant to them and worth the time
and effort it takes to receive, decode and attach meaning to

39

it. How does God address relevance issues in the communication process? His messages are always put in terms of the receptor's needs or concerns. For instance, when God spoke to Noah, Noah was a righteous man in the midst of an unrighteous society of people. That had to have been a concern for Noah. When God spoke to Noah, he couched his message in those terms: the people are wicked and I must do something about it. That would have been extremely relevant to Noah. What was God going to do, how was he going to do it, and how would it effect Noah and his family?

Abraham provides us with another example of relevant communication. In the ancient Middle East, having a large family was very important. To not have children was considered a punishment from God. Or, if not an outright punishment, being childless was at least considered as a withholding of divine blessing. Abraham and Sarah were childless. So of course, when God spoke to Abraham of having descendants, Abraham was very interested. The relevancy factor was high.

During the times of the Judges, when God spoke to Israel, he spoke of their sins as the reason for being oppressed by foreign nations. The reason for social and political oppression being related directly to the behavior of the nation was a relevant message to a people who were suffering and wanting to know why and how to change their circumstances. A similar explanation applies to God's communication during the times of the prophets. As it had so many times in the past, sin would result in oppression and suffering if behavioral changes were not forthcoming. The message was relevant because it was rooted in past realities, present conditions, and future possibilities.

When John the Baptist began his ministry people were looking forward to the coming of God's messiah. When John began to prophesy the coming of one of whom the prophets had spoken, the people were interested. The message seemed relevant to them. When John spoke of God's judgment against sin, the people understood a connection between his preaching and their lives. Again, the message seemed relevant to them.

There are many more examples but these are sufficient. God, as a good communicator working within the framework of human communication, took the receptor's needs for relevancy seriously in each communication context.

In each case, God paid careful attention to the communication needs of his receptors. He took into consideration their worldview assumptions, the cultural considerations of their society, their language requirements and relevance issues. God did all the same things a human communicator must do to enhance the communication process and increase the opportunity for effective communication. God entered the human communication context, using the same communication conventions humans use when communicating with each other. Understanding that effective communication is receptor-oriented, God focused his attention on his receptors, accommodating their communication needs. Following the rules of good communication, God made it possible for effective communication to occur.

The Divine-Human Communication Process is Relational in Nature

Just as effective communication is receptor-oriented, it is also relational in nature. If a communicator is going to effectively address the receptors' communication needs (worldview assumptions, cultural considerations, language requirements, and relevance issues) he or she will need to have enough of a relationship with the receptors to have insight into those needs.

41

Relationship in the Communication Process

Communicators have to know people pretty well to understand their worldview assumptions. To understand how to use language effectively in a specific cultural context, and to understand how to make messages relevant, communicators must have a relationship with their receptors. Relationship enhances communication. Individuals who enjoy a close relationship have fewer communication misunderstandings because they know enough about each other to understand how words will be used, applied and interpreted.

The Divine-Human Communication Relationship

If relationship is a factor in effective human-to-human communication, it is also a factor in effective divine-human communication. Communication is a two-way process that is rooted in the two-way give and take realities of relationship. In the divine-human communication context that means that God knows us and we know God. The problem is that some of us don't know God. Some people know *of* him or know *about* him, but they don't really *know him*. They have no relationship to draw on to help them understand what he is trying to get across to them. That lack of relationship is a communication hindrance. God attempts to overcome that hindrance by knowing his receptors so well (even those who do not know him) and meeting their communication needs so thoroughly, that effective communication will still be possible even if the relationship is somewhat one-sided.

God Knowing His Receptors

There is a great deal of evidence in Scripture indicating that God fully appreciates the relational nature of

42

effective communication. In the ancient world, God spoke to and through Noah, a man with whom God enjoyed a close relationship (Gen. 6:9). Later, God spoke to and worked closely with and through Abraham, a man referred to as the friend of God (2 Chron. 20:7). The Lord explained to Jeremiah that he had known him before he was born and had selected Jeremiah to be his spokesman. In Psalm 139, David explained how completely God knew and understood him. Like Jeremiah, the apostle Paul was known and selected by God before he was born (Gal. 1:15).

There are yet other examples that could be cited, but these are sufficient to illustrate that God knows the people to whom he speaks. He knows them well enough to understand them and meet their communication needs (worldview, cultural, linguistic, relevance) so he can communicate effectively with them.

God Making Himself Known to His Receptors

God was not satisfied knowing people that did not know him. He wanted people to know him as fully as human beings can know the Almighty God. Part of the problem was that as Almighty God he seemed rather unapproachable—too holy, beyond comprehension. He had spoken through prophets on many occasions, making himself available as he interacted with humans, entering into agreements with them, instructing them about life and holiness. One of the reasons he had done those things was to reveal himself, to make himself accessible. But most people still did not know him very well. What could he do to make himself more approachable, more knowable? He could become a human being. People could then see him, feel him, talk with him, experience him as they experienced everything else in their world—with their physical senses. They could observe him acting, interacting, and reacting. They could observe him living life as a full participant of society, living out his

43

worldview, engaging culture just as they did. When they could experience him more fully they could know him more fully.

So God became a human being. In the person of Jesus, God was born into this world and lived as a full-fledged, one hundred percent human being—a first century Palestinian Jew, living out his Jewish worldview, in a Jewish culture. Of course, while he was 100% human he was still 100% God, retaining all the essence of God, his divine nature, his eternal perspective. But still, he was fully human, completely accessible, essentially knowable. His goal in becoming human was to offer himself as a sacrifice of atonement for the sins of humanity, making reconciliation and relationship possible, thereby enhancing effective *relational* communication, which in turn serves to deepen the relationship.

This relational factor in the divine-human communication process is highly significant. It is the basis for effective communication between God and humans. God always knew his human children thoroughly. He created them and the world in which they live. So naturally he understood them. But understanding them was not enough. To communicate with them in an effective way God had to enter human culture and speak to humans from a human point of view. This is what is involved in relational communication— speaking to people from their point of view, taking into consideration their worldview assumptions, their cultural needs, their linguistic requirements, and relevance issues. God did all of this, and his having done so is what makes effective divine-human communication possible. His having done so also impacts our understanding of the process of inspiration.

The fact that God entered the human communication context and communicated with humans as humans communicate with one another involves significant implications for the concept of inspiration. It does not change the fact of inspiration. God's communication to us in the Scriptures is inspired. But God's communication methodology (receptor-oriented and relational) does impact the way inspiration is understood. This, in general terms, is the topic under consideration in the next chapter.

CHAPTER 3

THE DIVINE-HUMAN COMMUNICATION COLLABORATION

As I made clear in the beginning, the inspiration of the Scriptures is not in question in this material. I believe the Scriptures are inspired. They are God's communication to us. But understanding and applying God's message to us correctly requires more than acknowledging the divine origination of the message. If God's message is to be properly understood and applied, the process by which it was communicated must be understood. The nature of the Scriptures is an important issue in the interpretation of the Scriptures. The hermeneutical (interpretive) process applied to the Scriptures must be consistent with the communication process used by God in giving us the Scriptures. This is the subject under consideration in this chapter.

The Divine Origin of the Message

As noted earlier, when Paul reminded Timothy that the [Hebrew] Scriptures were *God-breathed* he was asserting the divine origin of the Scriptures, not explaining the process of inspiration. Likewise, when Peter said that the messages spoken by the prophets did not originate with the prophets but with God, he, too, was discussing origin not process. Peter refers to the prophets being moved by the Holy Spirit. Again, origin, not process, is Peter's point. The Spirit was the one who actually conveyed God's message to the prophets. He motivated them, moved them to speak and write. He gave them the message of God which they, in turn, passed along (recommunicated) to the people. From God to the Spirit to a prophet to the people, the point Paul and Peter were making was origin not process. The message that ended up with the people had originated with God. It was inspired—*God-breathed.*

The prophets themselves made it very clear that the things they said and wrote originated with God. They were messengers of God, recommunicating to the people that which God had communicated to them. The oft repeated phrase, *"Thus saith the Lord,"* was intended to provide both authority and relevance that would enhance receptivity on the part of the people. It is difficult to read the Old Testament without getting the distinct impression that not only are you reading the history of God's interaction with the Hebrew people, but also receiving specific messages that originated with God. It is also difficult to read the New Testament without getting the distinct impression that one is reading something that did not originate with the human authors, but with God.

The human authors of the Old and New Testaments claimed that their messages originated with God. Jeremiah, for instance, received messages from God which he passed on to the people of Judah (Jer. 1:1-3). Paul referred to having been taught spiritual truths by the Holy Spirit which he then taught to believers (1 Cor. 2:13). The Scriptures are replete with claims as to its divine origin.

The Human Conveyance of the Message

The origin of the message contained in the Scriptures is divine. But the conveyance of the message involved human beings. The Scriptures are the result of a *divine-human communication collaboration,* or we could refer to it as *a divine-human inspiration collaboration.* Just as the inspiration of the Bible is not being questioned, neither should the divine-human collaboration that produced the Scriptures being questioned. That the Scriptures include a human element should not be questioned by anyone. The Bible did not fall out of heaven in complete form without any human influence. The question is, *how much human influence was involved* in the production of the Scriptures and what impact does that have on the hermeneutical process.

Peter's Thoughts on the Divine-Human Collaboration

It is interesting to note that in commenting on Paul's writing, Peter (2 Pet. 3:15-16) does three significant things: 1) he equates Paul's work with the Hebrew Scriptures, 2) he thinks of Paul's writing as Paul's, and 3) he says that Paul wrote *out of the wisdom* God gave him. Paul's letters were likely gathered into a collection and copied and distributed, if only in limited editions, around AD 90 (Thompson 1971:933). Peter's equation of Paul's work with the "other Scriptures" ranks it along with the Old Testament as inspired Scripture. But as far as Peter is concerned, Paul's letters are his work. Paul authored them. It was Paul who wrote some things that, for Peter, were hard to understand. In what sense, as far as Peter was concerned, was Paul's work his own? What kind of a process may have been involved in the divine-human collaboration between God and Paul in producing the Pauline corpus?

The key to understanding Peter's view of the process involved in the divine-human collaboration is the phrase, *"according to the wisdom God gave him."* Paul wrote according to the wisdom God gave him. What does that mean? Not many scholars, conservative or progressive, have commented on the implications of the phrase. Duane Watson (1998:359-360), Raymond Kelcy (1972:161), and Richard Bauckham (1983:329) (to mention only three) casually link the phrase to the process of inspiration but make no attempt to explain it in any meaningful way. It is unfortunate that this crucial concept has been overlooked. *I believe Peter is describing a process in which Paul's relationship with God through Jesus, enhanced by the indwelling of the Holy Spirit, is the crucial factor in the inspiration of the Scriptures.*

In his letter to the believers in the region of Galatia, Paul insisted that he received directly from Jesus the content of what he preached (Gal. 1:12). In his letter to the believers in Corinth he stressed the Spirit's role in what he had been taught (1 Cor.2:13). Paul was the recipient of revelation and instruction from God. God, through Jesus and the Holy Spirit, communicated with Paul using the human communication conventions described in the previous chapters. The communication was rooted in the relationship Paul and God enjoyed. The more communication there was, the deeper the relationship got. The deeper the relationship got, the better, easier, and more effective the communication became. Out of that intimate relationship, Paul came to know and understand God's will. He acquired a depth of spiritual wisdom that allowed him to address spiritual issues in a way that was entirely consistent with God's wishes. *When the Holy Spirit prompted Paul to write a letter, Paul wrote according to the wisdom he had received from God. God did not need to put words into Paul's mouth. He had put spiritual wisdom into Paul's heart. Paul was perfectly capable of selecting his own words in order to recommunicate to the believers in Corinth (or anywhere else) that which God had communicated to him.*

This, I believe, is what Peter was talking about when he referred to Paul writing according to the wisdom God had given him. Peter, of course, had experienced the same process and had written according to the wisdom God had given him. So Peter understood quite well how the process worked.

Some will wonder how the words Paul wrote can be *God-breathed* if they are Paul's words and not God's. The focus should not be on the individual words, but on the message and its origin. As an ambassador of Christ (2 Cor. 5:20), Paul was empowered to speak for God, representing him in spiritual matters. God had selected Paul, appointed him as an apostle, and had given him the spiritual wisdom and insight he needed to speak on his (God's) behalf. That's what ambassadors do. They speak on behalf of the one they represent. They are empowered and entrusted and their authority and ability to negotiate is assumed and respected. When Paul spoke and wrote according to the wisdom God gave him he was speaking for God with God's full authority. The source or origin of what Paul said (even if Paul selected his own words) was God. Thus, the message Paul delivered was inspired. It was *God-breathed*, for God was the originator of the message. The letters written by Paul were the result of a divine-human communication collaboration.

Paul's Thoughts on the Divine-Human Collaboration

Peter's comments about Paul's writing are highly significant as one attempts to develop a biblical theology of inspiration. Paul's thoughts on the divine-human collaboration are also significant. He considered himself to be one who had been entrusted with the message of God. In his own account of his conversion experience he explains what Jesus had said to him: *"The God of our ancestors has chosen you to know his will and to see the Righteous One and hear him speak. You are to take his message everywhere, telling the whole world what you have seen and heard"* (Ac. 22:14-15). Paul was selected to *know* the will of God. If he knows the will of God, he is capable of explaining it to others in his own words. In his letter to the believers in Thessalonica, Paul said, *"For we speak as messengers who have been approved by God to be entrusted with the Good News"* (1 Thess. 2:4). Paul had been selected to be a messenger and had been *entrusted* with the message. God trusted Paul to deliver the message accurately. Because Paul was Jewish he could deliver the message accurately and in a culturally appropriate way to Jewish people. Because he was a Hellenistic Jew, Paul could also deliver the message accurately and in a culturally appropriate way to Hellenistic people. Could God have delivered the message accurately and in a culturally appropriate manner himself? Certainly. But he chose to communicate directly with selected individuals and then have them recommunicate the message to others. Those selected individuals (such as Peter and Paul) were trusted ambassadors who knew God. They had received wisdom from God and knew his will. They were able to effectively and accurately recommunicate his message and will to others without God having to select their words for them.

In 1 Thessalonians 2:13, Paul expressed his appreciation to the believers in Thessalonica because they believed his message to them was of divine origin rather than human origin. It was the word of God. Regardless of the particular linguistic choices Paul made in delivering the message to them, his message was the "word" of God because the message originated with God. It was *God-breathed*.

In 1 Cor. 2:13, Paul reminded the believers in Corinth that what he had taught them while he was with them, and what he was teaching them in his letter, was spiritual truth which originated with the Spirit (that is, with God). It was not human in origin, but divine. Many people seem to believe that Paul's focus in this text is the source of the individual words he used as he spoke and wrote, suggesting that Paul's point is that the Spirit tells him (dictates to him) each word he is to use when he speaks or writes. When those individuals want to argue a specific theological point, especially when their argument is rooted in the definition of a specific word, they point out that the Holy Spirit selected that specific word and that it's precise meaning, therefore, must be highly significant. But who selected the precise words with which he communicated the truths he taught is not Paul's point in this text. The context of 1 Corinthians 2 (and into chapter 3) is a contrast between worldly wisdom and spiritual wisdom. The believers in Corinth were not sufficiently spiritual. Communicating with them on a mature spiritual level was difficult. Paul's point in 2:13 is that the message he is discussing with them is not human in origin, but divine. He is talking about spiritual things. He is using spiritual language (words) to discuss spiritual truths. Where did he learn these spiritual things he is trying to teach them? From the Spirit.

A brief survey of how different scholars and translation committees translate Paul's thoughts in this text may be helpful.

Jerusalem Bible: *Therefore, we teach, not in the way in which philosophy is taught, but in the way that the Spirit teaches us: we teach spiritual things spiritually.*

Phillips Modern English: *It is these things that we talk about, not using the expressions of the human intellect but those which the Holy Spirit teaches, explaining spiritual things to those who are spiritual.*

In the footnote of the New Living Translation, two alternate translations are listed as: *explaining spiritual truths in spiritual language,* or *explaining spiritual truths to spiritual people.*

My own translation of this text, based on the context of this section is: *The things we are telling you are the things God has given us. His Spirit teaches us the spiritual truths he wants us to pass on to you.*

A careful exegesis of the passage based on the context makes it clear that Paul's point concerns the origin of the material he is passing on to the believers in Corinth. It is of divine origin. Paul is not suggesting that every word he speaks is dictated to him by the Holy Spirit.

Another Pauline text which gives us a great deal of insight into the divine-human inspiration collaboration that resulted in the production of the biblical text is 1 Corinthians 7. In the course of these comments Paul makes a number of statements that illustrate the kind of interaction going on between himself and God as he deals with problems not previously addressed in the Scriptures or by Jesus in his ministry.

The first illustration of the divine-human interaction that is part and parcel of inspiration is in vs. 6, where Paul says that what he has said about the frequency of sexual relations in marriage is his suggestion and not an absolute rule. Paul was not making a law, though he had the authority to do so (Philemon 8-9). He was suggesting a framework for healthy sexual relations.

Verses 8, 10, and 12 contain an interesting combination of comments. In verse 8, Paul speaks to believers who are unmarried or who are widowed. In verse 10, he speaks to believers who are married. But he adds that what he is saying was a command from Jesus himself. Then, in verse 12, Paul speaks to "the rest," (who would be believers who are married to unbelievers) acknowledging that he has no direct commandment from Jesus regarding their situation and responsibilities. Most scholars take this to mean that Jesus himself had not discussed issues related to believers married to unbelievers. Therefore, Paul is providing legislation on the matter. The apostle differentiates between those things Jesus himself addressed during his ministry and those things for which he (Paul) provided guidance. In verse 6, Paul had been careful to say that he was not making a law. However, in verses 8 and 12, Paul makes no distinction between the instructions given by Jesus and those given by himself. In one case (verse 10) Jesus himself issued instructions and in the two others cases (verses 8 and 12) the instructions were coming from Paul. Paul understood his instructions to be as binding as those of Jesus.

In verse 17, Paul notes the rule or ordinance he has established in all the churches, namely, that individuals not be required to make changes in their personal status when they become believers. Paul is very clear that this is his ordinance. His words are authoritative.

In verse 25, Paul again acknowledges that Jesus gave no specific instructions regarding the marriage opportunities or obligations of single young women. Paul, however, wanted to make another suggestion. He did not want to make it a binding obligation, but wanted them to take his advice seriously. He said, therefore, *"the Lord in his kindness has given me wisdom that can be trusted, and I will share it with you."*

In verse 40, Paul gives his "judgment" (opinion, suggestion) about the status and marriage opportunities of widows. The reason his opinion should be weighed carefully is that, *"I am giving you counsel from God's Spirit when I say this."* Paul understood that his relationship with God, and the special wisdom he had been given as an ambassador of Christ, gave him the spiritual insight necessary to dispense valid *and authoritative* spiritual advice. This is clearly evident in Paul's comments to Philemon regarding Onesimus. Paul says, *"that is why I am boldly asking a favor of you. I could demand it in the name of Christ because it is the right thing for you to do, but because of our love, I prefer just to ask you"* (verses 8-9). As an ambassador of Christ,

Paul had the authority to speak for God. To use Jesus' phraseology as he spoke to his apostles, *"Whatever you prohibit on earth is prohibited in heaven, and whatever you allow on earth is allowed in heaven"* (Mt. 18:18).

Paul had been given wisdom from God and out of that wisdom he spoke and wrote. Paul refers to this in his letter to the believers in Colosse: *"So everywhere we go, we tell everyone about Christ. We warn them and teach them with all the wisdom God has given us, for we want to present them to God, perfect in their relationship to Christ"* (Col. 1:28). Out of the wisdom Paul received from God he preached the Gospel and taught believers how to live as God would have them live. The Holy Spirit did not need to dictate to Paul the words he should use. Paul was perfectly capable of selecting his own words. And when he did, that which he communicated was authoritative and trustworthy. Paul collaborated with God in a divine-human process that resulted in Paul's authoritative teaching and writing.

Jeremiah and the Divine-Human Collaboration

One of the best examples of how the divine-human collaboration worked is found in the book of Jeremiah. The opening verses of chapter 36 set the stage for evaluating the events described in that chapter.

> *During the fourth year that Jehoiakim son of Josiah was king in Judah, the LORD gave this message to Jeremiah: "Get a scroll, and write down all my messages against Israel, Judah, and the other nations. Begin with the first message back in the days of Josiah, and write down every message you have given, right up to the present time. Perhaps the people of Judah will repent if they see in writing all the terrible things I have planned for them. Then I will be able to forgive their sins and wrongdoings." So Jeremiah sent for Baruch son of Neriah, and as Jeremiah dictated, Baruch wrote down all the prophecies that the LORD had given him* (Jer 36:1-4).

55

God, through the Holy Spirit, had been communicating with Jeremiah for quite sometime when the events of chapter 36 occurred. Jeremiah had lots of *"messages against Israel"* to remember and write down. Through the Spirit, God prompted Jeremiah and gave him instructions as to what to do. Jeremiah was to write down the content of previous communications from God, putting in writing all that God had said regarding the sins of Israel, Judah, and other nations, and God's threats of punishment if change was not forthcoming. Jeremiah called Baruch and dictated his words to Baruch. But was the Holy Spirit dictating words to Jeremiah? Or was God simply allowing Jeremiah to remember the content of their conversations and the messages Jeremiah had delivered to the people based on his conversations with God? From the first four verses of the chapter it is difficult to tell. Jeremiah is simply told to write down all the messages he had received from the Lord. However, in the last section of the chapter, verses 27-32, after the scroll had been destroyed, Jeremiah and Baruch sit down again and rewrite the messages.

The last sentence of the chapter tells us that this time Jeremiah added even more messages. He included more in the second scroll than he had in the first. What might that infer? It might infer that Jeremiah was not receiving dictation from the Holy Spirit but was remembering the messages he had received from God. This does not mean that the Holy Spirit was not somehow involved in the process. Of course he was. Peter was emphatic that the Holy Spirit was involved with the prophets as they spoke and wrote. The issue is not the Spirit's involvement. The issue is the level or nature of his involvement. Did the Spirit select the words Jeremiah used or allow him to select his own words? Is it not possible that Jeremiah was remembering his encounters with God and writing about them in his own words? When he had to rewrite his scroll, he remembered additional material and included it in his second draft. Could the Holy Spirit have been involved in assisting him to remember that additional material? Certainly. But is there any evidence that the Spirit told Jeremiah word for word what to write? There does not seem to be.

I believe this sequence of events coincides with what we discussed earlier regarding Paul receiving wisdom from God and writing according to that wisdom. Jeremiah had received messages (wisdom) from God regarding the people of Israel, Judah, and other nations. He had delivered those messages verbally. God then wanted Jeremiah to write the messages down so the people would experience the impact of a written judgment against them. God did not need to reveal once again that which he had already revealed to Jeremiah. God simply needed to tell Jeremiah to write it down. Jeremiah had been faithful in delivering the verbal messages and would be faithful in delivering the written messages. The prompting for the writing came from the Holy Spirit, as had the original communications containing God's judgments. The origin of the messages was clearly divine—from God, through the Holy Spirit, to Jeremiah. But putting them down in ink was human. The *origin* was divine, the *transmission* was human. The two aspects combined added up to a divine-human collaboration that resulted in the scroll of Jeremiah—which probably became the basis for the Bible book we know as Jeremiah.

Culture and the Divine-Human Collaboration

What has this concept of a divine-human communication collaboration to do with the role of culture in the production of the biblical text? One of the ways God saw to it that his communication with humans was culturally appropriate was to partner with human authors in the delivery of his message. This is not to suggest that God himself could not have made the message completely culturally appropriate. He could have. But he chose to involve humans in the process, not merely as passive vehicles in a mechanical process, but as active participants in a dynamic process.

All communication, even God's communication to his human children, is *culture-bound* and *culture-laden*. That is, it occurs within the context of a culture and is filled with and based on cultural references. God understood this and chose to communicate in culturally appropriate ways with his prophets and apostles (and a few other ambassadors he selected to participate in the process, such as Luke, Mark, James and others) who were then permitted to use the wisdom God gave them to speak and write on his behalf in culturally appropriate ways. The Holy Spirit was an active participant in the process as well, but not as one who selected each word to be spoken or written. He was the presence of God giving the writers the wisdom they needed to speak and write as ambassadors of Christ. As the writers selected their own words and arranged their material to suit their purposes (as did the writers of the Gospels, for instance), they did so within the context of their culture. Their messages were not bound to the limits of their respective cultures, but were delivered within the framework of those cultures so that they were intelligible to the people of those cultures.

One of the ways God decided to make his messages to humans culturally appropriate was to partner with humans using them in an active, dynamic way in the communication of those messages. The biblical writers said what God wanted them to say, but God gave them the freedom to say it the way they wanted to say it. That is what the divine-human communication collaboration is all about—God and humans working together to get God's message across in a way that was culturally appropriate to the people of those ancient cultures.

Dictation Theology in Disguise

Many believers try to avoid the word *dictation* when explaining their theology of inspiration. A mechanical form of dictation is so problematic that it has been abandoned (at least formally) by most believers. It simply does not make sense that the Holy Spirit dictated a letter to Paul which said, *"Paul, called to be an apostle of Christ Jesus by the will of God, and our brother Sosthenes"* (1 Cor. 1:1), as if the letter was from Paul and Sosthenes. If the Holy Spirit dictated the letter then it was not from Paul and Sosthenes, it was from the Holy Spirit.

Along the same lines, if the Holy Spirit dictated the gospels to Matthew, Mark, Luke and John, why would he have dictated different versions of the same story to each of them? Why would he have arranged the material in each gospel differently? Why would he have omitted some details in one version of the story and added details in another version of the story?

The fact that nearly everyone has formally denied the viability of dictation as the way to explain inspiration demonstrates how problematic it is. However, even if a dictation methodology has been formally set aside, it continues to be advocated in subtle ways. Many preachers still engage in theological arguments based on the specific meaning of specific words, declaring that since the Holy Spirit selected that word it must be highly significant. To suggest that the words of the biblical text are the direct result of the Spirit's influence is to advocate a dictation methodology. Either the Spirit selected the specific words of the text or he did not. If he did and gave (dictated) those specific words to the writer who then wrote what he was told to write, that is the dictation method. It makes no sense to deny the dictation method on the one hand and then advocate it on the other.

Who selected the words of the biblical text, the Holy Spirit or the human authors? I believe that many believers cling to a dictation theology of inspiration because they are afraid that if the human authors selected the words of the text the text is no longer trustworthy, no longer divinely inspired. That is a mistaken assumption. As we have already noted, the biblical claim that it is inspired has to do with the origin of the message, not the process by which the message was transmitted. The message of Scripture originated with God. The process of transmitting that message to humans allowed for the human authors to select their own words. But their selection of words grew out of the wisdom God had given them. They were trusted servants whom God had prepared to participate with him in the recommunication of his message. The message is inspired because it is not of human origin. It is time we learn to be comfortable with the human side of the divine-human communication collaboration.

The historical controversy over the nature of Christ serves to illustrate the problem. For over 450 years (between 325 and 787) Christians argued over the exact nature of Christ. He was both divine and human, but in what combination or proportion? Which of his two natures was dominant? How can one be equally God and human? For some people the answer to the dilemma was to minimize the human nature of Christ. For others it was to minimize the divine nature of Christ. Neither of those reactions was acceptable. Jesus was both fully God and fully human. It may not be possible for the human mind to fully understand how such a thing can occur, but because it is impossible for humans to fully understand does not mean that it is impossible.

God is not limited to or by human comprehension. It may be difficult for some to see how the Bible can be the result of a divine-human collaboration and still be completely inspired, authoritative, and dependable, but being difficult for some to understand does not make it impossible.

The biblical writers were participants with God in the divine-human communication process. They worked as his partners. He gave them the wisdom they needed to do the job he wanted them to do. He trusted them. There is no reason we should not trust them. The Bible is God's inspired, authoritative communication to his human children. But all humans live within the framework of human culture. To be appropriate and relevant God's communication to humans had to occur in, and in relation to, the cultures of the people to whom God spoke. To assist him in accomplishing his communication purpose, God decided to partner with human speakers and writers in the delivery of his messages.

Recommunicating God's Message—Then and Now

God communicated with his prophets, apostles and others he had selected to be his spokesmen. He communicated with them in ways that were, for them, culturally appropriate and relevant. Once God had communicated with them they were to *recommunicate* his message to others. They had received a message within their specific cultural context and would recommunicate it to others within a specific cultural context—usually their own, the one they knew and understood the best. An exception of this would be Jonah, who was called to go preach to the people of Nineveh. That was obviously a cross-cultural experience for Jonah. Normally, however, speakers and writers recommunicated God's message to people of their own culture, or another culture with which they were very familiar. Paul, for instance, as a Hellenistic Jew was comfortable and effective working in the Hellenistic culture.

It is important to understand that *as God allowed each of his ambassadors to determine exactly how they would recommunicate his messages to the people of their culture, which included expressing the messages in ways that would be culturally familiar, that the messages would reflect the particular worldview and cultural perspectives of the society receiving the messages.* When we read the Bible we experience God's messages constructed not in the cultural framework of our contemporary Western society, but constructed in the cultural framework of ancient peoples and societies. Such is the unavoidable reality of God communicating with humans within the context of their culture—which is, as we have discussed, the only way to engage in effective communication.

Cultural Relativity

Does this mean, then, that everything is culturally relative? No. *Everything* is not culturally relative. Absolutes exist. God is an absolute. The qualities that flow from his nature and character are absolutes. Positive absolutes are qualities or behaviors that are in harmony with God's character. These would include (but not be limited to) love, kindness, helpfulness, mercy, and so forth. Negative absolutes are qualities or behaviors that do not flow from God's nature, or that are opposed to or opposite to God's nature. These would include (but not be limited to) murder, adultery, hate, brutality, greed, and so forth. God's existence and character are absolute and create absolute moral standards that transcend all human cultural values. God is *supracultural*, that is, he is above culture (Kraft 1979:121). The absolutes that flow from his nature are also supracultural[4]. They transcend all cultural standards and define right and wrong.

God's communication to his human children makes it clear that moral absolutes exist. Everything is not culturally relative. But to recognize that everything is not culturally relative is not to suggest that *some* things are not culturally

---

[4] The term *supracultural* is used by Charles Kraft to describe those things which are "above and outside culture" (1979:120).

relative. For instance, anger itself is not wrong. God becomes angry when people engage in sinful, hurtful behavior. Anger itself is a valid emotion. Uncontrolled anger is bad and can lead to terrible results. But as an emotion, anger is not wrong. However, in Namibia, a country on the West coast of Southern Africa, displaying anger is considered a terrible sin. People who live in Namibia must control themselves. Even though God may not consider properly controlled anger to be sinful, the Namibians do. God does not have a rule against it, but the Namibians do. It is simply unacceptable in their culture to display anger. Namibian culture, therefore, defines acceptable or unacceptable behavior in relation to anger. Italy, however, has no such cultural taboo against displays of anger. Emotional outbursts are commonplace. Drivers angry at one another may get out of their cars and shout, waving their arms wildly in the air, shaking their fists at one another as they criticize and blame the other person for their vehicular transgressions. However, the anger rarely lasts long or escalates into anything serious, such as physical violence. The frustration subsides and drivers get back into their cars and drive away. No harm done. That which is terribly sinful in Namibia is perfectly acceptable in Italy. In some cases, culture determines whether or not a specific behavior is acceptable. This is an example of acceptable cultural relativity.

There are a number of European cultures, however, where it is accepted that a married man will take a mistress. Adultery, in those cultures, is not looked upon as unacceptable, sinful behavior. God, however, does look upon marital unfaithfulness as sinful behavior. His character includes honesty and faithfulness. Behaviors opposed to honesty and faithfulness, such as adultery, are simply unacceptable, regardless of what a society may conclude. Adultery cannot be justified as acceptable behavior simply because it is culturally acceptable. It is a violation of the moral absolutes that flow from God's nature.

There are moral absolutes. There are some things that are always right, no matter what. There are also some things that are always wrong, no matter what. These moral absolutes are universal, transcending all cultural boundaries. But there are also things that do not rise to the level of universal moral absolutes. There are things that are right or wrong depending on cultural perspectives. Such things are considered culturally relative. Biblically speaking, there are a number of things that fall into this category: head coverings for women during prayer, the holy kiss, foot washing, and so forth. And *while it is vital to acknowledge that God's communication to us contains universal moral absolutes, it is also vital to acknowledge that the Scriptures contain some things (things that may actually be given in the form of a command, such as the command to greet one another with a holy kiss) that are culturally relative.*

The difficulty, after acknowledging the presence of things in Scripture that are culturally relative, comes in attempting to determine the difference between those things that are universal absolutes and those things that are culturally relative. This difficulty will be discussed in more detail in Part Three. Before turning to that discussion, however, it is important to remember that the original or primary recommunication of God's original messages was completed roughly between 3000 and 2000 years ago in cultures very different from our contemporary Western culture. As we interpret and recommunicate God's messages today, we must keep the original cultural context clearly in mind. In Part Two we will examine the ancient cultures present in Scripture in an attempt to understand the cultures in which God's messages were first delivered.

Summary

The Bible's claim to be inspired is not in question. But we must remember that the claim has to do with the origin of the message not the process of transmission. The Bible is the result of a divine-human communication collaboration. Just as Jesus' human nature does not detract from, minimize, or in any way jeopardize his divine nature, neither does the human part of the divine-human inspiration collaboration detract from, minimize, or in any way jeopardize the divine origin and trustworthiness of the Scriptures.

Peter and Paul both understood that their writings were their own, but were also "inspired" because they had been given wisdom from God and were his trusted ambassadors. Through their relationship with God, they knew God and his will for his human children. They knew what God wanted and were able to recommunicate his will to people without the Holy Spirit having to dictate to them exactly, precisely, word-for-word what to say.

Jeremiah (chapter 36) provides a marvelous example of how the prophets were moved by the Spirit to recommunicate God's message to people.

People can only understand that which is part of their cultural frame of reference. God understood this. So he communicated his message within the cultural contexts of the people with whom he wished to communicate. All communication, even God's communication to his human children, is *culture-bound* and *culture-laden*. That is, it occurs within the context of a culture and is filled with and based on cultural references. God chose trustworthy people to communicate with who would then be able to recommunicate his messages in culturally appropriate ways.

Our challenge today to is understand this cultural component of the inspired Scriptures and sift through what is there to differentiate between the cultural and the

65

supracultural, between that which is absolute and that which is culturally relative.

PART TWO

THE ROLE OF CULTURE IN THE PRESENTATION OF THE BIBLE[5]

---

[5] In this section I have made use of a few popular sources. For my academic colleagues who find this annoying or unacceptable I offer my sincere apology. However, the historical information offered by the scholars I have referenced is reliable regardless of the audience for whom it was originally prepared. Accuracy and reliability rather than audience ought to be the primary concern.

CHAPTER 4

THE BIBLE'S ANCIENT MULTICULTURAL CONTEXT

The Bible tells a story that unfolds across the pages of human history. The main part of the story, which begins in Genesis 12, tells of events that occurred over 4000 years ago. As the story unfolds, people from many different cultures are involved in different ways. Abraham, for instance, one of the main characters in the story, is from Ur, an ancient Sumerian city. Obeying God's instructions, Abraham left Ur and traveled northwest, first to Haran, then down into Canaan. From there he traveled into Egypt and later back into Canaan. Reading about Abraham's travels in the biblical text, one encounters four different major cultures.

Throughout the biblical text there are at least nine major cultures and several less significant cultures that are crucial to the telling of the story—cultures that impact the people involved, the story itself, and the telling of the story. The most recent of those cultures, first century Roman and first century Jewish Palestinian cultures, are over 2000 years old. The oldest cultures involved in the Biblical story (Mesopotamian cultures) are over 5000 years old.

Obviously, the Bible is an ancient book that tells a story rooted in antiquity. It is absolutely essential to understand that the ancient cultures in which the events unfold impacted the people involved in those events. Those cultures, then, impacted the story itself, and they impacted how the story was told—for story-telling (communication) is culture-bound and culture-laden.

As contemporary readers read the biblical story, they are brought into contact with many ancient cultures, cultures rooted in what appear to be odd perspectives and strange practices. *The reader's task is to understand the cultural context in which the story unfolded and differentiate between the essence of what God was communicating and the cultural context in which it occurred.*

Ancient Near Eastern Literature

In order to understand the biblical story in any detail, it is essential to have some familiarity with the ancient cultures in which the events unfolded. To accomplish this, it is helpful if the reader is familiar with the similarity between biblical literature and other literature of the Ancient Near East (ANE). Samuel Kramer, noted Mesopotamian historian, discusses the benefit of archeological research in the Near East as it relates to our understanding of the Bible:

> One of the major achievements of all this archeological activity in "Bible lands" is that a bright and revealing light has been shed on the background and origin of the Bible itself. We can now see that this greatest of literary classics did not come upon the scene full-blown, like an artificial flower in a vacuum; its roots reach deep into the distant past and spread wide across the surrounding lands. Both in form and content, the Biblical books bear no little resemblance to the literatures created by earlier civilizations in the Near East. To say this is not to detract in any way from the significance of the Biblical writings, or from the genius of the Hebrew men of letters who composed them. Indeed, one can only marvel at what has been termed

"the Hebrew miracle," which transformed the static motifs and conventionalized patterns of their predecessors into what is perhaps the most vibrant and dynamic literary creation known to man. . . To be sure, the Sumerians could not have influenced the Hebrews directly, for they had ceased to exist long before the Hebrew people came into existence. But there is little doubt that the Sumerians had deeply influenced the Canaanites, who preceded the Hebrews in the land that later came to be known as Palestine, and their neighbors, such as the Assyrians, Babylonians, Hittites, Hurrians, and Arameans (1981:141-142).

Kramer's point is that the Bible did not simply appear as a finished product, but was produced in specific cultural contexts. Those cultural contexts impacted its production. It is important, therefore, to understand as much as we can about those ancient cultures.

Major Ancient Cultures Represented in the Scriptures

This section will include a brief introduction and overview of each of the major cultures represented in the biblical text[6]. An excellent additional resource for material about cultures represented in Scripture is *Life in the Ancient Near East* by Daniel Snell.

Mesopotamia

The land between the Tigris and Euphrates rivers (in present-day Iraq) is known as Mesopotamia. *Mesopotamia* is a Greek word which refers to the land *between the rivers*. In Northern Mesopotamia, Assyria eventually became a significant power; in the South, Babylon became significant.

---

[6] It should be noted that in this material I am not engaging in scholarly interaction with historians on the most recent research or theories regarding the ancient cultures discussed below. Rather I am utilizing respected (though not always the most current) scholarship regarding these ancient cultures in an attempt to provide a cultural and historical overview for the readers of this present work.

Assyria and Babylon will be discussed separately after a general overview of Mesopotamia.

Scholars agree that the earliest forms of "civilization" appeared in Mesopotamia between 3500 - 3000 BC with the arrival of a people known as the Sumerians. Chester Starr explains that "civilization" as used by archeologists and historians refers to a number of specific features including:

> [T]he presence of firmly organized states which had definite boundaries and systematic political institutions, under political and religious leaders who directed and also maintained society; the distinction of social classes; the economic specialization of men as farmer, trader, or artisan, each dependent upon his fellows; and the conscious development of the arts and intellectual attitudes... [which includes] the rise of monumental architecture and sculpture, the use of writing to keep accounts or to commemorate deeds, and the elaboration of religious views about the nature of the gods, their relations to men, and the origin of the world (1991:27).

People had begun to live together in groups and cultivate crops in other locations. Jericho, for instance, was a walled city whose inhabitants engaged in agriculture between 9,000 and 6,000 BC (Bahn 1996:248-249). But their society was not organized and developed to the level of a civilization as scholars define the concept. When the Sumerians arrived in Mesopotamia their society evolved into a fully functioning civilization. It was a way of living life that had not previously existed among humans.

However, the Sumerians were not the first people to live in Mesopotamia. According to Samuel Kramer, the earliest inhabitants of southern Mesopotamia were a people known as Ubaidans. That name was given to them because the location where archeological evidence of their society was first found is known as Tell al-Ubaid (1963:41-42). By 4000 BC, their culture was well established in the region. Since writing had not been invented at that time, no one knows how the Ubaidians referred to themselves. They

71

were, however, a capable and industrious people, engaged in agriculture and building, including expansive temples made of mud-brick. The impact of their culture extended to some degree throughout the ANE from the Mediterranean to Caspian Sea.

The Sumerians, who probably came from Central Asia through Iran into southern Mesopotamia, arrived around 3500 BC[7] and began building what would become the first civilization—a civilization so creative and influential that aspects of it have become permanent fixtures of Western culture. For instance, Sumerian arithmetic, which was sometimes based on a unit of 10 and sometimes on a unit of 60 (a sexagesimal system), is the source of our 60 second minute and our 60 minute hour, as well as the reason for our speaking of a circle in terms of 360 degrees (De Blois and Van Der Spek 1997:12).

The Sumerians were accomplished farmers. Even though the climate conditions in southern Mesopotamia are not the most hospitable and the soil leaves much to be desired, the Sumerians excelled agriculturally, growing barley, wheat, dates, flax, apples, plums, and grapes. Eighty to ninety percent of the Sumerian population engaged in farming, using crops for bartering goods and to pay taxes (Starr 1991:33). They made extensive use of irrigation canals to water crops.

Though most Sumerians were farmers, all were not. There were various kinds of craftsmen: there were leather workers, potters who worked in clay, those who transported goods, and various kinds of merchants. "By 3300 B. C., when writing began, the Sumerians already used sailboats, wheeled vehicles, and animal-drawn plows. They invented the first industrial machine providing continuous rotary

---

[7] Some historians (Roberts 1993:42) suggest a Sumerian presence in southern Mesopotamia as early as 5000 BC. Most, however, differentiate between the earlier Ubaidian presence and the influx of new peoples around 3500 BC known as the Sumerians.

motion: the potter's wheel which spins the clay as the craftsman shapes it" (Bickerman 1972:57).

As was common at that time in that part of the world, their culture was a male dominated, patriarchal society. However, J. M. Roberts points out that even though the society was patriarchal, Sumerian women were held in high esteem, enjoyed significant rights and could expect equitable treatment under the law (1993:45). Along with patriarchy, polygamy was a common practice, as was slavery. It is crucial to understand that these and other cultural elements that became features of Israelite culture existed in that part of the world long before Israel did.

The greatest contribution of Sumerian civilization was the invention of writing. As early as 3,000 BC Sumerian scribes were using writing in the educational process (Kramer 1963:229). Leo Oppenheim suggests that the Sumerians may have borrowed an alphabet and writing from an earlier lost civilization (1977:49). Most scholars, however, attribute the invention of writing to the Sumerians. Their earliest efforts involved the use of *pictographs*, simple pictorial symbols. A pictogram might easily represent a cow or a sheep, a person or some item. As Kramer points out, however, it was difficult to communicate the idea of thinking or a thought using a pictogram. It became obvious to the Sumerians that they needed a more sophisticated method of written communication. That need resulted in the development of *cuneiform* writing, a series or group of wedged shaped symbols that could be used in combination to represent sounds and syllables in words.

Their writing served to advance their civilization by allowing business transactions to be recorded, to record political and social events, to create a unified code of law, to record legends, and to write stories and poems. The world's oldest agricultural manual may be a Sumerian "farmers' almanac" explaining how to grow barley (Kramer 1963:104-105).

The invention of writing required schools where *scribes* could learn to write so that the new invention could be used. The schools developed by the Sumerians were *professional* rather than academic in purpose in that their goal was to train scribes to serve as officials for record keeping in both the private and public sectors (Kramer 1981:4).

Politically, the Sumerians were very advanced. In their earliest days their leaders were elected by an assembly of free citizens. Later a heredity kingship became the accepted practice (Kramer 1963:74), but initially Sumerian society was a democracy, predating Greek democracy by hundreds of years. As early as 3000 BC, the Sumerians met in a congress comprised of two houses, a senate and a lower house, to debate the merits of going to war. The king had veto power, which could send a decision back for extended debate. But the process was rooted in democratic discussion and voting not in dictatorial decision (Kramer 1981:30-31).

Sumerian cities were walled cities with narrow, winding streets lined with mud-brick houses. A typical city, such as Ur, may have covered as many as 150 acres and sustained a population of 24,000 (Starr 1991:31). Many of the houses were two-story with perhaps six or seven rooms, including an entryway, a work room, a storage room, a guest room, an area for slaves, a kitchen, and a lavatory, all surrounding an open courtyard. The bedrooms were upstairs. Some of the houses had walls six feet thick. In Ur, houses of this type, approximately 4000 years old, have been excavated, providing a model of the kind of home in which Abraham may have lived before leaving Ur to become a nomad.

As Sumerian society evolved into a full-blown civilization it became clear that laws to govern society were necessary. The earliest known law code is the code of Ur-Nammu (ruler of Ur) dated at 2100 BC. It served as the model for law codes produced later, such as the Babylonian code of Hammurabi—discussed in more detail in the section on Babylonia.

Religiously, the Sumerians were polytheistic, believing that the good fortune of their civilization was the result of the favor of the gods, whom they sought to honor and, if necessary, to placate. Mircea Leiad suggests that there were three main deities: An, En-lil, and En-ki. An, named for the sky, was their supreme, sovereign high god. En-lil was the god of the atmosphere. En-ki was their *Lord of the earth* (1963:112-164). Starr, however, suggests that there were four main deities: An, the high god, En-lil, the "active force of nature often manifested himself in the raging storms of the plains," Nin-khursag, the goddess of the earth, and En-ki, the god of waters who fertilized the ground. Along with these key deities were a group of 50 other "great gods" and many deities, demons and spirits, most of whom were visualized in some human form (1991:37-38).

Each city in Mesopotamia had a temple where the gods were thought to live (Durant 1963:Vol. 1, 128) and where priests administered daily rites. Sacrifices of meat and vegetables as well as libations of water were made to the gods. The average citizen had little to do with those worship activities. The populace, however, participated in regularly scheduled festivals and a number of monthly feasts designed to honor or appease specific deities. As with all pagan religions, Sumerian religion represented an attempt to cope with life. The gods had power the people did not have, exercising control over aspects of nature and life that the people could not control. Being able to approach the gods for favors, or to appease them if there had been a possible offense, gave worshippers a connection to powers far beyond their own that could be manipulated to their own advantage.

Around 2276 BC, Sargon, an Akkadian (from Akkad) began a dynasty that would last 150 years. The Akkadians were a semi-nomadic Semitic tribe who lived in the northern region of the Mesopotamian plain (Harrison 1970:50). De

Blois and Van Der Spek note that, "the Akkadians borrowed much from the Sumerians, including their script, their religious imagery, scientific principles and literary styles. But their culture also contains elements of their own devising because they continued to worship their own deities (which were, however, identified with Sumerian gods) and to use their own language" (1997:13). If Abraham was born after the beginning of the Sargonian dynasty began (as some chronologies suggest) he would have spoken Akkadian as his native language.

Babylonia

As the Sumerian-Akkadian civilization was coming to an end (marked by the fall of Ur in 2004 BC), a significant Amorite dynasty began forming north of Ur at Isin. This was the beginning of the Babylonian civilization (Grayson 1992:Vol. 4, 759). The Amorites were Semitic-speaking semi-nomadic people who migrated East from Syria-Arabia into Babylonia. The people of Babylon (Sumerian-Akkadians) did not appreciate the primitive manner of the Amorites. Some of the Amorites came peacefully. Others, however, banded together and arrived in force, capturing strategic Babylonian centers, thereby gaining control.

Even though the Amorites gained control, establishing their own succession of rulers, they adopted the culture of Babylon. They learned the language and became part of the great Mesopotamian culture that was by that time over 1000 years old. And although there may have been slight cultural modifications (all cultures change and evolve to some extent over the years), the culture of Babylonia continued to be an extension of Mesopotamian culture.

Other than Nebuchadnezzar II, the best known Babylonian king was Hammurapi (or Hammurabi) who became king in 1792 BC and ruled for nearly fifty years. The *Code of Hammurabi* is the best known ancient law code beyond the biblical recode of the Law of Moses. It is a compilation of nearly 300 laws that provides a revealing portrait of life in ancient Mesopotamia for perhaps two or three thousand years (Kramer 1963:82-88).

The Babylonians, for instance, like most ancient cultures, took a dim view of adultery. If a man and woman were caught in adultery they were to be bound together and cast into the water. If a builder did not build a sufficiently strong house and it collapsed, killing the owner, the builder was to be put to death. The code reveals a society in which law and order were valued, and all citizens, even the poor, were entitled to protection under the law.

Babylonian society included an aristocracy, a large middle class, and a slave population. It was not uncommon to find several slaves in the average household, some of whom were Babylonians who sold themselves into slavery, perhaps for debt relief. The life of a slave was not always as brutal as one might expect. Slaves were legally entitled to participate in business, to borrow money and to purchase their freedom. As is always the case, the large *middle class* (for lack of a better term) of citizen tradesmen/craftsmen were the foundation of Babylonian society: builders (which included carpenters and brick makers), farmers, merchants, fishermen, herdsmen and so forth (82-83).

After the death of Hammurabi (1750) the Babylonian power began to decline. Around 1595, a foreign people known as the Kassites (illiterate nomads from central Asia) invaded Babylonia and held control throughout the region for several hundred years. After the fall of their dynasty (1133), Nebuchadnezzar I (not the biblical Nebuchadnezzar II) came to power establishing the second dynasty of Isin. From 1000 to 748 BC Babylonia and Assyria existed side by side, with Assyria gradually gaining in strength (Grayson 1992:760-763). During all this time the basic Mesopotamian culture developed by the Sumerians remained, for the most part, unchanged.

Assyria

In northern Mesopotamia is the region known as Assyria. Assyria's major cities included Asshur, Nineveh, Arbela, and Calah. The ancient geopolitical boundaries of Assyria proper lay within the area today known as Iraq. But their military and political strength (by the 7th century BC) was felt as far West as the Mediterranean coast and Egypt, and in the East to the border of Media. Kramer (in a popular work based on his earlier academic material) describes the Assyrians during the Middle Assyrian Empire (1132-1036 BC) as "more belligerent than the Babylonians—who placed greater emphasis on cultural achievement than they did on warfare—the Assyrians at about this time embarked upon a policy of ruthless conquest that would ultimately make them masters over nearly all of the Near East" (1978:56).

Grayson notes during the early days of this Middle Empire, the introduction of iron weapons and armor had a significant impact on warfare, as much as the horse-drawn light chariot had in earlier centuries (1992:Vol. 4, 739).

Religiously, the Assyrians carried on the traditions of the older Mesopotamian culture. A few new gods (or gods that had been lower in the pantheon) were given more attention than the old ones, but generally speaking the religious culture of Assyria was a continuation of Sumerian religion (Oppenheim 1962:Vol. 1, 262-304). Durant, in describing Assyrian religion, notes that its "essential function. . . was to train the future citizen to a patriotic docility, and to teach him the art of wheedling favors out of the gods by magic and sacrifice" (1963:276).

Assyrian religion, however, did little to minimize their tendencies toward brutality. Durant suggests that they seemed to find satisfaction in torturing their captives. There are records of Assyrians skinning people alive, roasting them in kilns, caging them for amusement, even blinding children while forcing their parents to watch. Ashurbanipal boasts of burning people alive, dismembering people, including cutting tongues out, and otherwise executing thousands of people (275-276).

In the southern regions of Mesopotamia (Babylonia) commerce was more common than agriculture. To the north, however, in Assyria, agriculture was more common. A wealthy Assyrian nobleman supervised the agricultural production of his grand estate. Mining was also a significant industry, as was glass, textiles, and pottery. "Houses were as well-equipped in Nineveh as in Europe before the Industrial Revolution." Lead, copper, silver and gold were used as currency and lenders charged as much as 25% interest on loans. One of the earliest examples of official coinage can be traced to the Assyrian king Sennacherib around 700 BC— a half-shekel minted of silver (Durant 1962:274).

Assyrian society was a stratified society made up of five classes: nobles, craftsmen, unskilled but free workers, serfs attached to the land of an estate, and slaves captured in battle or attached because of debt. Because Assyria was a military state, large families were encouraged. More sons meant more soldiers. Abortion was illegal—a capital crime. Women who attempted to abort their babies, even if they died in the attempt, were impaled on a stake (274).

Women could become powerful in Assyria through marriage or manipulation, but generally speaking did not enjoy significant status, as women did in Babylonia. They could not be seen in public without a veil and marital infidelity was simply not tolerated. Husbands, however, were allowed concubines. A husband whose wife was unfaithful was within his rights in killing her lover. Prostitution was not only tolerated, it was regulated by the State (274).

Though this brief sketch has not done it justice, the Mesopotamian civilization, under Sumerian and Akkadian rule, was an intricate cultural tapestry far beyond anything the world at that time had ever seen. The subsequent civilizations of Babylonia and Assyria adopted that culture and were, therefore, extensions of that great Mesopotamian culture. Because Abraham is a key biblical character and was from Mesopotamia, and because when the Northern and Southern tribes of Israel were carried into captivity they were captives in Mesopotamia (Assyria 722 BC for the northern tribes, and Babylonia 606 and 586 BC for the southern tribes), Mesopotamian culture plays a significant role in the story told in the Old Testament Scriptures. In fact, the day-to-day lifestyle (culture) of Israel was very similar to Mesopotamian culture in many ways. Just as an American can travel to Great Britain and experience a level of cultural familiarity (there are minor differences to be sure, but generally speaking there is a great deal of similarity) so ancient Israelites would have been able to travel to Mesopotamia and other Middle Eastern countries and experience a similar kind of cultural familiarity.

Egypt

G. Herbert Livingston notes that settlements began to spring up in the Nile Valley as early as 5000 BC (1974:24). However, Egyptologist Lionel Casson notes that there were organized settlements along the Nile before 8000 BC (over 10,000 years ago). Archeological evidence indicates that people lived in Egypt 33,000 years ago, though probably not in what could be termed as organized settlements (Wendorf and Close 1992:Vol. 2, 331-333). It is in the Neolithic period (between 5000-3100 BC) that evidence allows for more precise information regarding the mixture of peoples who populated the Nile Valley (Starr 1991:54, Harrison 1970:99-101). Those people may have migrated to the region from Nubia in the south, Palestine and Syria in the North, and Libya in the west (Starr 1991:54).

As early as 4000 BC, the people who settled along the Nile lived in communities with an established government (Durant 1963:146). During this time, wheat, barley, and flax were cultivated and burial traditions (such as positioning a body on its side facing west and including provisions of food and equipment for hunting) were established practices. The Egyptians were well on their way toward a society that could accurately be described as a *civilization* by 4000 BC (Freeman 1996:16). They were not a unified people, however, until 3100 BC, putting the development of their civilization a few hundred years behind the development of Mesopotamian civilization. The unification of Upper and Lower Egypt was not so much an event as it was a process, occurring over the last centuries of the 4th millennium BC (Kadish 1992:342). Tradition, however, credits Menes as the ruler who unified the two kingdoms, establishing Memphis as his capital (Casson 1975:4).

Society in Egypt, as in Mesopotamia, rose to the level of a civilization with the invention of a system of writing, which appeared in Egypt around 3000 BC, a century or so after it was developed in Mesopotamia. Roberts suggests that the Egyptians may have learned from the Mesopotamians how to organize themselves into a civilization (1993:50), but Starr believes civilization arose independently in Egypt without outside influence (1991:51). With help or without, the Egyptians developed a civilization that was not only unique to them, but equal to the Mesopotamian civilization, and in some particulars (medical procedures, for instance) even surpassed it.

Egyptologists divide Egypt's past into chronological stages: the era before the beginning of the dynasties (protodynastic) 3200-2700 BC, the Old Kingdom 2700-2200, the First Intermediate period 2200-2052, the Middle Kingdom 2052-1786, the Second Intermediate Period 1786-1575, the New Kingdom 1575-1087, and the Post-Empire era after 1087 BC (Starr 1991:55). This cultural overview will not attempt to follow a chronological timeframe, but it is helpful to know how the historical timeframes fit together.

Agriculture was one of the cornerstones of Egyptian civilization. The Nile would flood its banks annually, not only watering the dry desert soil, but depositing a rich layer of silt that fertilized the land. With simple hand tools at first, then later with plows pulled by oxen, Egyptian farmers prepared the soil for planting. Fields would be divided up into square sections, with irrigation canals running between them (Casson 1975:35-41). After the seed was spread over the field in broadcast fashion, domesticated animals were used to trample the seeds into the soil. After the harvest, threshing was accomplished by driving sheep, goats or cattle over the grain that had been spread on the threshing floor (Baines and Malek 2000:191). Crops and produce included Emmer wheat, flax, barley, castor oil, grapes, sesame, and dates.

Another major product of Egypt was papyrus paper. Papyrus reeds (the stems of which could be 7-10 feet long) were harvested from the banks of the Nile, peeled, cut into strips, and through a complicated process made into paper. Not only did the Egyptians use this paper, they exported to other parts of the world for centuries.

Their pictograph form of writing, referred to as *hieroglyphics*, originally utilized pictorial symbols to stand for words or thoughts. As written communication evolved, hieroglyphs were used to denote sounds, and multiple hieroglyphs drawn in succession spelled out words. Twenty-four hieroglyphs were selected to represent twenty-four consonants. Vowels were never added, however, so an alphabetic form of writing using traditional hieroglyphics was not possible. This was acceptable as long as hieroglyphics were carved into stone. But when paper was invented and began to be used for a writing material, it was apparent that a more flowing form of script writing was needed—a writing style that could be used with a reed pen and ink, or a brush. A script form of writing was developed around 700 BC, (Baines and Malek 2000:198-201; Casson 1965:142).

As it had in Mesopotamia, the invention of writing required that people be schooled in its use. Scribal schools were established and the sons of important people were sent to master the skill. Boys as young as twelve years old completed school and began their careers as scribes, often in their father's business or profession.

Egypt's government rested on the shoulders of the pharaoh, the absolute ruler, the god-king. One of the most important gods in the Egyptian pantheon was Re, the sun-god. Eventually the pharaoh was considered the son of Re, the human incarnation of the deity. As the representative of the gods, the pharaoh was responsible for the rise and fall of the Nile, for a good crop, for a healthy economy, for the well-being of the army, and for peaceful relations with neighboring countries.

To maintain a unified kingdom was no small task. To assist him the pharaoh appointed a vizier, who was second in power to the pharaoh. Generally speaking, the vizier ran the country. He was the chief officer of the State, responsible for people, animals, crop production, building, taxation, trade, and all other civil affairs. In the Bible, this is the position which was granted to Joseph after he correctly interpreted the pharaoh's dream regarding the seven years of plenty and the seven years of famine.

Generally speaking, life in Egypt was good. Aristocrats lived well, but so did the average citizen. During the Old Kingdom (2700-2200) the population of Egypt may have been 2 million. By the period of the New Kingdom (1575-1087) population may have increased to between 3-4 million. Such increases in population would have been possible only if Egypt's agricultural and economic output could sustain them. There were probably three social classes in Egyptian society: 1) Aristocrats, which included royalty and those appointed to powerful government offices, 2) a middle class, which included less important officials, priests, high-ranking scribes, military officers, wealthy landowners, and skilled artisans, and 3) a lower class, including low-ranking officials, scribes, craftsmen and tradesmen, farmers, laborers, serfs, and servants. This lower class was the largest.

The family was an important social structure in Egypt. Society was patriarchal in structure so the father was the head of the family. Women, however, enjoyed significant prominence and power in society. They were probably illiterate and were, therefore, excluded from official positions. However, they were able to own land and engage in business. They could file lawsuits. A woman could own property separately from her husband, and while property was normally passed on from father to children, a woman who owned property could pass it on to her children independently of her husband. Women were responsible for home and family life. In wealthy families the wife supervised household servants. In middle class families she would have supervised and participated in household chores, such as cooking and making clothes. In lower income families with no servants the wife did all the work herself or may have worked outside the home to earn additional income (Silverman 2002). There was a limited amount of polygamy, but monogamy was expected. Adultery was frowned upon, especially a wife's (Baines and Malek 2000:204-205).

Children did not wear clothing of any sort until they began to mature, perhaps in their early teens. Clothing for mature people of either sex consisted of a short white linen skirt. Neither men nor women covered their upper body (Durant 1963:169). The Egyptians were very forthright about sex, with women often asserting their sexuality, initiating sexual encounters.

The Egyptians loved music. The musical instruments found in excavations include: flute, double clarinet, double oboe, trumpet, harp, lute, lyre, and drum. Wealthy Egyptians enjoyed owning beautiful objects and using various kinds of toiletries, including combs, ointment spoons, decorative containers for eye makeup, vases and mirrors. They owned elegant furniture such as chairs, stools, beds, chests, tables, and boxes, and valued fine clothes, jewelry and wigs. They enjoyed social functions involving food, drink, music, and dancing (Baines and Malek 2000:196-197).

The games and amusements of ancient Egyptian children involved simple toys—horses carved of wood for example. Adult children were responsible for caring for their aging parents, for burying them properly, and for proper maintenance and ritual connected with their tombs.

Servants were an important part of Egyptian society, especially among the aristocracy. In a presentation intended for a popular audience Casson notes that:

> Servants were essential to the well-run, noble Egyptian household. Some, trained in personal service, worked as maids, played musical instruments about the house, or tended to banquet guests. Others were employed outside the main house, cooking, baking, washing the laundry or working in the fields. Servants were frequently foreigners, Nubians and Asiatics taken in war. Others may have been bought in slave markets (1965:107).

Religion in Egypt was polytheistic and impacted virtually every area of life. John Wilson notes that, "the world of the ancient orientals was thoroughly saturated with the presence of the gods, so that every phenomenon and every process in man's life could be attributed to the agency of the gods. There was no separation of life into the religious and the secular" (1962:Vol. 2, 56). The Egyptians (along with all other ancient people) did not believe in the modern concept of cause and effect, which allows for "natural" causes to generate "natural" effects. Everything that occurred happened because a god wanted it to happen.

In every society there is the official religion or "theology" associated with it. Then there is the *folk religion* lived out on a day-to-day basis by average people. Historians know little of Egyptian folk religion since their homes were mud-brick and over the centuries were washed or blown away. There is, however, a great deal of information available on the official religion of ancient Egypt, for official religious events, beliefs, and practices were carved into stone and have resisted the ravages of time.

Wilson notes that the deities of Egypt can be categorized into three groupings: 1) gods or goddesses associated with specific locals such as Ptah of Memphis, or Khnum of the First Cataract, 2) gods or goddesses associated with the cosmos, such as Nut, the goddess of the sky, Geb, the earth-god, and Re, the sun-god, or 3) gods or goddesses responsible for specific functions, such as Ma'at, goddess of truth and justice, or Bes, goddess of the household and childbirth (1962:56). Baines and Melek's text include drawings or photos of actual idols representing twenty-six local and universal gods of the Egyptian pantheon. It is not an exhaustive listing.

The distinctive feature of Egyptian religion was its emphasis on immortality. As is the case with many religions (including the Christian faith), death was looked upon as a transition to another phase of life. This "theology" took time to evolve, but in time became the common belief of all Egyptians. Casson explains:

> At the beginning of the Old Kingdom, only pharaohs were entitled to an afterlife. But by the time of the New Kingdom, 11 centuries later, life after death was the expectation of all Egyptians. They carefully prepared for a hectic hereafter in which, according to one Egyptologist, "The dead man is at one and the same time in heaven, in the god's boat, under the earth, tilling the Elysian fields, and in his tomb enjoying his victuals."

For the wealthy, elaborate embalming and well-stocked tombs assured a house for the Ka, or soul, and the Ba, or physical vitality, which fled a body at death. But a dead man still went forth to be judged by Osiris, god of the underworld. Osiris, weighing his virtues and faults, could then mete out either a renewed life in eternity—or a second death of extinction (1965:81).

Note the works orientation of Egyptian "theology." A similar orientation still permeates much religious thought today. If one's good deeds outnumber or outweigh one's bad deeds, then one can be granted eternal life. This represents a common pagan perspective[8].

The ancient Egyptian civilization was well-advanced in areas of mathematics and medicine. Mathematically, the Egyptians used arithmetic and developed basic concepts in geometry. They also understood the use of fractions. Medically, some of the earliest known medical texts were produced by Egyptians, dealing with internal medicine, surgery, pharmaceutical remedies, dentistry, and veterinary medicine (Silverman 2000).

Familiarity with Egyptian culture is important in understanding the story that unfolds in Scripture, for Egypt played a significant role in the lives of individuals in the story (Abraham, Joseph, Moses), and in the development of the nation of Israel. The four hundred years the people of Israel spent in Egypt impacted their worldview, that is, their way of understanding the world. Even if the people of Israel kept somewhat to themselves and were not fully assimilated into Egyptian society, the presence of Egyptian culture all around them for generations would have impacted their way of thinking and living. For instance, the Wisdom Literature of the Hebrew people (the book of Proverbs, for instance) bears a striking resemblance to the "wisdom literature" of other Near Eastern cultures, including that of Egypt, which is

---

[8] Unfortunately this also represents the perspective of many Christians who have a legalistic understanding of Christianity.

considerably older than Hebrew wisdom Literature (Garrett 1993:19-26). The Israelites were, in part, the way they were because of the influence of Egyptian culture.

Generally speaking, Israelite culture was more like Mesopotamian culture than Egyptian culture, but there were similarities between Israel and Egypt. Many day-to-day features of Egyptian culture also became common features of Israelite culture. It is essential to remember the impact of ancient Middle Eastern culture in general on the specific cultural development of the nation of Israel. It is important to remember that God worked with Israel within the framework and context of that general culture as he communicated with his people.

Canaan

Canaan is the region along the Mediterranean coast north of Egypt, west of the Jordan River, extending north to the southern border of Syria. Since it lies between Egypt and Mesopotamia it was part of the well-traveled trade route between those two centers of ancient civilization. Humans have lived in Canaan, as they have throughout the entire Near Eastern region, since the Stone Age. The earliest evidence of an organized culture in the region is the ancient city of Jericho. Archeological evidence suggests that people were living at the site of Jericho as early as 9000 BC. Between 8500-8000, Jericho became a walled city, making it one of the oldest cities yet discovered (Holland and Netzer 1992:Vol. 3, 723-740). By 3000 BC, the people who came to be known as Canaanites inhabited the region known as Canaan, speaking a Western Semitic language (Haldar 1962:Vol. 1, 494-498).

The origin of the names *Canaan* and *Canaanite* are difficult to ascertain. Some have linked them to the red or purple dye marketed widely by the Canaanites. The color of the dye was called Canaan and some have suggested that the geographic region was named after the color of the dye that originated there (McCarter 1993:98). Others have linked the name to the Phoenicians who were renowned traders of the ancient world. Since a secondary meaning of the word Canaan or Canaanite is *merchant* or *trader*, it is thought that the term Canaanite may have been used to refer to the Phoenician traders who settled along the Mediterranean coast. Schmitz notes that the name may trace its roots to the Western Semitic language (the language the Canaanites spoke) and that it may have come from the word meaning "to bend, to bow." Thus the Canaanites may have been named for their social custom of bowing (1992:Vol.1, 828). The true origin of the names Canaan and Canaanite may never be discovered.

Some scholars have suggested that the terms Canaanites and the Amorites are two terms describing the same people. Others speak of the Amorites as one of the Canaanite tribes (Bright 1972:114 and Haldar 1962:Vol. 1, 115). Biblically speaking, the name *Canaanite* is used of a specific tribe of people (Ex. 3:8), or as the generic name of the many people groups that inhabit the region (Josh. 13:1-6). In this section, the term Canaanite will be used in the generic sense to refer to the many tribes of people who inhabited the geographic region known as Canaan.

The Canaanite culture more closely resembled the civilization that developed in Mesopotamia rather than the culture of Egypt. The Phoenician culture also impacted Canaanite culture. The Western Semitic language spoken by the Canaanites may have Phoenician roots and their renown as merchants and traders may be traced to the Phoenicians as well. However, since there were a number of individual tribes that peopled the region of Canaan, their "culture" was something of a heterogeneous conglomeration of many local traditions rather than a single unified society. There are, however, some general similarities that can be noted.

The Canaanites lived in walled cities in smallish houses made of mud bricks. The layout of the cities does not suggest a great deal of planning was done before building began. The cities were busy, congested places of international trade where their purple dye was marketed along with olive oil, wine, ivory, various kinds of metal, cedar logs, and various kinds of agricultural produce (Gray 1964:53-103).

While most of the Canaanite houses were smallish, a few were large affairs, built around a large courtyard. This likely indicates a feudal society where a few nobles owned the land and peasants worked it for them. These would have represented opposite ends of the socioeconomic spectrum with a class of tradesmen and craftsmen in between.

Weddings were important social events, as was the birth of children. Celebrations were connected with both. Marriages were arranged and the custom was for the groom to pay a bride price for his bride. The society was patriarchal and polygamy was acceptable for those who could afford multiple wives. Death was understood as a "season of passage" (Gray 1964:115), perhaps reflecting some Egyptian influence in their thinking.

Both Mesopotamian and Egyptian influence can be seen in political traditions. Canaanite kings were thought to have a special relationship with their gods, so much so that the king was "regarded as the special channel of divine power and blessing to the community" (105-107). Mesopotamian influence became the dominant cultural influence in Canaan largely through the introduction of writing. As it had in Sumer, the availability of writing for political, economic, social, religious and literary concerns allowed for the development of a formal civilization, even though it was not a homogeneous society (Haldar 1962:Vol. 1, 496).

Canaan was predominantly an agricultural society. The industrious household farmers produced wheat, barley, grapes, olives, beans, maize, and other fruits and vegetables. There were also those who kept flocks and herds. There were scribes, artists, and craftsmen of various types. There were professional soldiers who commanded the military. Citizens paid taxes and the kings could "draft" people into public service in building or maintaining roads, fortresses, temples, or to work on royal lands (497).

Canaanite religion included a crowded pantheon that was headed by El, the supreme god who was the "final authority in all affairs human and divine" (Gray 1964:121). He was known as the *Father of men*, and as the *Kindly* and the *Merciful*. He was also referred to as the *Bull*, probably denoting his strength, and as the *Creator of Created Things* (121). As the most high god, El was beyond the reach of any evil power. El's mistress/wife was the goddess Athirat. Through her, El fathered the gods Shabar, the dawn, and Shalem, the dusk.

Though El was the Canaanite high god, Baal was the *active expression* of El. Baal was constantly engaged with the powers of chaos. In each case he emerged victorious. Baal was envisioned as young and vigorous, and was known as the Mighty, the Mightiest of Heroes, or the Prince. He is lord of the fertility cult and the god of vegetation. Known as the *rider of the clouds*, Baal was responsible for bringing the rain that made the ground fertile (Day 1992:Vol. 1, 831).

Baal had two consorts, Anat, who was completely devoted to him and constantly at his side, and Astarte. In some ancient documents Astarte was not as prominent as Anat, yet in the Bible Astarte (called Ashtoreth) appears as Baal's mistress (832).

Though El was the most high god, Baal was considered the king of Canaan. His enthronement was celebrated annually by Canaanite Feast of Tabernacles, similar to the Hebrew Feast of Tabernacles, which commemorated Israel's wandering in the wilderness (833).

Sacrifice was an important feature of Canaanite religion, including human sacrifice, often in the form of child sacrifice. When animals were sacrificed (sheep, cattle, etc.), the blood would be offered, along with internal organs and the fat surrounding them—sacrificial methodologies virtually identical to those practiced later by the Israelites under the Mosaic Covenant (Gray 1964:125). Sacred prostitution was also practiced. Young women would be dedicated for a time to sacred prostitution and engage in various kinds of sexual activity as acts of worship (Day 1992:Vol. 1, 834). The Canaanites also made and paid vows in their religious observances, and sought divine guidance, as did the Israelites (Gray 1964:125-126).

It is interesting to note that the God of Israel, before he revealed his personal name, *Yahweh*, was referred to as *Elohim*, a name derived from El, and is known variously as El-Shaddai, El-Olam, El-Roi, El Elohei Israel, El-Eyon, and so forth, all derivatives of El. The similarity of Israelite religion to Canaanite religion indicates that God was interested in using existing local religious forms to communicate with his people in ways that were familiar and understandable to them. Some of the Canaanite religious practices were absolutely unacceptable to God, such as human sacrifice and sacred prostitution. Those and other unacceptable practices were rejected by Yahweh. But practices that were not objectionable were utilized by Yahweh as he established and ordained Israelite religious practices. Yahweh utilized aspects of the existing religious and social cultural context to facilitate effective communication and comprehension.

Understanding the Canaanite culture is vital to understanding the context in which the Old Testament was produced. The Israelites were influenced by the Canaanite culture, often in detrimental ways. Some aspects of the Canaanite culture were unacceptable to God. Others were acceptable. Understanding the general worldview and the subsequent sociocultural perspectives of those people provide us with important insights into why the Israelites behaved as they did. The ancient Israelites, like all people, were products of their cultural context. God had to take their cultural context into consideration in order to communicate effectively with them. That included accommodating some of the cultural perspectives that were common in that day—perspective he was not thrilled with, but which he was able to tolerate: such as slavery, polygamy, and patriarchy, to mention only three.

Persia

Another major culture that plays an important role in the story told in Scripture is that of Persia, roughly equivalent to modern-day Iran. In his article on the Persian Empire, Pierre Briant notes that:

> In the third quarter of the 6th century B.C., the political geography of the Middle East underwent a profound change. Divided around 550 between powerful contemporary kingdoms (Babylonia, Egypt, Media, Lydia), it would be, in the decades that followed, unified by the conquests of the Persians, a small group practically absent from historical documentation until the time when, under Cyrus the Great (560/59-530), they began their indomitable expansion. Under the reigns of the first three representatives of the new "Achaemenid" dynasty, the territory controlled by the Persian armies continued to extend in all directions at a very rapid pace (1992:Vol. 5, 236-237).

Little is know about the Persian people before the reign and military campaigns of Cyrus the Great. They came, evidently, from Central Asia around 1000 BC and settled in the region known as Susa, the land of the Elamites (237). Under Cyrus' competent leadership the Persians quickly conquered Media in 550, Lydia in 547, and Babylon in 539 (Starr 1991:276-277).

One of the unique features of Cyrus' rule was that he decreed that peoples displaced by previous kingdoms could return to their ancestral lands if they so desired. The Israelites, who had been displaced by Nebuchadnezzar of Babylon and had spent seventy years away from their homeland, were allowed to return to Palestine.

Another unique feature of Persian rule (begun by Cyrus and developed more fully by Darius) was the division of the vast empire into twenty manageable administrative units (provinces) called *satrapies*. Each satrap administrator was given a fair amount of autonomy as long as taxes and tribute were appropriately paid (Dresden 1962:Vol. 3, 742). Traveling inspectors were appointed by Persian kings to inspect provincial administrations and be the king's "eyes and ears" throughout the extensive empire (Starr 1991:279).

The Persians, for the most part, survived as farmers and cattle breeders. The land was arid so substantial resources went into irrigation operations. "Culturally the Persians were far less civilized than most of their subjects of the Fertile Crescent, and they showed originality only in the field of religion" (280). That religion is Zoroastrianism.

Zoroastrianism was founded by the Persian prophet Zoroaster, also known as Zarathushtra. Some historians doubt that Zarathushtra was an actual person, but others find enough evidence to confirm his existence (Eliade 1978:302-303). The sacred book of Zoroastrianism is called the *Avesta*. Only a small portion of it survives today. According to Mary Boyce, Zoroastrianism became the official State religion of the first Persian Empire, founded by Cyrus in the 5th century BC (1997:237). R. C. Zaehner, however, says that it became the official State religion of Persia during the second great (Sassanian) Empire dated in the 3rd century BC (1988:201). Even if Zoroastrianism did not become the "official" religion of Persia until the 3rd century BC, it appears to have been a significant force in Persian culture in the 5th century BC when Zarathushtra lived and taught. The *magi* who came from the East to acknowledge Jesus' birth were Zoroastrian astrologers (Boyce 1997:237).

Before Zarathushtra came on the scene, the Persians were thoroughly polytheistic, worshipping many gods by means of rituals common to pagan cults (Zaehner 1988:201-206). Zarathushtra was a priest within Persia's existing religious system. He challenged their traditional beliefs, however, by insisting that there was only one eternal God (a capital "G" God as he understood him). For Zarathushtra this God was *Ahura Mazda*, who was completely wise, good and just, though not all-powerful. Ahura Mazda had an Adversary, *Angra Mainyu*, who was the Evil Spirit. It is unclear whether Angra Mainyu is also thought to be eternal, as was Ahura Mazda, or is the created counterpart of *Spenta Mainyu*, the Holy Spirit. Boyce suggests that Angra Mainyu was believed to be uncreated (1997:243), but Zaehner and Eliade argue that if it was believed that Ahura Mazda was the one eternal God, then Angra Mainyu, the Evil Spirit, would have been understood as a created counterpart to Spenta Mainyu, the Holy Spirit (Zaehner 1988:204, Eliad 1978:310). This explanation seems preferable. According to Zarathushtra, Ahura Mazda was the one eternal God who created other spirits. Angra Mainyu and Spenta Mainyu were two of them. Each had free will and one, Angra Mainyu, exercising his freedom of choice, chose to do evil. This choice put him in conflict with Ahura Mazda, initiating the cosmic struggle between good and evil.

For Zarathushtra, the basic struggle between good and evil had to do with monotheism (good) versus polytheism (evil). He taught that to choose *Asha* (Truth or Justice) was good, and to choose *Drug* (Lie or Deceit) was evil. Zarathushtra taught that worshipping the many gods of the Persian pantheon was evil because it was rooted in a lie. Since there was only one eternal God, worshipping him alone represented truth. The choice between good and evil was the choice between who and how one would worship (Eliade 1978:310).

This very brief overview of Zoroastrianism is sufficient to illustrate how different it was to the standard polytheistic pagan religions of centuries past. It is also sufficient to illustrate how similar in some points Zoroastrianism was to the truths Yahweh had revealed to his people Israel. As the Israelites lived out their time in captivity (which was punishment from Yahweh for participating in the polytheistic idolatry of Canaan) they would have become aware of the teachings of Zarathushtra. The similarities had to have made them think, and perhaps explore the truths of their own faith and theology more deeply. Their own prophets had warned them of the evils of worshipping other gods. Finding themselves captives in a foreign land and hearing a very similar message from a foreign prophet had to have impacted them.

Obviously, much of what Zarathushtra taught is not in harmony with what Yahweh has revealed in Scripture. Yet Zarathushtra did hit upon some truth: 1) that there is one eternal God, 2) that people are free to choose between good and evil, 3) that there is an evil presence in the world that has made himself an adversary of God, and 4) that there is a holy presence in the world that is an ally of God and all that is good. Without a doubt, Christians would explain these concepts differently than Zarathushtra did, but the similarities between his teachings and those of Yahwehistic monotheism are undeniable. Surely the Israelites noticed this as they reflected on their past behavior and the unhappy circumstances that resulted. The cultural context in which they found themselves included a spiritual context that would have impacted the way they thought about their relationship with God and their behavior as people of faith.

I would not suggest that the Israelites adopted aspects of Zoroastrianism and incorporated them into the faith. I do not believe that anything Jesus taught grew out of anything

Zarathushtra taught. I do believe, however, that Zarathushtra may have had a few genuine spiritual insights (perhaps revealed to him by God) upon which the Israelites could have reflected in positive ways. Zarathushtra's insistence upon abandoning the pagan cults and worshipping the one true God (even if Zarathushtra did not know who that one God was) could have impacted the Israelites in a positive way while they were in captivity.

Whether one acknowledges this possibility or not, one thing is certain, when the Israelites returned from captivity they no longer engaged in idolatrous practices. They abandoned the "lie" of polytheism and embraced the "truth" of monotheism. There is little doubt that the main impetus for their abrupt about face was Yahweh and his prophets—Ezekiel, for instance. But their temporary cultural context may have been helpful as well.

What has Persia got to do with Israelite culture and God's communication with his people? The Israelites were captives in Persia for many years. The experience impacted them as a people. While in Persia their language changed. They probably developed the synagogue system while there—a major change in their worship practices. They changed their thinking and behavior regarding polytheism. When the possibility of returning to their homeland presented itself some took advantage of it, some did not. Why not? Because for many of them, Israel was not their home. Few, if any, were still living who actually remembered it. They were now the people of another culture, another language, another perspective. They were still God's people, but they were culturally different. The ones who returned were different as well. They were not the same people, culturally speaking, who had been carried away into captivity because of idolatrous behavior. They were so culturally different that when they did return and the Law of God was read to them it had to be translated and explained. The old ways of communicating did not work any longer.

Israel after the captivity was a very different society than it had been, say, in Jeremiah's day.

Greece

The culture of ancient Greece is one of the most significant civilizations in the world, ancient or contemporary, and is important in understanding the role of culture in the production and presentation of the Scriptures (especially the New Testament) because of its pervasive influence throughout the ancient world. Civilization had developed in Mesopotamia 2000 years before the Greeks even began to think like civilized people. But as Greek culture and civilization developed and reached its peak, it became, in many ways, the most influential civilization the world has ever known.

Before the Greeks began building their civilization, the Minoan civilization of Crete dominated the islands and the lands surrounding the Aegean Sea. Their presence was felt from 1600 to 1400 BC. During the same time the people of Mycenae (on the Greek mainland) built a rich civilization that flourished until 1200 BC. The Mycenaeans were a wealthy people who delighted in building. Some of their palaces had walls ten feet thick. They were an industrious people with a highly evolved society. Records discovered by archeologists indicate a royal bureaucracy that included "tax assessments, land holdings, agricultural stores, and inventories of slaves, horses, and chariot parts." They list over 100 occupations present in Mycenaean society, including: goldsmiths, shipwrights, masons, bakers, cooks, woodcutters, messengers, longshoremen, oarsmen, saddlers, shepherds, dry cleaners, doctors, heralds, potters, foresters, carpenters, bowmakers, weavers, bath attendants, and unguent boilers" (Bowra 1965:32). They were also a warrior society.

Over a period of years the Mycenaean society gradually disintegrated. Civil strife, economic disruption, and successive waves of invasion and infiltration by a group of people from the North called the Dorians, proved to be more than the Mycenaean civilization could withstand. The Dorians became a formidable presence in Greece (on the mainland and throughout the Islands), though they were not able to subjugate all of the native Greeks. Athens, for instance, was able to stand against their invasion (33-34). The fall of the Mycenaean civilization plunged Greece into 450 years of social darkness. From 1200 to 750 BC, "the Greek world passed through a Dark Age from which only scattered legends and unrewarding artifacts survive" (32). But when that Dark Age past, the Greeks began to define themselves more clearly (Starr 1991:205). The City-State evolved and the political, social, and philosophical foundations that made Greece great were laid.

Greek City-States were originally ruled by kings. Each city (*polis*) was an independent entity. But those independent, local kings were gradually replaced in each polis by a counsel of aristocrats—wealthy Greeks who thought themselves superior to those not of their own socioeconomic class. The citizens of a polis would assemble periodically to elect officials and vote on issues (208). Bowra notes that Greek citizens assembled 40 times each year to deliberate on important issues (1965:108). Greek society was not egalitarian, but all citizens, regardless of social standing, were protected by law and enjoyed justice.

The splendor of Greek society—their beautiful works of art, their political and philosophical contributions—have been the focus of much attention for centuries. Yet the mundane permeated their society as well. Freeman has noted that "the majority of Greeks spent most of their time as farmers. . . 90 percent of the population of ancient Greece cultivated the land and had no other option if their city was to survive" (1996:169). Two factors beyond their control

99

made their agricultural endeavors a backbreaking task to be endured: poor soil conditions and unpredictable rainfall. Primitive tools did not make the job any easier, and the ever-present possibility of insufficient rainfall, resulting in a poor crop, lent itself to a constant anxiety. Maintaining a surplus of grain and other produce was essential for survival in drought years as well as for trade and dowries for daughters.

Planting and harvesting were busy times. During slack times, after planting in early spring and during the summer and early fall before harvest, the Greeks would busy themselves with their athletic games (170).

As is always the case, the Greek agricultural economy involved caring for animals. Sheep and goats required pasture. Shepherds would move herds across the lands outside the polis. No one owned the land. Herds were moved from place to place depending on grazing and water (171).

Even though farming provided the foundation of Greek society, there was a manufacturing aspect as well. Sheep were sheared for wool; iron, and clay were mined and sold. These enterprises were small scale, but contributed in a meaningful way to the economy (171).

Though the Greeks have become renowned for their advanced thinking in some areas (democracy, the rule of law, philosophy, the importance of the individual), in other areas their thinking was limited (as it is for all people) by their worldview and cultural assumptions. Their thinking regarding slavery was one of these areas. It is estimated that in 430 BC the population of Attica, a polis not far from Athens, was 315,000. About 115,000 (over 36 percent) of them were slaves (Bowra 1965:94).

The most common form of slavery was "chattel" slavery. The slave was owned outright by his or her master and had no rights whatsoever. Slaves worked in the mines, on farms, in workshops, or in households in various capacities. Household slaves might be involved in cleaning and cooking and other household chores. Some household slaves served as teachers or household overseers. Their daily lives may have been quite comfortable compared to those who worked in other capacities.

Not all Greeks advocated slavery. Bowra points out that the playwright Euripides referred to slavery as evil by its very nature, for it required a kind of submission that was beyond that which should be expected of anyone. Aristotle, however, attempted to defend slavery by suggesting that some people were naturally inclined to servitude (1965:95).

Another aspect of Greek society where otherwise enlightened people seemed to be operating in the dark had to do with the place of women in society. Greek society was patriarchal to the extreme. Greek boys were educated. Greek girls were not. Greek men were required to be involved in society. Greek women were not permitted to be involved in matters outside the home to any significant degree. In the older ages of Greek society women enjoyed greater freedom, though were never allowed to engage in politics. As centuries passed, however, their freedoms were limited. Their place was in the home and their role in society was to have children and to keep silent (95). Property was owned by men and inheritance was patrilineal. In families where there were no sons to inherit, the daughter who inherited would be married to a near kinsman (effectively allowing him to inherit) so property would remain in the family.

The city of Sparta appears to have provided an exception in these matters. Sparta had been dominated by Dorian attitudes and was more interested in warfare than other Greek cities. The men of Sparta were often away on military campaigns leaving their wives to manage affairs on the home front, thus allowing them greater social and economic latitude.

The most important day in a woman's life was her wedding day. Greek women (girls) would be married between the ages of ten and fifteen to husbands in their late twenties or early thirties. A young woman would go directly from her father's house to her husband's. Marriages were arranged. Dowries were paid. And while it is not entirely accurate to say that women in ancient Greece were thought of as property, for all practical purposes that is the way life was lived (Freeman 1996:177-178).

The wedding ceremony consisted of a purifying bath for the bride followed by a ride with the groom and his best friend in a cart to the groom's house. Upon arriving at the groom's home the new wife would be welcomed to the family by her mother-in-law before being taken to the bedroom where she and her husband would consummate the marriage (178).

Religion in ancient Greece was polytheistic. "The aim of Greek cult [religion] was to protect mankind during its life and to secure continuation of the group. Problems of individual survival after death, of individual ethics, or even of the origins of the world emerged only partially and were not always to be answered in religious terms" (Starr 1991:238). Religious rituals and sacrifices were conducted at the altars outside of local temples. Prayers to the various deities were offered inside the temple. Twelve gods or goddesses were eventually elevated to primary positions— the gods of Mount Olympus. Zeus was the father, Hera was his wife, Poseidon, Hestia, and Demeter were his brothers and sisters. Zeus' children were Athena, Artemis, Aphrodite, Apollo, Hermes, Ares, and Hephaestus. In addition to these primary gods and goddesses there were numerous other local deities worshipped throughout the Greek world.

It was to these gods and goddesses, and other powerful supernatural creatures, that the Greeks prayed and offered sacrifices in order to assure a plentiful harvest, safe passage during travels, profitable business, victory in battle, and whatever else may have been perceived to be in the hands of the gods. Prayer, of course, was an important element in Greek worship. The central feature, however, was an animal sacrifice offered by the family father on their behalf. The animal (usually a sheep or goat) was slaughtered and bled. The blood, along with the fat around internal organs would be burnt in sacrifice. The meat of the animal would be cooked and consumed in a ritual meal by the family offering the sacrifice. If all of the meat could not be consumed it would be sold in the marketplace.

One of the reasons Greek culture became such a dominant force in the ancient world was that in spite of some of its shortcomings it was an excellent civilization. They did things well. The other reason was Alexander the Great. The Greek City-States eventually came under the control of Philip of Macedonia. When Philip died in 336 BC, his son, Alexander, at the age of 20, became king in his father's place. Bowra notes that "when Alexander ascended the throne at the age of 20, Macedonia's power was so firmly established, and Philip's policy of expansion so well developed, that the young king with his dream of a unified world needed only to pick up where his father had left off" (1965:157). Alexander set out to consolidate his control of Greece and did so without too much difficulty. Only Sparta successfully resisted Alexander's dominance. Rather than engage in a protracted war with the powerful Spartans, Alexander allowed them to remain independent.

Once Alexander had solidified his control over nearby regions, he set his sights on the Persian Empire. The Persian Empire was gradually weakening and since 401 BC the Greeks had known they could defeat the Persians. A Persian renegade named Cyrus had been determined to take the throne of his brother Artaxerxes II. He hired an army of Greek mercenaries as his invading force. Cyrus was killed and the Greek army was held off but not defeated. In fact, they defeated the left wing of the Persian forces and were able to make their way safely back home through Persian territory. Knowing he could defeat the Persians, Alexander began his campaign.

Aristotle had been Alexander's teacher. He instilled in Alexander a love for all things Greek. As Alexander began his push south and east his plan was to civilize the world by establishing a Greek empire. In each region his army conquered, Alexander established Greek cities. Soldiers were allowed to settle and become residents, marrying local women and establishing Greek culture (Freeman 1996:273).

Spreading Greek culture was one of Alexander's goals. He wanted to unite East and West in one grand culture that was Greek through and through. That meant speaking the Greek language, understanding Greek philosophy, attending the theater and stripping naked to exercise at the gymnasium. It meant, for those who were willing, thinking and acting like a civilized Greek in every respect. Alexander, however, and those who came after him, were wise enough to allow for cultural variation due to local and religious traditions. Jews, for instance, were not going to strip naked and exercise at the gymnasium, and they were going to continue the practice of circumcision—a practice considered barbaric by the Greeks. Generally speaking, however, Alexander accomplished his goal. The known world, so Greek in its outlook, was truly a *Hellenized* world (Freeman 1996:274-283).

There is little doubt that the Hellenization of the ancient world had a tremendous impact on the production of the Scriptures. After all, the New Testament was written in Greek. Christian concepts were explained from a Greek point of view. While most of the men who wrote the New Testament were Jewish, the man who wrote most of it, Paul, was a *Hellenistic* Jew whose writing reflects more Greek influence than Hebrew.

There is a very obvious difference between the "feel" of Paul's writing as a Hellenistic Jew and the writing of

James, Peter and Jude, whose work has a very Jewish feel to it. This is one reason Peter referred to Paul's writing as containing some things that are hard to understand. For Peter, who had a thoroughly Jewish worldview, Paul's writing, which reflected a Hellenistic worldview, felt unfamiliar to him. Reading something written by someone with a different worldview is like putting on a new pair of shoes. The shoes may fit and you may be able to walk in them, but they certainly do not feel like your comfortable old slippers. Paul's letters were like new shoes (sandals?) to Peter rather than an old pair of slippers because Paul's letters were written from a Greek perspective rather than a Jewish perspective.

Why would God have arranged things so that so much of the New Testament was written by Paul from a Hellenistic perspective rather than from a Jewish perspective? Because most of the people in that time and place were not Jewish. Most of the people Paul wrote to were Hellenistic. They needed letters written to them that were culturally appropriate for them. By utilizing Paul the way he did, God was meeting the cultural needs of believers in that time and place.

So pervasive was the Hellenistic culture on Christianity that although the Christian faith sprang from Jewish roots (and in its earlier days was an entirely Jewish movement) by the end of the first century Christianity was, for the most part, not associated with Judaism. Christianity had been shaped by the dominant culture of that time and place--Hellenism. This was, of course, what God had planned. This is why God selected and commissioned Paul—so he could spread the Gospel in the Hellenistic world. The old Jewish ways, which would have hindered the spread of the Gospel in the Hellenistic world, were set aside, replaced with culturally appropriate ways of thinking, communicating and doing. As Jesus explained, you can't put new wine in old wineskins.

Rome

According to legend, Rome was established by Romulus, one of the twin sons of Mars, the god of war. In fact, the city of Rome was most likely established by the Etruscans, a people who migrated to the northwest coast of the Italian peninsula from Asia Minor perhaps as early as 1000 BC. The indigenous people of the region were dominated by the powerful Etruscans. Moses Hadas notes that the Etruscans were highly civilized with a love for music and dancing. They were capable warriors and politicians (1965:35). They were also very religious and sought divine guidance in affairs of daily life. Many of their gods (approximately two-thirds) appear to have been borrowed from the Greeks (Freeman 1996:305). Greek culture appears to have had a significant impact on Etruscan civilization.

Small pastoral settlements in close proximity to each other along the Tiber River probably merged into a village, growing eventually into the city of Rome. During the 6th century BC, many different people groups inhabited the region now known as Italy: Etruscans, Greeks, Ligurians, Veneti, Carthaginians, Italic, and Messapii Iapyges (Hadas 1965:37). Under Etruscan leadership, Rome emerged as a dominant force in the midst of the sociopolitical interaction and intrigue of these various people groups.

According to tradition, the last Etruscan king of Rome was Tarquin The Proud, whose reign came to an end in 509 BC. The end of his reign marked the end of a monarchy and the beginning of a republican form of government in Rome. While Hadas notes that the transition from monarchy to republic "was accomplished with relative ease," he also notes that, "the history of the early Republic is the history of the struggle of the common people for a larger voice in the government and for social equality" (36).

In the early days of Roman society there were two basic classes: patricians, the aristocratic upper class, and plebeians, the common people (36). By the first century, a slightly different social structure had evolved. There were still upper class patricians—nobles who held pubic office. There was also an *equestrian* middle class of businessmen who were similar to knights. Finally there was the large common class of plebeians, which included liberated slaves who, though free, were not full citizens (79). There was also a huge number of slaves. Freeman notes that by the end of the first century as much as 40 percent of the population of the Roman Empire may have been slaves (1996:455-456).

The earliest Romans were farmers.

> The earliest Romans were farmers in a hostile land, and no matter how urbanized Rome later became, Roman roots remained firmly fixed in the soil. From their pioneer forebears Romans inherited respect for strength and discipline, for loyalty, industry, frugality and tenacity... Strength clothed with dignity was the Roman ideal, (Hadas 1965:12).

The Romans preferred enduring strength over delicacy, power over agility, mass over beauty, utility over grace. They were a straightforward, practical people. Problems were analyzed and solutions were developed and carried out efficiently and effectively.

The family was the basic social unit of Roman society. It was a patriarchal society with absolute control of the family resting with the husband/father (Adkins and Adkins 1994:339). Marriages were often arranged, with parents selecting partners for their children. However, mature couples also married on the basis of mutual consent. Monogamy was the *official* expectation for married people. The Romans defined marriage as "a union of man and woman, a partnership of all life, a sharing of rights human and divine" (Hadas 1965:80). The egalitarian language notwithstanding, women had few rights within a marriage. A newborn child would be brought to the father and laid at his feet. If he picked it up, signaling his acceptance of the child, all was well. If, however, he did not pick the child up the child would be exposed to die or sold into slavery. The wife/mother had no say in the matter. A husband could divorce his wife for adultery, but the wife had no such recourse. Regardless of the official attitude toward monogamy, it was understood that a husband could take a mistress or make use of a slave or a prostitute for sexual satisfaction. There was no religious or social stigma attached to divorce and the practice was widespread. In the case of a divorce, children remained the property of the father. Unwanted pregnancies would be terminated by abortion (Adkins and Adkins 1994:339-340).

As noted above, slavery was common and even "middle class" families could own two or more household slaves. Slaves and their children were the property of their owners. Some were treated better than others, but slavery was still slavery. "There is evidence that slaves on agricultural estates were chained, working in gangs in the fields in the daytime and locked in prisons at night, particularly in southern Italy and Sicily. They could also be branded or wear inscribed metal collars so that they had little chance of successful escape" (342).

If a father picked up the newborn child laid at his feet, accepting responsibility for that child, it would be given a name nine days later in a birth celebration. It was the father's obligation to educate and train his children. In the early days of the Empire, parents may have been personally involved in teaching their children. As time passed, however, the well-to-do of the Empire hired educated Greeks (or utilized educated Greek slaves) to educate and care for their children.

The educational path for boys was different than for girls. Both boys and girls were given a basic education, learning together reading, writing, arithmetic. At age twelve or thirteen girls would no longer attend classes. They returned home and received further education by a private tutor. Roman women were very well educated, many of them better than their male counterparts. Boys continued to receive their secondary education in a formal setting. At about age sixteen they enjoyed a coming of age ceremony and were granted citizenship. Their education would then continue as they learned composition and oratory at an advanced (college) level (Hadas 1965:81-82).

Describing the religion of Rome, Hadas notes that:

> It was, to begin with, a religion of form, of ritual, with little emphasis on the spiritual. The Roman made a compact with his gods—you do something for me and I will do something for you—and his religion was largely a meticulous observance of that bargain. Second, it was an external, communal affair, rather than an internal experience (1965:121).

The earliest forms of Roman religion were animistic. As their ancestors had for thousands of years in the lands of their origins, Romans worshipped spirits who inhabited trees, rocks, and animals, or who existed independent of material creation, interfering in the world of humans as they pleased. Those spirits, called *numina*, had to be respected and worshipped. They were not to be offended. Offending a spirit could result in great misfortune. If an offense occurred, a sacrifice designed to appease the offended spirit was necessary.

As Greek influence became more pervasive in the developing Roman culture, the more ancient animistic forms of religion were superceded by a more formal or highly developed approach. The Greek gods and myths surrounding them were adopted and worship was directed toward them rather than to local spirits. The basic pagan concept, however (described above by Hadas), remained the same even though sacrifices were being offered in a more formal structure to gods rather than to spirits.

As noted above, many of the Roman gods were Greek gods the Romans appropriated and renamed: Their high god Jupiter evolved until he became identical to Zeus. Venus became Aphrodite and Hera became Juno. Some Greek gods, such as Apollo, were adopted into the Roman pantheon without the benefit of a name change (Hadas 1965:124). Adkins and Adkins list 223 gods worshipped by Romans. The list includes the gods and local spirits not just of the Greeks, but of people groups throughout the Empire. As Roman religion evolved, becoming more formal on the State level, individual families continued to honor local *numina*. As far as they were concerned, there was no point in risking an offense by failing to honor a local god or spirit. The consequences for such an offense could be serious. Such is the nature of pagan worship: honor all who might be able to make life difficult. Don't leave anyone out.

The Romans, as all ancient people, understood the world from a supernatural, holistic point of view. That is, they did not think in naturalistic, scientific, compartmentalized terms as do contemporary Western people. For them, all of life was holistically integrated; and everything had a connection to the supernatural world. There were, therefore, gods and goddess for just about everything. There were numerous gods and goddesses for war, fertility, rain, harvest, and so forth. They were responsible for the important and foundational concerns of life. But there were also highly specialized gods and goddesses associated with more mundane concerns. For instance, Forculus was the god of doors, Cardea was the goddess of door hinges, Limentius (or Limentinus) was the god of the threshold, Spiniensis was the god who presided over the digging up thorn bushes, and Sterculinus was the god of manure-spreading (1994:256-273).

The city of Rome was a noisy, dirty, smelly place. Wealthy patricians lived out of the city in country villas, avoiding the city as much as possible. The crowded streets of the Imperial city were filled with hungry, bored people who were out of work—perhaps 150,000 unemployed citizens—dependent on the State for a daily ration of bread. One of the ways the Caesars kept them distracted was with numerous official holidays (over 180 per year) and circuses filled with amazing and violent spectacles. The Colosseum could hold 50,000 spectators, and the much larger Circus Maximus could hold 260,000 people assembled to cheer on the chariot racers. The brutality and carnage witnessed during these events served as an outlet for the people's pent up frustrations—frustrations that might otherwise have materialized as aggression toward the State (Hadas 1965:45).

"One of the key elements of the expansion of the Roman world, and its subsequent consolidation and control, was efficient communications, which allowed effective policing of the provinces and encouraged trade throughout the empire" (Adkins and Adkins 1994:169). Travel had always been a difficult and dangerous task. The Romans set out to minimize both the danger and the difficulty. One of the most important things they did was to build a series of interconnecting roads across their vast empire. Initially, the roads were built to facilitate the movement of troops. However, the roads, with maps and routes posted at regular intervals and inns and way-stations along the way for rest, refreshment, and even medical care if necessary, made travel for business or personal reasons safer and faster. By the time of Diocletian's reign (about 285 AD) there were 372 main roads that stretched for over 53,000 miles (Adkins and Adkins 1994:172).

Latin was the official language, but Greek (thanks to Alexander the Great) was the common spoken language throughout the empire. A common language and roads patrolled and maintained by the Roman army made travel, whether for government, business or personal reasons, safer and easier than it had ever been in the ancient world.

The Implications of the Bible's Multicultural Context

Religion has an enormous impact on a society's culture. But culture also has an enormous impact on a society's religion (Dearman 1992:3). Many specific cultural practices of ancient Israel, the culture in which the Scriptures (for the most part) were produced, developed as a result of the Law of Moses. That law was the civil and religious, social and moral code given by God to the people of Israel. It was designed to produce a *holy* society that reflected their relationship with the Holy God, Yahweh. But many of the things God incorporated into that covenant were standard, existing, typical cultural practices in that part of the world at that time. And while the covenant provided legislation for most aspects of daily life, it did not provide detailed legislation for *every* aspect of daily life. In those cases, God's people were allowed to decide for themselves what to do and how to do it.

For instance, God did not tell the Israelites what crops they had to grow and what agricultural techniques to use to grow them. Neither did God tell the Israelites what style of clothing to wear, what language to speak, how to go about the task of educating their children, how to write or what to write on, how to sing or what kind of music to enjoy, or how to dance. On and on the list could go but this is sufficient to make the point: there was a great deal of Israelite culture that did not develop as a result of specific legislation from God. Where, then, did it come from? The Israelites borrowed much of their culture from the people with whom they came in contact, which, over the centuries included: the Mesopotamians, the Egyptians, the Canaanites, the Persians, the Greeks, the Romans, and a number of less significant cultures.

What does this cultural borrowing have to do with the Scriptures? The Scriptures are a divine-human collaboration. Human culture is everywhere in the

Scriptures. God communicated his message to selected humans who in turn recommunicated it (verbally and in writing) to others. The people with whom God communicated were, as are all people, products of their cultural context. God communicated with them within the framework of their culture. That is the only way humans can communicate. As God's messengers recommunicated God's message to others, they did so within the framework of human culture—the ancient Israelite culture, first-century Jewish culture, or in the case of several of Paul's letters, first-century Hellenistic culture. The communication took place within the context of human culture and human culture is laced throughout the communication—because communication is culture-bound and culture-laden.

The presence of human culture in Scripture is not surprising, but it is challenging. Since none of the cultures in which and for whom the Scriptures were produced still exist, it is necessary for us to determine which aspects of Scripture were uniquely tied to those original cultures and which ones extend beyond the bounds of those original cultures to people in other places and times. We need to determine which parts were cultural and which were supracultural.

The implication and challenge of the multicultural context of the Scriptures has to do with developing a process for separating the supracultural message of God (the eternal message that transcends time and culture) from the cultural context in which it was delivered. Before this can be accomplished, however, it is necessary to look more closely at the various developmental stages of Israelite culture.

CHAPTER 5

ISRAELITE CULTURE

The people of Israel did not yet exist when the cultures of ancient Mesopotamia, Egypt, and Canaan evolved into civilizations. The people of Israel and the cultures that emerged throughout the different stages of their life as a nation of people came into existence with the call of Abraham and the birth of his son, Isaac. Isaac's son, Jacob (whose name was changed to Israel), became the father of a large family that, over many generations, grew into the nation of Israel.

Stages of Worldview and Cultural Development

To understand the worldview and earliest cultural forms of the people known as Israel, it is essential to understand the cultures of the ANE—Mesopotamia, Egypt, and Canaan.

Abraham was born in the Mesopotamian city of Ur likely in the twenty-second century BC, perhaps between 2170 and 2160 BC. It is especially important, therefore, to understand Mesopotamian culture during that time, for it was that cultural context that shaped Abraham's worldview, providing him with a framework for thinking and living.

114

Life in Ur in the twenty-second century BC was civilized and metropolitan. Abraham and his family lived in a comfortable two-story mud-brick house. Abram (as he was called then) may have been a livestock breeder, that is, a keeper of flocks and herds. He would have recorded his business transactions on clay tablets in the Akkadian language. The society of Ur was orderly, governed by written laws. As noted earlier, the oldest known law code is from Ur, dated very near the time Abraham lived there. The culture of ancient Mesopotamia was rooted in a holistic, supernatural view of the world. The gods controlled everything and every aspect of life was connected to every other aspect of life. There was nothing similar to our modern Western naturalistic, compartmentalized view of life. Religion was polytheistic. Society was patriarchal. Slavery was commonplace. Nomadic peoples were considered uncivilized.

At some point, Terah, Abraham's father, moved his family from Ur to Haran, an important city in Northwestern Mesopotamia. Abraham's life in Haran was probably very much like it had been in Ur, breeding and selling livestock. After Terah died, Abraham (prompted by God) moved his family down into Canaan where, except for a brief sojourn into Egypt, he lived for the rest of his life.

Canaanite culture had been deeply impacted by Mesopotamian culture. So even though Abraham left his native Mesopotamia to live in Canaan, the cultural context was not entirely unfamiliar to him. The major cultural (lifestyle) shift for Abraham was that he no longer lived in a walled city in a brick house. He became semi-nomadic (which socially was a major step down—his friends in Ur would have considered him uncivilized), living in a tent, moving his herds and flocks where water and pasture were abundant. The semi-nomadic lifestyle adopted by Abraham when he left Haran became his family's way of living for at least three generations, until their move to Egypt resulted in changes in their status and lifestyle.

From the time of Abraham to the coming of Christ and the establishment of the church, God's people lived in many different cultural contexts. This chapter will provide an overview of the many cultural changes the Israelites experienced over the centuries and the implications of those changes for interpreting and applying the Scriptures in our contemporary cultural context.

A Canaanite Semi-nomadic Pastoral Culture

Though Abraham lived in a tent and moved about with his flocks and herds, he was not a true nomad. According to De Vaux, a true nomad (or Bedouin) is a camel breeder who moves about the desert (1961:3). A more correct designation for Abraham is *semi-nomadic pastoral*. He was not able to live in the same harsh desert climate with his sheep as a true nomad could live in with his camels. Abraham's sheep and goats required more grass for grazing and more water. They could not move as far between grazing and water as camels. Abraham could not venture out into the harsh desert east of the Jordan, but needed to stay in the more moderate climate of the Palestinian hills between the Jordan and the coast of the Mediterranean Sea.

Adjusting to a New Way of Living

Abraham's adopted semi-nomadic lifestyle in Canaan resulted in a very different day-to-day routine than he had enjoyed in Ur. Abraham's native language was Akkadian. The people of Canaan spoke a Western Semitic language which Abraham would have had to learn to communicate effectively with his new neighbors. He no longer enjoyed the security of living in a walled city or being part of a homogenous group of people whose written laws guaranteed certain rights, freedoms and protection—all of which he would have enjoyed as a citizen of Ur.

While the Canaanite culture was similar to Mesopotamian culture, the people among whom Abraham lived in Canaan were not his people. Their customs were not his customs. Eventually, when Isaac was grown and needed a wife, Abraham sent his servant back to Northwestern Mesopotamia (probably the region of Haran) to obtain a suitable wife from among relatives. Why? Because the Canaanites were culturally different. Because Abraham and Sarah wanted a wife for their son who understood their language, their customs, who would be able to "fit in" with their family.

One of the main differences between Ur and Canaan had to do with religious practices. While it is clear that Abraham knew and worshipped Yahweh (though Abraham did not know him by that name), it should not be assumed that Abraham was not also very familiar with the gods of his homeland. The religious practices of the Mesopotamians were ancient by the time Abraham was born and he would have lived as a full participant in that religious context. That Yahweh had revealed himself to Abraham does not mean that while in Ur and Haran Abraham did not worship the Mesopotamian gods. We do not know when or how Abraham became acquainted with Yahweh. Once Abraham came to know Yahweh, he worshipped and obeyed him. At some point (either in Mesopotamia or in Canaan) Abraham began to worship Yahweh exclusively. But there is no reason to believe that Abraham did not believe in the existence of the many gods of the Mesopotamian pantheon. When he arrived in Canaan, he encountered a new pantheon of gods and goddesses and different customs associated with their worship, all of which would have been very foreign to him.

Ancient Worldviews

Abraham's assumptions about life (his deep-level underlying worldview assumptions) would have been similar (though not identical) to those of the Canaanite people. All the people of the Near East during those centuries held similar assumptions about the nature of life in this world. As noted above, their worldview was fundamentally supernatural and holistic. These two factors affected every other aspect of their lives. As far as relationships were concerned, ancient Near Eastern people were group or family oriented. This is in contrast to contemporary Western people who are individualistically oriented. Concerns for punctuality did not govern the daily schedule of ancient Near Eastern people. They were more concerned with the quality of an event than with its duration. Every aspect of life was fully integrated with every other aspect of life. The gods controlled all things and it was absolutely essential that they be honored regularly to avoid incurring their wrath. If an offense did occur, it was essential to offer an appropriate sacrifice to appease the offended deity and guarantee his or her continued blessing. Abraham would have shared these common assumptions with the Canaanites. Eventually Abraham began to worship Yahweh exclusively, but his basic assumptions about how things worked in a world controlled by supernatural forces would have remained the same—honor God to ensure his continued blessings.

Generally speaking, as a Mesopotamian, Abraham shared the same basic worldview assumptions as the Canaanites. However, the same basic assumptions held by different groups of people can manifest themselves in different forms of behavior, or different cultural practices. So even though Abraham shared a common view of life with his Canaanite neighbors, Abraham's customs were different. The differences between himself and his new neighbors required some adjustments on Abraham's part.

Abraham's Culture

There are several aspects of Abraham's culture that deserve specific mention. The polytheistic nature of his culture has already been noted. Another is that Abraham's culture was thoroughly patriarchal. Patriarchal cultures are built on the foundation of male dominance. In a patriarchal culture, when a woman married she became a part of her husband's family. She had few rights and lived entirely according to his will. She called him Master or Lord (Perdue 1997:181). If he died, it was necessary for her to be cared for by another male—a mature son or another male member of her dead husband's family. Every aspect of a woman's life was dominated first by her father, then by her husband.

In most patriarchal societies, descent is reckoned through the father's line and property is passed on through the father. These are referred to as patrilineal societies[9]. *Patriarchal and patrilineal practices are products of human culture, not of divine planning. They were invented by humankind after sin entered the world. They are present in the Bible because Abraham was from a patriarchal, patrilineal culture, not because God ordained them as his preferred method of human interaction.*

In Abraham's culture it was also permissible to marry one's close kinsman. Sarah was Abraham's half sister. They had the same father, Tarah, but different mothers. When their son, Isaac, need a wife, Rebekah, his cousin was chosen to be his wife. Another cultural feature related to marriage was the practice of polygamy. Abraham's father had multiple wives. So did Abraham. It was a common cultural practice that God saw fit not to condemn. It is unlikely that God's original intention for human marriage included polygamy. But once sin entered the world,

---

[9] In contrast, the Navajo Indians are a matrilineal society. Descent is reckoned through the mother.

polygamy, like polytheism, patriarchy, and slavery soon followed. While God did not intend for these things to happen, he allowed them to happen. He accepted them as part of human culture and they became part of the biblical story. *It is important that we understand the origin of these practices. God did not ordain patriarchy any more than he ordained slavery, polygamy or polytheism. These practices were products of human culture—practices that God saw fit to accommodate until humankind matured, outgrowing such foolish behavior.*

An Egyptian Captivity Culture

Abraham passed his culture on to his son, Isaac, who passed it on to his sons, Esau and Jacob, who passed it on to their children. In the biblical story, it is Jacob who becomes the prominent figure because it is through Jacob that God's promises to Abraham will be fulfilled. For four generations (Abraham, Isaac, Jacob and Jacob's sons) the culture of God's chosen people remained essentially the same: they were a semi-nomadic pastoral people. They were patriarchal and patrilineal, with a holistic, supernaturalistic, family/group orientation. They were a polytheistic people. They believed in the existence of, though did not worship, many gods. They were a polygamous, slave-utilizing clan of people. They were products of their particular cultural context (and of the larger ancient Near Eastern cultural context) and God's association with them occurred within the framework of that cultural context. But then everything changed. Joseph's brothers became jealous of him and sold him into slavery. Joseph ended up in Egypt. Eventually Jacob's entire family ended up there. It was a social and cultural change that allowed (perhaps *forced*) a single clan of people to grow into a nation of people. In the 400 years they lived in Egypt, at first as free people, then as slaves, Jacob's family became the nation of Israel.

The people of Israel could not escape the cultural impact of their time in Egypt any more than they could escape the cultural impact of Abraham's native Mesopotamia or his adopted Canaan. The Israelites were who they were because of their history as a people. They were not Mesopotamian or Canaanite. Neither were they Egyptian. But they were influenced by all three of those powerful cultures. In what ways did their time in Egypt impact them?

Egyptian Culture

A previous section has dealt with Egyptian culture and it is not necessary to duplicate that material here. But a brief summary may be helpful. Egyptian culture was ancient by the time Jacob's family arrived there as guests of the pharaoh. Egyptian knowledge of medical procedures was unsurpassed in the ancient world. They were the first ancient society to have a highly developed expectation for an afterlife. Religion permeated every aspect of Egyptian life, for the gods controlled every aspect of Egyptian life. Their system of writing and record keeping promoted effective business transactions and political procedures. A good standard of living was available to not only to the aristocrats but to common people as well. Egyptians enjoyed a love of music, dancing, and food. Though Egyptian society was patriarchal and patrilineal, women enjoyed a prominent position in society. They were able to own property and pass it on to heirs separate from their husbands. Egyptians, like all ancient peoples, made use of slaves for manual labor (farming and building) as well as household chores. While there was a significant emphasis on building (temples, pyramids, and so forth) Egypt was very much an agricultural society, depending on the Nile to water and fertilize the desert soil.

The Israelites as Slaves in Egypt

John Bright notes that there is little extra-biblical evidence regarding the Israelite sojourn into Egypt. However, even for scholars who do not accept the biblical record simply because it is the biblical record, the biblical material regarding Israel's stay in Egypt is so unique and, in many ways so unflattering, that one is swayed toward acceptance of the material. As Bright asks, who would make up such a story about themselves, (1961:119)?

For a period of time, Jacob's family lived as honored guests of Pharaoh. They lived in the land of Goshen, somewhat removed from major Egyptian population areas. The Egyptians did not think highly of livestock breeders, so even though the Israelites were welcomed guests, they were not expected (or allowed) to assimilate into Egyptian society. It is likely that in those early days of their move to Egypt they continued to live in their tents. However, as years and generations passed, and as their status changed from guests to slaves, they abandoned their tents in favor of Egyptian style mud-brick homes.

Making the shift from semi-nomadic tent living to brick houses—a significant cultural shift—would have been accompanied by other subtle changes. There is a permanence associated with living in a brick house as opposed to a tent. It involves a resignation that *I am here to stay*. That may have been difficult for the Israelites for several reasons. First, they were simply not accustomed to settled living. Second, they had been told for generations that the land of Canaan would one day be theirs. Settling in Egypt would have appeared to run counter to that expectation. Third, settled life in Egypt, even if the Israelites remained somewhat separate from mainstream Egyptian culture, would have been different from life in Canaan. Canaan had been influenced more by Mesopotamian culture than by Egyptian culture. The Egyptian language was different.   Egyptian clothing was very different.   So was religion.   The food was different.   Burial customs were different.   Climate, though not radically different, was not what the Israelites had been used to.   Since the Egyptians did not appreciate livestock breeding as a profession, living among them and doing business with them must have been difficult for the Israelites.   All of these differences, and hundreds of other minor cultural differences would have made life in Egypt, at least initially, something that required adjustment and change.

The most dramatic change, however, came when the Israelites were no longer considered guests.   The details of exactly what happened and when are not available.   The biblical record simply tells us that a pharaoh who did not know Joseph came to power and subjugated the Israelites.   Their status changed from resident aliens to slaves very quickly and there was, apparently, nothing they could do about it.

One of the tasks they were given was that of making sun-baked mud-bricks.   They may also have been utilized as laborers in building monuments, temples, and royal cities and residences.   However, we know that when Israel left Egypt they took their herds and flocks with them.   Whatever else they were required to do, they were evidently allowed to continue breeding their livestock.

The specific work to which they were assigned is not as important as the fact of their slavery.   As slaves, they had no rights.   They lived where they were told to live and did what they were told to do.   They lived and died at the whim of the pharaoh.   Such is the lot of the slave.

For over 400 years (according to Scripture) the people of Israel lived among the Egyptians.   They would have absorbed much of the Egyptian way of thinking and living.   Clearly, they did not simply become Egyptian.   They were not completely assimilated into Egyptian culture.   But it is not possible that they remained unaffected by Egyptian

123

worldview assumptions and social customs. Like all people, they were impacted by the world in which they lived, by the people among whom they lived.

A Desert Semi-nomadic Pastoral Culture

The book of Exodus records God's intervention in the national life of Israel, freeing them from slavery in Egypt. Upon leaving Egypt they entered the Sinai desert, where, eventually they wandered for forty years, reestablishing the semi-nomadic pastoral cultural similar to that of their ancestors Abraham, Isaac and Jacob.

The biblical record provides a great deal of detail regarding Israelite culture during their wilderness wandering. When they left Egypt, the Israelites took with them their herds and flocks. They lived in tents and moved about in search of water and grazing on their way to the mountain of Yahweh, where they would receive his law as they entered into a covenant with him. That covenant would become the foundation of much of their culture from that time forward. However, as semi-nomadic pastoral people of the ANE, they held certain worldview assumptions that were common for that place and time. Their worldview was holistic, supernaturalistic, polytheistic, group oriented, event oriented. Polygamy was an accepted practice, as was slavery and patriarchy.

To this foundation of common worldview assumptions and social practices, God attempted to add concepts and behaviors that reflected his interests for his people. He wanted them to be a holy people. He wanted them to live by a higher standard, to think and behave differently. To accomplish this, God entered into a formal covenant relationship with the Israelites and gave them a detailed law to live by. The law he gave them was both religious and civil. It covered not only such things as when, where and how to worship God, but provided rules for daily living, including property rights, civil liability, sexual behavior, marriage, civil policing, a system of taxation referred to as tithing, and so forth. A portion of Israelite culture grew out of the law God gave them during the semi-nomadic days of their wilderness wandering, making it a hybrid culture that was a blend of practices that grew out of God's expectations for them as his holy people and typical cultural practices of the ANE.

A Pre-Monarchy Agrarian Culture

After the end of their forty years in the wilderness, Israel entered the promised land—the land of Canaan. Abraham had immigrated to Canaan from Mesopotamia by way of Haran hundreds of years before. The Phoenicians as well as the Mesopotamians had left their cultural mark on the Canaanites. The Canaanites spoke a Western Semitic language, utilized an alphabetic system of writing, worshipped a group of gods unique to their geographic region—worship that often included sexual immorality and occasionally human sacrifice—carried on trade in distant locations, lived in walled cities, and made and drank beer and wine. They were primarily an agricultural people. When the Israelites displaced them, they took possession of private compounds, walled cities, brick houses, plowed fields, vineyards, olive groves, wells, threshing floors, and more. In a relatively brief span of time, Israel went from being a semi-nomadic pastoral people to being a settled *agropastoral* people. That is, they no longer lived in tents, but in the brick houses, compounds and walled villages built by the Canaanites. They maintained their flocks and herds, but also engaged in agricultural practices. The blending of agriculture and breeding and maintenance of livestock (agropastoral) is generally understood to be included the term *agrarian*.

Archeological evidence during this time in Israelite history is abundant and provides a reliable picture of daily life (culture) in Israel during the Iron Age (1200-586 BC).

Philip King and Lawrence Stager note that:

> For the Israelites, family and kin groups organized around agrarian activities provided the basic elements of daily life and generated the symbols by which the higher levels of order—the political and the cosmological spheres—were understood and represented. . . The family and household provide the central symbol about which the ancient Israelites created their cosmion, the world in which members of that society expressed their relationships to each other, to their leaders (whether "judge" or, later, "king"), and to the deity (2001:4-5).

At the ground level of Israelite society was the household, the *bêt 'āb*, literally, the *house of the father* (4). The physical house and grounds (the compound) was part of the household, as were the members of the family. The compound may have been equal in size to five or six standard city lots. It was a walled area large enough for perhaps two houses, a garden, a few trees, areas for firewood and hay, a place for watering the animals, and an area for grinding grain into flour, other food preparation activities, and cooking.

The typical Israelite house during that time is referred to as a pillar house (Meyers 1997:14). It was rectangular in shape, made of sun-baked mud-bricks. Two rows of pillars running the length of the house separated the large central room from the additional rooms on either side of the rows of pillars. The houses were two-story and had three or four rooms. A door at one end of the house opened into the main room of the house. A ladder led to a second story room where the family slept together. A stairway on the outside of the house led up to the flat roof which served as a place for drying various kinds of produce, or for outdoor sleeping on hot summer nights. The roof could also be used for other utility functions, such as bathing, or an out of the way place to eat or meditate.

The typical Israelite did not have furniture as we think of it. Each individual had a "bed" that consisted of a thin *mat* that could be rolled up and carried from place to place. There were cooking utensils and storage jars. There may have been a small table and a chair or two. There could have been a lampstand, or small oil lamps could have sat on the table and/or on a ledge built into the wall (King and Stager 2110:28-30).

It is in the structure of the family unit that we encounter the basic assumptions of Israelite society— *assumptions that permeated the ANE long before Israel existed as a people or before God gave them his law*[10]. King and Stager describe the ancient Israelite family as: "endogamous, patrilineal, patriarchal, patrilocal, joint, and polygynous" (38). Examples of each of these practices can be found in the Old Testament.

Endogamy refers to a preference for marriage between close blood relatives. *Patrilineal* refers to property being passed from one generation to another through the father's line of descent. *Patriarchy* refers to male dominance and control in the family. *Patrilocal* refers to the practice of a new couple living with, and the bride becoming part of, the groom's family (in contrast to *matrilocal* where the new couple lives with and the groom becomes part of the bride's family). *Joint* (or joint family) refers to the multigenerational makeup of the family. Normally three

---

[10] This is an important point. If a particular behavior or way of thinking (polygamy, patriarchy, slavery, or polytheism for example) existed generally throughout the Near Eastern world two thousand years before God gave his law to the Israelites, it is difficult to trace those ways of thinking and behaving to God, suggesting that he specifically wanted his people to think and behave in those ways. The assumptions that led to those behaviors and the behaviors themselves were products of human culture and not part of God's original ideals for the way humans ought to interact with each other and with him.

generations (grandparents, parents and children) would make up the family unit. *Polygyny* (or more commonly referred to as polygamy) refers to the practice of having more than one marriage partner (38).

There were provisions in the Mosaic Covenant (or a lack of legislation against them) that allowed for each of these typical cultural practices. But these were practices of God's people, and of people of the ANE, long before God demonstrated his willingness to tolerate them by making allowances for them (or accommodating them) in his law.

Eighty to ninety percent of the population of Israel lived in rural family compounds during the early days of their settled life in Canaan (King and Stager 2001:21). Self-sufficiency, therefore, was highly valued (Blenkinsopp 1997:53). In addition to self-contained family compounds, small villages dotted the Israelite landscape. Populations in these villages may have varied from between 50 to 150 (Meyers 1997:12).

Though Israelite society was patriarchal, women played a prominent role in society. In addition to giving birth to children, and raising them through infancy and childhood, women were responsible for providing the family with food and clothing. They engaged in crafts of various kinds (spinning wool, making baskets, tapestries, mats and so forth) and shared in the management and upkeep of the compound. They participated in community activities, including worship. While leadership roles were normally reserved for men, women did occasionally hold prominent positions. Deborah served as a judge over Israel. Huldah was a prophet. Miriam, Moses' sister, enjoyed some prominence as a leader. Hannah, though not a leader in the public sense, is portrayed in Scripture as a very significant person, used by God to accomplish his will.

Marriages were arranged and a bride-price paid to the bride's father as compensation for the loss of a daughter. Marriage was viewed as a civil contract rather than a religious ritual (Collins 1997:107-110). Brides went to live with and be a part of the groom's family. The wedding ceremony itself was probably quite simple. The groom and his friends may have gone to the bride's home to accompany her to his house. She would be attired in her finest clothing, veiled so she could not be seen. She would be escorted to her new home amidst singing and dancing. If the distance was too far to be easily walked, she would ride in a cart with her groom and his friend—the *best man*). Upon arrival at her new home (her father-in-law's compound) the bride would be greeted by family and perhaps additional friends. The most important person to greet her would be her new mother-in-law, who would officially welcome her into the family. After appropriate introductions and greetings, the groom would escort his new bride into his room, or perhaps across the compound to his house, where the couple would consummate their marriage. A wife referred to her husband as *ba`al*, master, or *ādôn*, lord (King and Stager 2001:54-55).

The ancient Israelites ate three meals each day. Breakfast was light, a piece of bread or fruit. The midday meal was also light, perhaps some bread dipped into a vinegar-based wine. The evening meal was more substantial. It was a stew of vegetables sopped up with bread. Meat would only have been added to the stew on special occasions. Wine, the common drink, was consumed along with the meal.

Because the Israelite economy was agropastoral and households were self-sustaining, money (silver) was not the common means of exchange. A barter system where goods were exchanged for other goods allowed families to trade for what they needed. Items traded in Israel included: barley, wheat, olives, olive oil, grapes, wine, lentils, dried peas, pomegranates, beans, raisins, dried figs, dates, almonds, milk, cheese, butter, oxen, sheep, and goats. It wasn't until much later in Israelite history (during their exile) that Jews began to branch out into non-agrarian pursuits (193-194).

129

Children were a considered a blessing from God. Boys were especially valued for they would carry on the family name. This did not mean, however, that daughters were not valued as well. The concept of a bride-price involved compensation to the father of the bride for the loss of his daughter to his family. In an agrarian society every person is valuable, for every person contributes to the well-being of the family unit. Children in ancient Israel were probably given household responsibilities when they were five or six years old. Small children and girls were taught by their mothers. Older boys were taught by their fathers. Education included training in social and religious as well as gender specific responsibilities (Perdue 1997:172). Formal education did not develop for the average child until post-exilic times. In the early days of Israelite society most people were probably illiterate (173).

With the household as the central structure of Israelite society, it is not surprising to find that religion in ancient Israel was also family oriented. While God had given specific instructions regarding the priesthood and sacrificial system related to the tabernacle (which was eventually replaced by the temple), it should not be assumed that those corporate, national religious rituals and festivals constituted the entire religious life of ancient Israel. Religion, when it was practiced as God intended, was lived out within the structure of the Israelite household. Family worship revolved around the weekly observance of the Sabbath. From sundown Friday to sundown Saturday, the family rested and remembered Yahweh as creator and deliverer. The exact traditions of the Sabbath in the earliest days of Israel are unknown. Over the years traditions would have been modified. It is likely, however, that a special meal was prepared Friday evening. Wine was poured, a prayer was prayed. The meal was eaten. It was a family worship service.

In addition to the weekly Sabbath, there were annual holy feasts in which the entire family participated. They would travel to the tabernacle to offer sacrifices and worship as a family in the larger "family" of Israel. 1 Samuel 1 tells how Elkanah and Hannah went each year to the tabernacle in Shiloh to worship. There were three feasts each year that were to be attended by all Israelite men: the feast of unleavened bread, in April, known also as Passover; the feast of weeks, in June, later known as Pentecost; and the feast of tabernacles, in September or early October. While all men over twenty years old were required to attend these festivals, the entire family often traveled to the tabernacle (and later to the temple in Jerusalem) to worship together. Sacrifices were offered, prayers were prayed, meals were eaten, Yahweh was honored.

Politically speaking, Israel at this time was a loosely organized confederation of clans or tribes. They lived without the benefit of centralized leadership until a crisis arose, at which time God would raise up a judge to lead the people. The judges, however, did not function as government officials in the standard sense of the term. They were more like warrior-prophets than kings. When a judge died he was not replaced until another crisis arose that required the divine selection and appointment of another judge.

Life in Israel in those early years after the conquest of Canaan was a unique blend of ancient Near Eastern cultural practices and specific religious and civil behaviors ordained by Yahweh for his people. Part of the challenge of studying the Old Testament is distinguishing between those cultural practices which were common in the ANE and which ones owe their origin to God.

A Monarchy Agrarian Culture

The period of the monarchy in Israel begins with the reign of Saul, around 1050 BC and continues to the time of exile in 586 BC. During this time much of Israelite culture remained rural and family oriented, as described in the previous section. There is, however, a major change worthy of notice: the movement from a loosely organized tribal or clan society to an organized State under the central leadership of a king. This represents a significant cultural development.

The twelve tribes of Israel, referred to as pygmy States by De Vaux (1961:91), were small and must have felt quite vulnerable when compared to the vast empires of Egypt and Mesopotamia, and even to the smaller but politically organized States surrounding them—Edom, Ammon, Moab, Philistia, Tyre, Aram. Add to this feeling of vulnerability the desire to be respected and considered a political equal and you have the makings for political unrest and change. The Israelites wanted a king. The fact that they wanted a change in their societal structure indicates that they had begun to think of themselves differently. Their individual tribal mentalities had coalesced into a unified national identity, at least at a conceptual level. The loosely organized clan identity typical during the times of the judges took several generations to meld into the unified national identity finally achieved during the reign of David.

Most of the traditions of daily life remained unchanged during these years of political reconceptualization and reorganization. The people's worldview remained essentially the same: holistic, supernaturalistic, polytheistic, group and event oriented. They continued to practice patriarchy, polygamy and slavery. They remained an agropastoral people, living mostly in rural contexts. David's capture of Jerusalem and its establishment as the capital city of Israel may have spurred an interest (for a few restless souls) in a more urban approach to life. Beyond that, however, for the average person little of daily life changed in any dramatic way during the monarchy.

A Captivity Culture

If there were only moderate cultural changes during the pre-monarchy and monarchy periods of Israelite history (1200-586 BC), the period of their history that involved captivity in foreign lands brought worldview and cultural changes that shook the foundations of their society. The monarchy in Israel lasted technically until 586 BC, when Nebuchadnezzar of Babylon destroyed Jerusalem and the first temple. There had been, however, previous attacks and people had been taken captive in 606 BC. The prophecy regarding the length of Israel's captivity (70 years) is calculated from that invasion and deportation in 606 to 536 BC, when Cyrus of Persia decided that people displaced by previous imperial regimes could return to their homeland. During those seventy years in captivity the Israelites, for all practical purpose, became a different people. They did not stop being God's people, they did not stop being Israelites. But their thinking about themselves, about God, and about how to live (that is, their worldview) underwent significant change. When their worldview changed so did their culture.

First, the very fact that God had allowed them to be defeated and carried into captivity and had allowed his temple to be destroyed was a shock to their sense of who they were in relation to God. For some of them the question would have been, *How could God have let this happen?* For others the question was, *How could God have done this to us?* That God allowed such a tragedy to occur or that he actually caused it was both humiliating and demoralizing. Such a blow to a people's personal and national self-esteem erodes certainty and causes them to question deeply-held assumptions about the nature of things. It causes them to reevaluate things, creating an openness to new ideas and new influences. Cultural upheaval paves the way for dramatic cultural changes (Rogers, E. M. 1995:180-181).

What kind of cultural changes occurred among the Israelites in captivity? John Bright and Charles Pfeiffer both point out that the Israelites who were carried into Babylonian captivity were not forced to assimilate fully into Babylonian culture. They were allowed to form their own communities and live as they saw fit (Bright 1972:346; Pfeiffer 1973:422). The prophets told them to settle down and plan to stay a while. They did. They built brick houses and found ways to make a living. Many of them continued an agropastoral lifestyle, while some became merchants and tradesmen of different sorts. Their new trades may have included specialties such as carpentry, tentmaking, fishing, brickmaking, bricklaying, and so forth. None of these endeavors would have been unknown to the Jews. But to specialize in a trade more closely associated with an urban lifestyle rather than the farming activities of a rural lifestyle was a major cultural shift for the Jews.

Even though the deported Jews lived in their own communities where it was easier for them to maintain their group identity, it was still necessary for them to learn a new language so they could communicate with the people around them. To trade goods and services, to buy and sell, one must speak the *trade language*, which in that time and place was Aramaic. Learning a new language involves learning new thought patterns. It opens one up to all sorts of new perspectives and new ideas, which slowly and unconsciously become part of one's worldview.

Accepting the need to be adaptable is another result of cultural upheaval. Such acceptance may be conscious or unconscious, but it is imperative for survival. Israelite culture had not changed significantly for hundreds of years. Suddenly everything familiar was gone. They had to learn to adapt. They were in a new land, among a new people who had different ways of thinking and behaving. If the Israelites were to survive as a distinct people they needed some way to preserve their national identity. Their religion was one of the key features of who they were. They were the people of Yahweh. But Yahweh's temple in Jerusalem had been destroyed, his holy place lay desolate. This had happened because of the unfaithfulness of the Israelites, because of their idolatry. How could the Jews keep their faith intact? How could they rebuild their relationship with God? One way was to establish places in each Jewish community where God's law could be read and discussed and where their children could be taught about their heritage as God's people. Israelite adaptability manifested itself in the development of the *synagogue* system.

The synagogue system, which became a standard feature of Jewish culture, was probably established during the exile (Meyers 1992:Vol. 6, 251-252). With the temple in ruins and the priesthood unable to function in any meaningful way, the synagogue filled an important social and religious gap. It was a place of worship, education, fellowship and community activity. It became a key feature of Jewish life. Along with Sabbath observance, the synagogue helped the Jews retain their identity. Yet it had not been part of God's design for worship in the Sinaitic Covenant. It was an addition to what God had ordained. It was an exercise in adaptation, designed to meet new needs that arose out of new circumstances.

The religious thinking of the Jews was impacted in other ways as well. While the Jews were in exile the Babylonians were overthrown by the Persians. A Persian priest named Zarathushtra began teaching a system of belief known today as Zoroastrianism. As noted in a previous section, he proclaimed that the polytheistic ways of the old religions were wrong and that people should worship the one true God, whom he knew as Ahura Mazda. Zarathushtra also taught that humans had free will and determined their own destiny by the choices they made as they lived out their lives in the midst of a cosmic struggle between the forces of good and evil. While we would not want to suggest that the teachings of the New Testament regarding monotheism, good and evil, and the free will of human beings originated with Zarathushtra, it is difficult to deny that his teachings would have had an impact on the Jews in exile. As noted earlier, Zarathushtra's message in many ways was similar to the messages of the prophets (Ezekiel and Daniel) who condemned idolatry and blamed the exile on the poor choices the people of Israel had made. How could they not have noticed the similarity of Zarathushtra's message and considered the validity of what he had to say about free will and the struggle between good and evil?

Another change that had long-term effects on the Jews as a nation was the loss of their king and their status as a sovereign nation. From the time of their deportation, they never really regained their freedom and sovereignty. Though not slaves as their ancestors had been in Egypt, for hundreds of years, except for a brief time of independence between 143-63 BC, they remained a conquered nation, subject to the laws of those in power: the Babylonians, the Persians, the Greeks, the Seleucids, the Romans. Living as a subjugated people involves a very different corporate cultural consciousness than living as free, sovereign people.

The cultural changes prompted by life in exile (for those who continued to live in foreign lands and for those who returned to Palestine) took the Israelites in a new direction socially. They spoke a new language, enjoyed the benefits of a "trade class" of citizens, participated in a new kind of community worship, became thoroughly monotheistic, and began to entertain religious ideas far beyond anything their ancestors had considered in the years gone by. The Jews were still Jews after their forced exile ended, but they were also a very different people. They were the same but not the same. They had changed and would continue to change over the next several hundred years. Culture is not static. It is dynamic. It changes and evolves as time passes and circumstances change.

A Post-exilic Agrarian Culture

In 536 BC, the Persian king, Cyrus, decreed that all peoples displaced by previous regimes could return to their homelands. Many of God's people wanted to return to the land of their ancestors. One of the returning groups was led by Zerubbable, who initiated the rebuilding of the temple, which was completed in 516 BC. Another to lead a group of captives back to Jerusalem was Ezra, who, upon his arrival led the people in a spiritual revival.

The dedication of the newly rebuilt temple in Jerusalem ushered in a new era for the Jews. Scholars refer to this period of time in Jewish history as Second Temple Judaism. It covers the years between 516 BC when the new temple was built and 70 AD when it was destroyed by the Roman general, Titus.

Concerning this time in Jewish history Collins notes:

> The second temple period covers a span of some six hundred years, during which the Jewish people, like all peoples of the eastern Mediterranean, underwent great cultural upheavals. The Babylonian exile involved the demise of the monarchy, the interruption and reorganization of the temple cult, and the impoverishment of the population as a whole. The Hellenistic age brought exposure to a new culture and saw the rise of new forms of association, such as those we find attested in the Dead Sea Scrolls. It also brought increased urbanization, with the multiplication of Hellenistic cities, inhabited mainly by Gentiles, and the growth of Jerusalem, which was sparsely populated in Nehemiah's time, to a city of some eighty thousand at the turn of the era (1997:104).

The exiles who returned to Jerusalem were not the same people who had been taken captive generations before.

They were the grandchildren and great grandchildren of those who had once lived in Jerusalem. They were not returning home as much as returning to their *ancestral* home. When they arrived, they found Jerusalem in a shambles, the temple in ruins and a mixed race of people living in the region who did not want the exilic Jews moving in and taking over the land. But the Jews did move in; and they set about the task of rebuilding the temple and the city, including new homes for themselves. Most of them became farmers, maintaining the agrarian lifestyle that had characterized their ancestors. Some of them, no doubt, supported themselves with the trades they had learned while in exile.

A major cultural innovation in post-exilic Palestine was the introduction of synagogues. As noted earlier, it was most likely during the exile, without the temple and a functioning priesthood, that the people had established synagogues to serve as local centers for worship, education, fellowship and community activities. Along with the Sabbath observance, participation in the local synagogue became the fundamental expression of devotion to Yahweh. The people saw such a value in the synagogue system that even with the rebuilding of the temple and the re-establishment of a functional priesthood and sacrificial system they did not want to give up all that the system of local synagogues had to offer. Thus, local synagogues were built throughout Palestine. By the first century, the synagogue, from a very practical point of view, had become as important as the temple. The synagogue was a major cultural innovation that changed the way Jews interacted with one another and impacted the way they worshipped God.

Another significant cultural development of post-exilic Palestine was the spiritual revival led by Ezra the priest. While in exile the Jews had been "cured" of their proclivity toward idolatry, but they had not paid close attention to all of God's commandments regarding holiness and separation from non-covenant peoples. Most of them could not even speak Hebrew. One of their major transgressions was having married foreign people. When Ezra became aware of this he was deeply saddened. His remorse called attention to the sin and the people responded by deciding to send away their foreign wives and children (Ezra 9-10).

In addition, in the book of Nehemiah, we learn of a larger effort to reacquaint the people with God's law by means of a public reading and interpretation of the Torah (Neh. 7:73b-10:39). Because the people were no longer fluent in their own native language, the priests had to interpret and explain the meaning to the crowds as Ezra read from God's law. The people were saddened and remorseful that they had been so lax in their compliance with God's law and vowed to be obedient.

These very public (and to a degree *extreme*) displays of remorse and determination to be rigorously obedient to God's law deeply impacted the development of post-exilic Israelite culture. Social institutions basic to society had been disrupted, establishing precedents for further radical behavior. Throughout the remainder of their post-exilic history (to the end of Second Temple Judaism in 70 AD), radical responses (both political and religious) were common. Separatists such as those who lived at Qumran, and political activists such as the Zealots, were not uncommon.

The post-exilic culture of Israel was very different from the culture of their ancestors who lived during the pre-monarchy or even during the time of the later monarchy. They spoke a different language. Their weekly religious observances were different. They had a different understanding of God. Their socioeconomic and sociopolitical structures were different. The post-exilic Israelite culture of 500 BC did not resemble the Israelite

139

culture of 1000 BC any more than American culture today resembles the culture of North America in the 1500s.

A Roman Subjugated Agrarian Culture

After the death of Alexander the Great in 323 BC, there was no single individual who emerged to take control of the Greek empire. Instead, it was divided up among three of Alexander's generals: Antigonus I, who ruled sections of Asia Minor and the Middle East, Macedonia and Greece; Seleucus I, who ruled Babylonia and India; and Ptolemy I, who ruled Egypt. Because Alexander had established Greek outposts in so many places, effectively exporting Greek culture throughout the Near and Middle East, an umbrella culture called Hellenism impacted to varying degrees the indigenous cultures of those regions. While Antigonus, Seleucus, and Ptolemy (and their successors) ruled their kingdoms, an ambitious group of people in Central and Northwestern Italy began to exert their military power. After solidifying their control over the Italian peninsula (around 264 BC), the Romans began their conquest of the Mediterranean world. By 129 BC the Romans controlled the perimeter of the Mediterranean Sea. They had conquered; now the task was to control, to govern. This was easier in some regions than in others.

Because of the religious persecution of Antiochus IV, a Seleucid ruler, the Jews rebelled and in just over twenty years fought their way to a brief independence beginning in 144/143 BC (Rappaport 1992:Vol. 4, 433-439; Orlinsky 1962:Vol. 3, 197-201). Jewish independence under Hasmonean rule lasted until the conflict with the Roman general Pompey in 63 BC (Turner 1962:Vol. 2, 529-535). With the coming of Roman rule the Israelites were once again a subjugated people. There was a brief time (about four years, from 41 to 37 BC) when the Parthians were in power in Jerusalem. But from 37 BC, when Herod The

Great was installed as the local "King of the Jews," Rome was in firm control.

Herod ruled from 37 to 4 BC and was the king responsible for the slaughter of babies in Bethlehem in an attempt to kill the newly born messiah. When Herod died, his son, Archelaus, reigned from 4 BC to 6 AD. He was a brutal tyrant who was removed from office and exiled to Gaul by the Emperor in 6 AD. When Archelaus was removed from office, Judea and Samaria were incorporated into Syria for administrative purposes and fell under the authority of Roman governors (Levine 1998:360).

The Roman governors normally maintained their residence at Caesarea near the coast and only went to Jerusalem on important occasions. Given the political history of Palestine, however, a strong military presence was always maintained in Jerusalem. The best known Roman governor was Pontius Pilate, who governed Judea from 26 to 36 AD. To gain the cooperation of the Jewish population and to facilitate an orderly government in the absence of the governor, a Roman-appointed high priest worked to maintain peace. The high priest who held office the longest was Joseph Caiaphas, who presided from 18 to 36 AD (Ferguson 1993:391-392).

Social life during those years of political upheaval remained fairly constant. Most of the Jewish population remained agrarian, but a tradesman or middle class of merchants, scribes, low-level priests, small farmers, carpenters, leather workers and so forth had developed (Levine 1998:364). They were not part of the masses of poor, but neither were they rich. They were making a living. Together with the rich and poor they lived under Roman rule, left alone for the most part as long as they paid the oppressive tax levied against them and caused no trouble. The Romans liked everything peaceful and quite. Any hint of a disturbance would be met with a quick and powerful response.

Devout Jews living in Jerusalem participated in daily prayers at the temple. They observed the Sabbath, which included attending their local synagogue assembly each week. Many of them attempted to follow the rigorous standards of the Pharisees, keeping the ritual aspect of the law and Jewish traditions in even the smallest details. Not all Jews, however, felt compelled to live up to Pharisaic expectations. They were looked down on by those who did.

Jews who lived away from Jerusalem did not have daily access to the temple, but still participated regularly in their local synagogue. They tithed, observed annual holy days and festivals. They married, had children and buried their dead as people in that region of the world had for millennia. Their worldview remained holistic, supernaturalistic, and group and event oriented. They were monotheistic. Polygamy had ceased centuries before, but slavery (especially selling oneself or one's child into slavery in order to pay a debt) continued to be practiced. They knew Satan was active in the world and that his demons represented a serious threat. They knew the world of the supernatural was real and that supernatural things happened all the time. They knew that God was active in his world, involved in the lives of his people. They equated good fortune with blessing from God and difficulties or sickness with punishment for sin.

Jews who lived outside Palestine had a very different cultural experience than those who lived in Palestine, whether in Jerusalem or one of the outlying areas, such as Galilee. While Hellenism had impacted the Palestinian culture, its impact had, to a degree, been minimized. In the rest of the empire that was not the case. The Roman world was Hellenistic in perspective. The common language was Greek, which meant that people thought in Greek categories, from a Greek perspective. Throughout most of the known world, Greek culture had been adopted along with the underlying worldview assumptions that provided the foundation for Greek cultural structures. The way the Greeks thought about the world, about themselves, about religion, and about a whole host of philosophical and sociological issues was very different from the way people influenced by the cultures of Mesopotamia, Egypt, or Canaan would have thought about those things.

The degree to which Jews in the Hellenistic world had been assimilated into Hellenistic culture depended a great deal on the makeup of a local Jewish community and specific Jewish families. Some Jewish families were determined to maintain a completely separate lifestyle. Others, however, realized that to live effectively among non-Jewish people required some level of contact and interaction. That meant that strict Jewish customs could not always be maintained. Some Hellenistic customs and perspectives might even be adopted. Jews who lived in the Hellenistic world and accepted some of the Hellenistic ways of life were considered to have been *Hellenized*, at least to a degree, and were not well thought of by Palestinian Jews.

Hellenized or Hellenistic Jews probably did not follow the strict dietary regulations that were standard in Palestine. Neither were they able to maintain the strict rules of separation, that is, of avoiding contact with "unclean" or non-Jewish people that Jews in Palestine practiced. They still kept the Law of Moses, participated in their local synagogue, kept the Sabbath and observed holy days and religious festivals. But to an outside observer they would have appeared less fanatical about religious concerns than their Palestinian counterparts.

The underlying worldview assumptions and the surface-level cultural structures of Jewish society (Palestinian or Hellenistic) under Roman rule were, in many ways, very similar to those of their ancestors who lived 1000 years before them. At the same time, some aspects of their culture were very different from the culture of their ancestors. Understanding the differences between Jewish culture in 1000 BC and Jewish culture in 30 AD is important. Perhaps even more important is understanding the differences between Jewish culture (whether in 1000 BC or in 30 AD) and our contemporary Western culture. The differences are vast and the implications for biblical interpretation are staggering.

The Implications of Israelite Cultural Development on Biblical Interpretation

As this chapter has illustrated, it is not possible to talk about a single *biblical culture*. The culture which shape Abraham and in which he participated was very different from the culture David knew, which was very different from the cultural experiences of Ezra and Nehemiah, which were different from the cultural experience of Jesus, which was different from the cultural experience of Jews who lived in the Hellenistic regions beyond the borders of Palestine. What are the implications of the cultural diversity we encounter in the Scriptures? There are several. First, is the need to recognize that God's people lived in a human cultural context, and that as God communicated and interacted with his people, he did so within that human cultural context. All communication is culture-bound and culture-laden—even God's communication when he is communicating with human beings.

Second, the various cultural contexts in which God's people (Israel) lived were, to varying degrees, blended cultures, combining thinking and behaviors that were human in origin with those that originated with God. For example the ancient Israelites practiced polygamy. Polygamy was not part of God's original ideal for how males and females should interact with one another. It was a product of human culture. But God was not so opposed to the practice that he could not tolerate it. In fact, not only did he tolerate it, he participated in it by giving David Saul's wives when David already had four wives of his own (2 Sam. 12:7-8). Provisions that God included in the Law of Moses (the levirate law, for instance) also allowed for, and in some cases would have required, polygamy.

Polygamy was of human origin. In contrast, a strictly spiritual, transcendent concept of God that did not allow for any kind of material representation (any kind of an idol or other material/physical association of Yahweh) was of divine origin. Human tendency has been to create physical representations of the gods they worshiped. God was quite clear, however, that he wanted no such representations. Polygamy he could tolerate. Physical representations which tended to minimize his transcendence he could not tolerate. Thus, a transcendent view of God and polygamy were both part of ancient Jewish culture. It was a blended culture, involving some elements that originated with God and some that originated with humans.

Clearly, God did not ordain polygamy, but polygamy is part of the culture we encounter in the Old Testament—a part of human culture that God was willing to tolerate and accommodate until people realized for themselves that such practices were not the best way for people to relate to and interact with one another. It should not be surprising if there are other features of human culture that God was willing to tolerate and accommodate until people realized for themselves that such practices were not part of God's original plan for how people ought to relate to and interact with one another. Slavery would fit into this category. So would patriarchy.

Third, we must make every effort to differentiate between practices in Scripture which are human in origin and those which are divine. How one might go about doing this will be discussed in later chapters.

Fourth, we must not assume that human cultural practices allowed or accepted or tolerated by God were *ordained* by him as ways that all people in all places throughout all time ought to live. There is a great deal of difference between those things that God *allows* people to do and those things that he *demands* that all people do.

The development of the synagogue system and its incorporation into Jewish culture provides an illustration of this point. God had ordained a specific worship system for the Jews. The Law of Moses made God's expectations for how his people were to worship quite clear. The Israelites, however, failed to avoid idolatrous practices and subsequently found themselves in a situation where they could not worship Yahweh at his temple. Through creative innovation the Jews designed an alternative method for worship and fellowship with God and one another. The solution to their dilemma was the synagogue. The local synagogue met an important need in the spiritual and community life of the Israelites who lived in exile. When they returned from exile, the temple was rebuilt and the priesthood re-established. The "need" (in the strict sense of the word) for the synagogue no longer existed. Yet it had become such an important and helpful part of their spiritual and corporate life that they decided to keep it as a permanent feature of their culture. Synagogues were built throughout Palestine.

By the time of Jesus, the synagogue system that served the spiritual needs of God's people was several hundred years old. It was a feature of the culture in which Jesus grew up and in which he conducted his ministry. Jesus accepted it completely and participated in it without hesitation. Yet it had not been part of God's original ordained plan for how people should worship and interact with him and with one another. The synagogue was not of divine ordination, it was a human innovation. Yet there it is in Scripture. It was part of the world Jesus knew, part of the way he worshipped and enjoyed fellowship with others who were obedient to God.

Does the presence of the synagogue in Scripture mean that it was of divine origin? No. Does its presence in Scripture and its obvious divine approval (if Jesus participated in it God approved of it) mean that we must participate in the synagogue system? No. Because the Jews *could* utilize the synagogue system to help meet their spiritual needs does not mean that all believers in all places throughout all time *must* utilize it. Human cultural practices must not be confused with divinely ordained requirements. We are required to worship God. We are not required to worship God by means of the synagogue system.

The implications drawn from the multicultural nature of the Scriptures must be incorporated into our interpretive methods as we seek to understand and apply the Scriptures in our contemporary world.

CHAPTER 6

CONFLICTING CULTURES WITHIN THE FIRST CENTURY COMMUNITY OF FAITH

For about ten years after the church was established it remained completely Jewish in composition. The first believers were, for the most part, Palestinian Jews. As the story of Jesus, the Messiah of God, was told in Jewish communities outside Palestine, that is, among Hellenistic Jews, many of them also became followers of Jesus. During those early years there were also a number of proselytes to Judaism who became followers of Jesus. A number of gentiles who had been converted to Judaism, such as the treasurer to the Queen of Ethiopia (Ac. 8), believed when they heard the Good News. Jewish believers, however, had not proclaimed the story of Jesus to all people as Jesus had instructed them to do. Why had they failed to obey? Most likely, Jesus' Jewish followers had failed to obey him because they could not bring themselves to cross the cultural and social boundaries that, for centuries, had separated them from non-Jewish people.

Walls of Separation

God wanted his people to understand that he was holy and that as his people they, too, were to be holy. To live holy lives they had to understand the difference between holy and unholy. To help them understand the difference between holy and unholy on a conceptual, abstract level, he knew they would need to begin with concrete behaviors. So God gave the Israelites laws that had to do with clean (holy) and unclean (unholy) practices. These laws had to do with certain kinds of foods they were not to eat (Lev. 11: 1-23), sick people they were to avoid, such as people with leprosy or other illnesses (Lev. 14), and other behaviors that could result in uncleanness. For God, the point was not that some animals were literally unfit to eat. For instance, the Israelites were not to eat rabbit or pork. It was not that there was anything intrinsically wrong with eating rabbit or pork. God simply chose certain types of animals or food sources to be excluded from an acceptable diet for his people. Those exclusions were arbitrary selections by God designed to teach his people that just as some foods are acceptable and some are not, so some behaviors are acceptable and some are not.

To help the Israelites understand how serious he was about clean and unclean, God attached some very serious consequences to the concept of uncleanness. For instance, when a fellowship offering was being offered, if a person who was ceremonially unclean participated in the offering by eating some of the meat of the offered animal, that person was to be expelled from the community of the people (Lev. 7:20-27). Being expelled from the community of faith was a severe consequence and required sacrifices so the person could be forgiven and restored to good standing in the community. While one could be accepted back into the community, being expelled was a terrible event to be avoided at all costs.

Ceremonial contamination could result from a number of sources, including from contact with a person who was unclean. Unclean people included those who ate foods that were on God's list of foods that should be avoided. People who ate pork or rabbit were unclean because pork and rabbit were unclean. Therefore, not only were God's people to avoid eating pork or rabbit, they were to avoid contact with people who ate pork or rabbit or other unclean foods, or who engaged in other activity that made them unclean. Since non-Jewish people did not follow the regulations of the Sinaitic Covenant regarding clean and unclean foods, or other activities which resulted in their being unclean, the Jews, to avoid becoming unclean themselves, avoided interaction or contact with non-Jewish people.

This had been the custom of the Israelite people for nearly 1,500 years. God had told them to remain separate from foreign people so they would not be influenced by them or become ceremonially unclean. Many times over the centuries, however, they had disobeyed, interacting with foreign, pagan people who led them into sinful ways of living. Each time the consequences had been terrible. God had punished them for acting like pagan people. Finally the Jews realized that God was serious when he told them to avoid contact with non-Jewish people. Once they finally understood how serious God was about their holiness, they took proper precaution to avoid contact with non-Jewish people. They built social and cultural walls of separation between themselves and other societies. The problem was that when God decided to replace the Sinaitic Covenant with the New Covenant, eliminating the old laws about clean and unclean, bringing all people together into one united community of faith, the Jews failed to understand and failed to adjust. This is why Jesus' Jewish followers had not gone to non-Jewish people with the Good News about reconciliation and renewed relationship with God. They were still focused on the old traditions related to ceremonial cleanness and uncleanness. They avoided unclean food and unclean people, even though with the death of Jesus and the establishing of the New Covenant there were no longer unclean foods or unclean people.

Three Kinds of People in the World

To the Jews who lived in Palestine, there were three kinds of people who lived in the world: 1) Jews like themselves (Palestinian Jews) who kept themselves separate from all things and people who could cause uncleanness, 2) Jews who lived throughout the Roman world (Hellenistic Jews) who mixed more freely with non-Jews than they ought to, and 3) non-Jews. Palestinian Jews did not think highly of Hellenistic Jews because they did not maintain the strict ritualistic standards of non-contact practiced by Jews in Palestine. And of course, Palestinian Jews did not think highly (to say the least) of non-Jewish people. Some Hellenistic Jews tended to be more tolerant of non-Jewish people, but still, for the most part, did not accept them as equals or interact with them in unrestricted ways. As far as the Jews were concerned, they alone were God's chosen people. They had been given his sacred law and they kept it. That made them different from every other people.

If people from other ethnic groups wanted to be part of God's community of faith, they could do so by turning away from their ungodly society and becoming Jewish. This meant keeping the Law of Moses, being circumcised (if the individual was male), being baptized, and offering a sacrifice. The baptism and offering of a sacrifice were added later (perhaps in post-exilic days) by the Jews to enhance the ceremony of conversion. In the earliest days of Israel, an outsider could become one of the assembly of Yahweh simply by being circumcised. From a Jewish perspective, non-Jewish people had been joining the community of faith

151

by some combination of circumcision, obedience to the law, baptism and sacrifice for 1,500 years. Now that the messiah had come, outsiders were still welcome to join the people of God. The only thing that had changed, as far as the Jews saw it at the time, was that God had fulfilled his promise by sending his messiah. So from a Jewish perspective, non-Jewish people were welcome if they were willing to forsake their own native culture and become Jewish.

Their logic was certainly understandable. The problem was that after the death of Jesus this is not the process that God had in mind. Individuals of all ethnic groups were welcome to become part of the community of faith without becoming Jewish. To most of the Jews, this did not make sense. God had selected them and given them his law. He had punished them severely for not keeping it. Righteous people throughout the generations since Moses had received Yahweh's law had kept it. God's people kept God's law. So individuals who wanted to become part of the community of faith had to keep the Mosaic Law. It was that kind of logic that led to the cultural conflicts about which we read in the New Testament.

Culture Clash in Acts 10

The story Luke tells in Acts 10 is amazing. An angel of God visited Cornelius, an officer in the Roman army. Cornelius was a godly man who worshiped Yahweh. But he did not know the story of Jesus and how to be reconciled to God though faith in Jesus. The angel who visited Cornelius told him to send for Peter, who was in Joppa at the home of a man named Simon, who lived by the sea. Peter would explain to Cornelius what he needed to know. Cornelius obeyed, sending a group of soldiers to find Peter.

As the soldiers approached Joppa, Peter went up to the roof of Simon's house for a time of quiet meditation before the midday meal. During his prayer God sent him a vision. A large sheet suspended from its four corners came down out of heaven. In it were all kinds of animals—unclean animals that had been on God's "Do Not Eat" list. God told Peter to select an animal, kill it and prepare himself something to eat. The vision itself is not the amazing part of the story. The voice of God is not the amazing part of the story. The amazing part of the story is Peter's reply to a direct command from God. Peter refused God's order! *"No, Lord,"* he said. *"I have never eaten anything unclean."*

God's reply was, *if I say something is acceptable, do not say that it is unacceptable.*

This happened three times. How confused Peter must have been. He had always been a good Jew, just as God wanted him to be. Now God was telling him to do that which was detestable. Why? Was this some kind of test? What Peter failed to realize is that God had selected some foods to be unclean simply to make a point. Unclean foods had been an object lesson designed to teach that God's people must discern between good and evil practices. The food itself had never been the issue or the point. God had used food to illustrate a point: some things are acceptable and some are not. You must listen to God and obey him, avoiding those things that he says are unacceptable. Now God was using food again to make another point: that if God says a thing is acceptable you must accept what he says (even if it goes against your social and cultural conventions) and respond appropriately.

As Peter pondered the meaning of the vision, the Holy Spirit told him that there were men coming to meet him. Peter was to go with them. Imagine Peter's surprise when he went down from the roof to find a delegation of men looking to for him—Roman soldiers. Normally a Jewish man would not travel with a group of non-Jewish people. Just being near an unclean person could result in ritual contamination. But the Holy Spirit had told Peter to go with the men. Peter must also have begun to understand the meaning of the vision—that which was once unclean is no longer unclean. The vision had not been about food as much as it had been about people. Non-Jewish people should no longer be thought of as unclean or unacceptable to God. Peter invited the men to stay the night. The next morning he and several other Jewish men went with them as the Holy Spirit had instructed. By the time Peter and his friends arrived at Cornelius' home, Peter had figured out exactly what God had been telling him—that no person should be thought of as impure.

The implications of this for Jewish theology and culture were staggering. If people were not impure, even if they did not observe the ancient food and purification laws and the Jewish safeguards designed to prevent accidental contamination, then Jews could mix freely with non-Jewish people. They could do business with them and be friends with them. They could even eat with them! Even more, if non-Jewish people could eat whatever they wanted and not become unclean, could Jewish people also disregard the ancient dietary guidelines about clean and unclean foods? And if that might be the case, what other traditions might be open to review and reevaluation?

The events surrounding Peter's visit to Cornelius' home shattered Peter's Jewish assumptions about how God thought about and related to non-Jewish people. It required Peter to rethink all of his assumptions about Jews and non-Jews and how they should interact with one another, and about the basis upon which one is acceptable to God. Was salvation really by faith, or was it by faith *and* observing religious traditions, such as dietary regulations? Surely, as Peter pondered these concerns he remembered that Jesus had taught that it is not what goes into a person (food) that makes him or her impure, but those things (thoughts and behaviors) that flow from a person's inner self that make him or her impure.

The social implications of this for Jewish believers would be unsettling. Hundreds of years of avoiding or at least minimizing contact with non-Jewish people needed to change. Jesus had told his followers to go to all ethnic groups and it was time that they begin doing so. But changing deeply ingrained sociocultural patterns of behavior and thinking would not be easy. It could take several generations.

The events described in Galatians 2:11-21 illustrate just how difficult the process of social and cultural change would be[11]. Peter had received his vision from God and a message from the Holy Spirit. He had gone to Cornelius' home and witnessed God's acceptance of non-Jewish people—without their having to keep the Law of Moses. He had puzzled over the implications of it all and had realized that he could associate with and even eat with non-Jewish people. When he traveled to the region of Galatia he interacted freely with the non-Jewish believers there, eating with them in their homes—until some Jews from Jerusalem arrived. Peter knew that they held firmly to their old traditions and not only refused to have anything to do with non-Jewish people, but would be very critical of any Jew who did. Knowing this, Peter broke off his associations with the non-Jewish believers. He did not want to incur the wrath of those traditionalist Jews. When Paul saw what was happening he was disappointed and angry. He understood what was happening and why. And he was not going to tolerate it. Paul challenged Peter about his behavior, pointing out the theological inconsistency—and the sinfulness—of what Peter was doing.

---

[11] Scholars disagree as to the timing of the events described in Ac. 15 and those in Gal. 2:11-21. British scholars, for the most part, place the events described by Paul in Gal. 2 before the events described by Luke in Ac. 15. Many American scholars place the events of Ac. 15 before the events described in Gal. 2. I concur with many British scholars, such as F. F. Bruce (1954:298), that the events of Gal. 2 preceded the events of Ac. 15.

How can Peter's behavior be explained? The short answer is that old habits, deeply engrained patterns of behavior, are difficult to break. Old ways of thinking are not easily replaced. It is difficult to engage in behaviors that once generated repulsion—which is what the Jews felt at the thought of eating unclean food with unclean people. The fact that God had said that non-Jewish people should no longer be thought of as unclean made little difference to the Jew's emotional reaction at the thought of table fellowship with non-Jewish people. The Jews were being asked to cross sociocultural boundaries that they were not emotionally ready to cross. Social or cultural differences between believers or prospective believers can present serious difficulties in the church or in the church's outreach efforts.

Culture Clash in Acts 15

Acts 10 provides a partial framework for understanding the cultural context and dynamics of the first century church. Another text that adds to the framework is Acts 15.

Several years had passed since Peter had gone to Cornelius' house with the Gospel. Once that first step had been taken, other Jews (especially Hellenistic Jews who were more used to interacting with non-Jewish people) began sharing their faith with non-Jewish people, ignoring the social and cultural barriers that had previously stood in their way.

While some Jews openly and happily engaged non-Jewish people in conversation about Jesus, spending time with them, eating with them, being their friends, other Jews were not as enthusiastic about the unrestricted contact. Their feeling was that if non-Jewish people wanted to be part of the community of faith they could follow the centuries old prescription: circumcision, baptism, sacrifice, obedience to the Law of Moses. After all, these were the things God had asked of his people for ages. God was still God and people were still people. Now that the messiah had come and God's promises to his people had been fulfilled, it was crucial to be faithful to the old ways. This fellow Paul, therefore, teaching that Gentiles did not have to obey the Law of Moses (which really meant the Law of God), had to be stopped. Who ever heard of such a thing—not obeying the Law of God? How could such thinking be right?

Jewish believers (who happened to be Pharisees) traveled to Antioch where Paul was working and confronted him with his error. Paul, however, proved to be a formidable opponent and the controversy could not be settled in Antioch. So the whole group of them, the pharisaic believers along with Paul and Barnabas, traveled to Jerusalem to take up the matter with the apostles and church leaders there in Palestine.

The first order of business was for Paul and Barnabas to share their exciting news of what God was doing among non-Jewish people. These non-Jewish people believed and responded to the message of Jesus, changed their lives, and were helping to change the world (the non-Jewish world) in which they lived. When the Jewish believers heard what God was doing, which to them was an obvious sign of divine approval, they rejoiced. However, some of the Jews—those with a pharisaic background—remained unconvinced. They demanded that the Gentile converts be required to be circumcised and keep the law. What this amounted to was requiring non-Jewish people to become Jewish people in order for them to be acceptable to God. It was Peter, who may have still been feeling the sting of Paul's chastisement in Galatia, who spoke up in defense of Paul and the Gentiles. He reminded those present that it was through him (Peter) that God opened the door of salvation to the Gentiles by sending him to Cornelius' home. God had given those non-Jewish believers the same gift, the Holy Spirit, as he had given the Jews on the day of Pentecost. And he had given it to them on the basis of their faith, not on the basis of being circumcised and keeping the law. Non-Jewish believers were treated (by God) the same as Jewish believers even though the non-Jewish believers did not obey the Law of Moses or follow Jewish traditions related to ritual purity. Peter went on to point out that the Jews had never been all that successful in keeping the Law of Moses anyway. The Law of Moses had been given to the Israelites. If they had been unable to keep it, why were they now trying to bind it on non-Jewish people?

Peter's points were well made, effectively ending the debate. Paul and Barnabas told more stories of the supernatural things God had been doing among non-Jewish people, driving home the point that God accepts the Gentile believers on the basis of their faith without requiring them to keep the Jewish law. James, Jesus' brother (who had become a leader in the Jerusalem church), then spoke, suggesting that a letter be written to non-Jewish believers making it clear that the apostles and church leaders in Jerusalem would not be party to requiring non-Jewish believers to keep the law and live as Jews. Everyone agreed and the letter was written and sent with specially selected envoys.

Jewish Churches and Gentile Churches

What happened as this clash of cultures played itself out in the first century church? Churches were planted and grew that had a distinctly Jewish feel and flavor about them. And churches were planted and grew that had a distinctly Hellenistic feel and flavor about them. This simple fact is often overlooked as many people simply assume that all churches in the first century were alike. It is not uncommon to hear people refer to or describe *the* church in the first century from a singular perspective as if all churches were cookie cutter replicas of the first church in Jerusalem. Of course, there is a sense in which the New Testament refers to the one universal church. It is the universal community of faith that belongs to Jesus. But to recognize the oneness of universal church is not that same as suggesting that each individual community of believers looked, acted, and worshipped exactly as every other group. That is simply not the case.

There was probably a great deal of similarity between churches in one region and churches in another, but there would also have been subtle but significant differences as well. For instance, the church in Jerusalem was made up of Palestinian Jews who continued to observe Jewish cultural traditions. Acts 3:1 indicates that Peter and John, and presumably other believers, participated in the scheduled daily prayers offered at the temple. This was a Jewish custom. It was not a requirement in the Law of Moses. But pious Jewish believers observed the custom as part of their devotion to God.

Their continuing to observe Jewish customs was not something which occurred for only a short time after the beginning of the church. Years later, perhaps in the late 50s, Jewish believers were still observing Jewish customs, living as Jews had always lived. When Paul went to Jerusalem, the church leaders there were concerned about rumors that he was teaching Hellenistic Jews not to obey the Law of Moses. The church leaders seemed to understand that these were only rumors and that Paul was not teaching such things. Paul knew that it was perfectly acceptable for Jews to live as Jews, following the religious and social customs that had identified them as a group of people for 1,500 years. The charges against him were false. But if some of the Jews in Jerusalem believed the rumors about him there could be problems. The advice of the church leaders to Paul when he arrived in Jerusalem was that he participate with several other Jewish men who had taken a vow and were about to shave their heads in relation to that vow. The behavior in which they were engaging was very Jewish and very traditional. It was a religious practice rooted in Jewish antiquity that only the most serious and traditional Jews would have participated in. The fact that there were four believers in the church in Jerusalem that were doing this, and that Paul was encouraged to join them in the ceremony as a way of demonstrating that he remained a loyal traditional Jew, indicates that the Jewish believers continued to follow the cultural patterns of Jewish society (Ac. 21:15-25). Jewish believers continued to live as Jewish people had lived for centuries. When they came to believe that Jesus was God's messiah they did not stop living as Jews. Indeed, their belief that God had fulfilled his promises to them by sending his messiah would have served to confirm and intensify their religious zeal and their desire to live as he wanted them to live.

Churches comprised of Jewish believers were very Jewish. They observed Jewish customs and traditions. They had a Jewish look and feel about them. This was especially true of churches in Palestine. Churches comprised of Hellenistic Jews may not have looked and felt quite as Jewish. Churches comprised of non-Jewish people would not have had a Jewish flavor about them. Why would they? Hellenistic believers did not look, think, or act like Jews. This was the problem that sparked the conference in Jerusalem described in Acts 15. Palestinian Jews visited the church in Antioch, a Hellenistic church, and saw that it did not look, act, or feel like a good Jewish church. That's what upset them so. The church in Antioch was not a Jewish church. Paul's argument was that it did not need to be a Jewish church because non-Jewish people did not need to live like Jewish people in order to be pleasing to God. And of course, the church leaders in Jerusalem had agreed.

The cultural clashes between Jewish and Hellenistic believers that occurred in the first century church was significant enough to have prompted Paul to address the issue, encouraging unity between Jew and Gentile believers (Eph. 2:11-22). The church in Rome, as in other major metropolitan regions, may have been made up of a combination of Jewish and Hellenistic believers. The problems addressed by Paul in Romans 14 may have been a result of the sociocultural differences (in attitude and behavior) between Jewish and Hellenistic believers. Paul's advice to each group was *give people who think differently than you do room to be who they are.*

The Implications of Ancient Christian Cultural Conflicts for the Church Today

Bible students who are not trained in anthropology may not at first glance see the vast cultural variation that existed between Jewish and non-Jewish churches in the first century. But the variation is there. The conflicts that grew out of the cultural differences between Jewish and Hellenist believers in the first century church have significant implications for the church today. First, the cultural differences that existed in the first century church demonstrate that cultural differences are inevitable. People from different social and cultural backgrounds remain who they are (socially and culturally) when they become Christians. This is not to suggest that new believers do not change their behavior to conform to Christian standards. They do—or at least they should. But a person who has recently come to America from China and who becomes a Christian will still be very Chinese. Immigrants to America from India, Mexico, Columbia, or Indonesia who become believers will retain the cultural perspective and patterned behaviors of their native culture. They will be Christians, but they will be Chinese, Indian, Mexican, Columbian, and Indonesian Christians. Should they find themselves worshiping in Anglo churches they will struggle with cultural differences just as Hellenists believers would have

161

struggled with worshiping in Jewish churches. Such struggles are inevitable.

Second, the way the cultural differences that existed in the first century church were handled demonstrates that cultural differences between believers are acceptable. Cultural uniformity was not expected in the first century church and it was certainly not demanded. Unity does not require uniformity. Everyone does not have to be alike. They do not have to think the same or act the same. All believers must conform to God's standards of behavior, but within that divine standard there is considerable room for cultural variation.

Third, the presence of cultural differences in the first century church implies the adaptability of Christianity. Christianity's roots are Jewish. It was born in a Jewish cultural context. But it was designed to be carried across cultural boundaries to every ethnic group. There are only two ways that divine intention could be accomplished: either Christianity had to be structured in a very rigid way, requiring believers from every ethnic group to become Jewish in perspective and behavior, or Christianity had to be structured with a great deal of flexibility so that it could be adapted to fit the cultural patterns of different ethnic groups. Since it is clear that God did not require non-Jewish believers to become Jewish in their perspective and behavior, it is clear that God designed Christianity to be culturally adaptable.

Fourth, the presence of cultural differences in the first century church implies the need for being able to distinguish between those parts of Scripture that are related to the cultural practices of a specific ethnic group in a historical timeframe and God's expectations for all people— expectations that transcend time and culture. Bible students must be able to differentiate between those things in Scripture which were related to the cultural practices of a people, such as greeting one another with a holy kiss, and that which God expects of all people regardless of their cultural habits, such as abstaining from immorality.

Above all, the cultural conflicts experienced by the Christians of the first century make it imperative that we study and understand all we can about culture and its role in our lives and in God's kingdom. Too many people study the Scriptures from a monocultural perspective, not distinguishing between the many ancient cultures represented in the Scriptures and their own contemporary culture. The truths revealed in the Holy Scriptures are timeless and universal. But those timeless, universal truths were revealed within a number of ancient cultural contexts in relation to those cultural contexts. Those who would discover, interpret, and apply God's timeless, universal truths must be able to extract them from the cultural context in which they were given.

PART THREE

THE ROLE OF CULTURE IN THE INTERPRETATION OF GOD'S WORD

CHAPTER 7

CULTURE-RELATED ISSUES IN INTERPRETATION

A brief review of the history of hermeneutic methodology utilized in the interpretation and application of the Scriptures since the first century is necessary for a discussion of contemporary issues in biblical interpretation.

Richard Longenecker identifies four hermeneutic methodologies used by Jews of the first century in their attempts to interpret and apply the Hebrew Scriptures: *literalist, midrashic, pesher*, and *allegorical* (1999:14). A *literalist* approach, as the name implies, is a simple, straightforward way of trying to discover the plain meaning of a given text (14-17). A *midrashic* approach to the interpretive process looks for meaning beyond what is immediately obvious in a literalist approach. Midrashic methodology examines a text from every angle looking for the deeper spiritual meaning that might lie beneath the surface (17-24).

Pesher methodology was similar to midrash (looking beneath the surface for a deeper spiritual meaning), but was more focused on a contemporary application. The Qumran community made extensive use of pesher methodology, interpreting the prophecies of the Hebrew Scriptures in light of their contemporary perspective without a great deal of consideration to the historical context of a passage. *It is extremely crucial to note that Jesus and his followers used a pesher approach to interpret and apply the Scriptures* (24-30, 54-58).

An *allegorical* approach to the Scriptures is not satisfied with any kind of literal understanding of the text. Beneath the surface of the text is a deeper spiritual meaning. While midrash methodology was also concerned with the deeper spiritual meaning, it did not ignore the literal meaning of the text, but sought to go deeper than the literal meaning. Allegory, in its more extreme forms, often regarded the literal reading of the text as unimportant, preferring instead to assign a symbolic spiritual meaning—usually in a rather arbitrary manner (30-33).

As the population base of the church shifted from predominantly Jewish to predominantly Hellenistic, and as the apostles died, requiring the next generation of church leaders to fill the void, the hermeneutic methods used to interpret and apply the Scriptures eventually became more analytical in nature. This analytical approach, however, was, to a degree, a response to perceived interpretive abuses rooted in an allegorical approach to Scripture.

Origen of Alexandria (185-253) was a major proponent of the allegorical interpretive method. Generally speaking, he accepted the literal sense of the Scriptures, acknowledging the historicity of the events recorded there, but looked for deeper spiritual meaning and moral application to the contemporary context. The value of the allegorical method was that it emphasized that the Scriptures must be approached spiritually and applied in meaningful, practical ways. The difficulty with the allegorical approach was that in an effort to find deep spiritual meaning the text's connection to history was often lost (Bray 1996:99-103).

Origen's allegorical approach was considered problematic because it was not rooted in the literal historical settings in which the Scriptures were produced and about which they spoke. Opposition to the allegorical approach was led by the scholars in Antioch in the mid-fourth century. The Antiochene approach to hermeneutics was rooted in what those scholars referred to as *theoria*, which means *insight*. They upheld both the literal sense of Scripture and sought deeper spiritual meaning (insight) as well. However, for them, the deeper spiritual meaning had to be connected to, taken from, or grow out of the literal historical setting of the text. This analytical, Western approach to the text, rooted in the historical context of the Scriptures became the foundation for modern methods of interpretation (Klein, Blomberg, and Hubbard 1993:33-46).

Maintaining a clear focus on the historical setting of a text has become the central consideration in contemporary biblical interpretation—at least among conservative believers with a high view of Scripture. However, part of understanding the historical setting is understanding the *historical-cultural* setting in which the events recorded in Scripture occurred (172-183). History does not occur in a cultural vacuum. The cultural context in which events occurred is crucial to understanding what actually happened, why it happened, and how people were impacted by what happened. But how does the reader understand the historical-cultural context of a given text and incorporate that insight into his or her interpretation? What is the relationship between the reader and the historical-cultural biblical text?

Horizons, Spirals, and Responses

Anthony Thiselton has demonstrated the two-sided nature of the hermeneutical process by discussing it in terms of two horizons: the horizon of the text and the horizon of the reader (1980:10-16). Neither horizon can be ignored, for where they intersect each impacts the other. To do justice to the text the reader must attempt to understand the author's point, which includes the historical-cultural context in which the author wrote. But just as the author lived in and was impacted by a historical-cultural context, so, too, the reader lives in and is impacted by his or her historical-cultural context. The reader's contemporary context is just as much a part of the hermeneutical equation as is the biblical author's historical-cultural context. The reader must ask two questions: first, what did this mean to the original recipients? (which is the historical context, or horizon one), and second, what does it mean to me? (which is the contemporary context, or horizon two).

In their work entitled *Communicating God's Word in a Complex World* (2003: 83-95), R. Daniel Shaw and Charles Van Engen suggest four horizons that must be factored into the interpretation and communication of the Scriptures: the cultural context of the Old Testament authors, the cultural context of the New Testament authors, the cultural context of the individual interpreting the Old or New Testament material, and the cultural context of the people to whom he or she is recommunicating God's message.

Grant Osborne goes beyond the intersection of two (or four) horizons suggesting a continuous spiraling interaction between the biblical historical-cultural contexts and the reader's contemporary context (1991:6-7). The ongoing interaction between the historical text and the contemporary context allows interpreters to discover how the author's original intended meaning (as far as it may be ascertained) can best be contextualized to the contemporary context.

Osborne's explanation of an effective hermeneutic methodology is not essentially different from Thiselton's. Whether the process is viewed as an intersecting of horizons or a spiraling interaction, the essential elements remain the same: the interaction between the author and the reader. The importance of this interaction between author and reader, in which the reader is aware of the historical-cultural context of the author and its impact on what he wrote, has been called into question by some. A few postmodern philosophers have suggested that since the author's full original intent and meaning is unknowable that the reader's contemporary context and how he or she decides to interpret and apply the text (the *reader's response* to the text) is the only important consideration[12].

The fundamental mistake of reader response advocates is their failure to recognize that communication, oral or written, is a two-way process in which the receptor (the reader if we are discussing written communication) must attempt to understand the communicator's (author's) intended meaning. In a spoken conversation, if the speaker's meaning is not clear, the receptor can ask for clarification. Under normal circumstances a reader cannot ask the author for clarification. However, the author being unavailable for questioning does not relieve the reader of his or her responsibility to ascertain, as far as possible, the author's intended message. Reader response advocates assume that since the author is unavailable for questioning, his intent and meaning cannot be ascertained. Therefore, the reader is free to interpret the writing however he or she prefers. This may work on some level for reading poetry, but generally speaking it cannot lead to effective communication.

Fortunately, when it comes to interpreting the Bible, there is a great deal of historical information and internal hints regarding the author's communication intent that make interpretation a little easier. Many times a biblical writer will explain his purpose for writing. Knowing an author's reason for writing provides a good deal of insight into his

---

[12] See Rosenau 1992:25-41 for an overview of Postmodern hermeneutics. Postmodern hermeneutics, however, has to do with hermeneutical processes in general not specifically biblical hermeneutics.

reason for making specific statements. For instance, when the apostle John explains his reason for writing his gospel—so that readers may believe that Jesus is God's messiah (Jn. 20:30-31)—we understand that his purpose for writing impacted his choice of material to be included in his text. John's presentation is designed to provide his readers with enough information so that they can arrive at the conclusion that Jesus is the messiah. Specific questions within John's text about his meaning must be understood in light of his overall purpose.

Questions being answered in a text or problems being addressed can provide additional insight as to the author's intent and meaning. For instance, the believers in Corinth had evidently written Paul asking several questions about Christian doctrine and practice as it related to marriage (1 Cor. 7:1). Knowing Paul is answering questions he had been asked (at least in sections of his letter) provides readers with an interpretive framework for understanding Paul's intention and meaning. Regarding that same group of believers, Paul had heard some disturbing reports (1 Cor. 1:11). Some of what he wrote in his letter was designed to address those disturbing reports. Again, knowing what Paul was doing in a given section of his letter provides the reader with an interpretive framework. Purpose illuminates intention and intention guides interpretation and application.

Readers must attempt to understand the author's intended meaning. To miss or to ignore the author's intended meaning results in communication chaos. The responsible reader must interact with the author so that communication between the two can occur. At the heart of author-reader interaction is the historical-cultural context. Readers must not only understand the historical setting surrounding the writing, but the cultural context as well. Only when the reader understands the culture of the person doing the writing and the culture of the people to whom he wrote can the reader understand what is being said and how

170

the original recipients were mostly likely affected by what they read or heard. Those factors must be considered in interpreting and applying the text.

Avoiding Extremist Reactions

Human behavior is often perplexing. Why people react as they do in certain situations has been the subject of a great deal of study in the social sciences. Extremist reactions are especially interesting. However, as interesting as extremist reactions may be to psychologists, extremist reactions in biblical interpretation should be avoided. Two extremes that must be avoided are *simplistic literalism* and *absolute relativism*.

Simplistic Literalism

The tired old saying, "The Bible says what it means and means what it says," is an example of simplistic (naïve) literalism. Throughout the ages there have always been people who interpreted and applied the Scriptures in a simplistic literal way. As noted earlier, some Jews approached the Hebrew Scriptures in such naïve and literal terms.

Sometimes communication is simple and straightforward. Sometimes it is not. Sometimes that which appears to be simple, especially when historical and cultural issues must be factored into an interpretation, may not be as simple as it appears. Charles Kraft tells a story about his mission work in Nigeria that illustrates this point. One day a man from northeastern Nigeria came to him and asked, "What was wrong with Jesus?"

Kraft asked for clarification.

"The Bible says that Jesus was a shepherd?"

"Yes," Kraft replied. "He is referred to as The Good Shepherd."

"But he was a grown man?" the man asked.

"Yes."

"Then what was wrong with him?"

Kraft realized that there was something in the man's thinking that was creating a problem. He told the man there was nothing wrong with Jesus. But as Kraft continued to wonder about the man's question he noticed that in that region of Nigeria the only people tending sheep were young boys or men who were mentally incompetent.

The Nigerian man did not understand the cultural differences between his society and the society in which Jesus lived. So when he read the Scriptures in his simple, literal way without the benefit of all the historical and cultural information necessary to understand the text, he reached a conclusion that was completely without foundation—that there was something wrong with Jesus (Kraft 1996:25).

In America, as late as the mid-twentieth century, many women felt obliged to wear hats or scarves to church in order to conform to Paul's instructions in 1 Corinthians 11 regarding women covering their heads during prayers. Many Bible teachers and preachers had failed to ask questions regarding the historical and cultural circumstances that motivated Paul to issue such orders. They interpreted and applied the text in a simple literal way.

Eventually, more in-depth study revealed that Paul was concerned about their custom (cultural habit) of women demonstrating submission to men by covering their heads when they prayed or prophesied. As this became apparent and Christians realized that there was more to the text in 1 Corinthians 11 than was at first apparent, women stopped wearing hats and scarves to church. Even for Western women who felt that they needed to be submissive to their husbands, covering their heads was not an appropriate symbol of their submissiveness. In America, a woman covering her head did not mean she was submissive. It could have meant that she had not had time to fix her hair. It could have meant that she didn't want her head to get cold, or did not want the wind to blow her hair out of place. Or it could have simply been her fashion choice at that moment. Whatever else it might have been, wearing a hat or scarf to church for American women was not a sign of submission. They demonstrated their submission in other ways. To wear a hat or scarf to church without understanding the historical-cultural setting behind the command of 1 Corinthians 11 was to have misunderstood how to interpret and apply the text. It was an example of simplistic literalism.

The symbolic nature of language and communication must also be factored into the interpretive process. For instance, in Galatians 5:15, Paul says, *"But if instead of showing love among yourselves you are always biting and devouring one another, watch out! Beware of destroying one another."* If one approaches this text in a simple literal way, what it actually says is that the believers in Galatia were biting and eating each other! Were they? Of course not. Paul is speaking metaphorically about their unloving behavior toward each other.

Communication requires the use of linguistic symbols to communicate ideas. The words we use are verbal symbols. We paint pictures with those words to get our point across. For instance, Jesus said, *"Anyone who puts a hand to the plow and then looks back is not fit for the Kingdom of God,"* (Lk. 9:62). A simple literal interpretation of this comment from Jesus means that anyone who is plowing and looks behind himself is going to hell. Is that what Jesus meant? Probably not. So what one *says* and what one *means* are not necessarily the same. All communication requires interpretation. Communication is a subjective process. Often a simple literal interpretation of what is spoken or written is completely inadequate.

People who advocate a literal approach to interpretation have difficulty applying it consistently, for a

173

consistently applied literal hermeneutic would result in absurdities. Consider Jesus' comments in Matthew 5:29-30.

> *So if your eye--even if it is your good eye--causes you to lust, gouge it out and throw it away. It is better for you to lose one part of your body than for your whole body to be thrown into hell. And if your hand--even if it is your stronger hand-- causes you to sin, cut it off and throw it away. It is better for you to lose one part of your body than for your whole body to be thrown into hell.*

Gouging out an eye? Cutting off a hand? Is that what Jesus meant—literally? No. One's eye does not cause one to sin. Neither does one's hand. ("Bad hand, bad hand. Don't do that again!") Sin, we learn from James, comes from our inner sinful inclinations (Jas. 1:13-14). Literally cutting off one's hand will not keep one from sinning, for sin is a matter of the heart. So what was Jesus' point? His point was do whatever it takes to eliminate sin from your life, even if it requires drastic action. But his comments about cutting off hands and gouging out eyes were not meant to be taken literally any more than his comment that if one has faith as small as a grain of mustard one can move mountains. Exaggeration is a rhetorical device to drive a point home. That's what Jesus was doing. Jesus was not suggesting that believers would literally be able to move mountains.

To interpret such passages literally would result in people of faith gouging out eyes and cutting off hands, or being depressed because since they can't literally move mountains they must not have faith. Literalists, therefore, must be selective in which passages they will interpret literally and which ones they will allow to be explored for another perspective. They are inconsistent in their use of their chosen methodology. Literalism is an extremism that ought to be avoided.

Absolute Relativism

On the opposite end of the hermeneutical spectrum from simplistic literalism is absolute relativism. It, too, is an extremist response. Absolute relativism assumes that moral absolutes do not exist, that everything depends on circumstances or cultural context. With the rise of secular humanism came the idea that humans are the measure of all things. From the perspective of secular humanism, there is no authority higher than human authority. That which is morally and ethically acceptable is determined by human beings within the framework of their cultural context. Whatever a society decides is right, is right. Whatever they decide is wrong, is wrong. If, as the Nazis decided (and argued in their defense), that the presence of Jewish people in their society was unacceptable and that they must be exterminated, as a sovereign people they had the right to make such a decision. The difficulty with that line of reasoning was that the rest of the world, for the most part, did not agree with them. The Nuremberg trials stand as a powerful reminder of the unacceptable nature of absolute relativism. And yet, for all practical purposes many people in contemporary Western societies practice a form of absolute relativism. God and the Bible have been removed from the moral arena, and decisions about right and wrong, what is acceptable and unacceptable, are made on the basis of human cultural standards.

It is important to understand that to acknowledge the role of culture in the production, presentation, and interpretation of the biblical text does not have to lead to absolute relativism. To say that culture impacts some things is not to say that culture determines everything. To say that the Bible is God's inspired communication to his human children is to say that moral absolutes exist. God himself is an absolute. The qualities that flow from his divine nature (love, kindness, patience, self-control, gentleness, mercy, grace, truthfulness, justice, honor, love of life, and so forth) are the basis for the moral absolutes by which human ought to live. Those things which are opposed to the divine nature of God (lying, murder, dishonesty, hatefulness, unfaithfulness, and the like) define the immoral behavior human beings ought to avoid.

Absolutes exist. There is ultimate right and wrong. God's divine nature provides the standard for the moral absolutes we read about in the Scriptures. But those absolutes are communicated to us within the contexts of human cultures, from a human cultural perspective. They are part of a story that spans eons of time and many different cultures. To ignore the presence of moral absolutes in the Scriptures would be foolish. But it is just as foolish to ignore the impact of culture on the production, presentation and interpretation of the Scriptures.

Those who would advocate an absolute relativist approach in interpreting the Scriptures would suggest that whatever you might read in the Bible, a condemnation of homosexuality for example, would be confined to the cultural context of the time and place the condemnation occurred and should not be considered applicable today. For them, everything is culturally relative—which means that there are no moral absolutes. Such an extremist position is as unwarranted as the opposite extreme literalist approach.

A literalist approach attempts to interpret and apply the Scriptures without considering the role of culture in the process. An absolute relativist approach denies the existence of absolutes and makes everything culturally relative. Neither of these extremes is acceptable. How, then, does one acknowledge the presence of moral absolutes in Scripture and, at the same time, acknowledge the role of culture in interpreting and applying the Scriptures? That is the question that needs to be answered. Answering it begins with an examination of our hermeneutical assumptions.

Hermeneutical Assumptions

Hermeneutical assumptions have to do with the assumptions we make about the Scriptures as we read, interpret and apply God's word. Everyone has assumptions. We cannot function without them. It is vitally important that we understand what they are. Assumptions are *assumptions*. They are not facts that can be proven. They are things we believe, ideas we consider to be true and relevant. They are opinions. Sometimes we are aware of our assumptions, sometimes we are not. It is when we are not aware of our assumptions (or that our assumptions are just that—*assumptions*) that they can be problematic. Two possible hermeneutical assumptions need to be scrutinized closely: 1) assumptions regarding the nature of Scripture—whether it is prescriptive, descriptive or both, and 2) assumptions regarding the nature of the interpretive process—whether it is objective or subjective.

The Nature of Scripture:
Prescriptive, Descriptive, or Both

About seventy-five percent of the Scriptures are in narrative form. God's communication comes to us, for the most part, in story form. The Bible is a divine storybook. The story it tells is a true story, but a story nonetheless. That most of God's communication to us comes in the form of a story is highly significant, for a story is not interpreted and applied in the same way one would interpret and apply a list of rules and regulations. Within the narrative of Scripture there are lists of rules and regulations. But they occur within the context of a story that is being told—a story about ancient people in far away places. That fact has to be taken into consideration when interpreting and applying the lists of rules and regulations found in Scripture.

Within the basic narrative framework of Scripture, one finds a number of literary forms. In his book, *Models for Interpretation of Scripture*, John Goldingay notes that:

> Discussion of how we are to interpret scripture (and how we are to preach on the basis of scripture) has often implicitly assumed that there will be a single approach to the task, but that assumption takes no account of the diversity of the ways in which scripture itself communicates. Scripture utilizes many forms of speech: historical narrative, instructions about behavior, oracles of warning or promise, prayers and praise, manuals of theological teaching, accounts of dreams and visions. . . Our interpretation and our exposition of scripture need to allow for its diverse forms and to reflect them (1995:1).

Goldingay's point is that no one interpretive model can provide a satisfactory methodology for interpreting all the different kinds of literature found in the Scriptures, which as he recognizes, were, for the most part, delivered in narrative form.

In addition to assuming that there is a single interpretive model that can and should be used across the board to interpret Scripture, many people also assume that the Scriptures are entirely prescriptive in nature, that is, that they specifically and intentionally *prescribe* how humans are to behave. From this perspective, a narrative account of what someone did long ago, either good or bad, is considered to be a divine prescription of approval or disapproval. Acceptable behavior must be emulated, unacceptable behavior must be avoided.

While very few believes would deny that some parts of Scripture are specifically prescriptive, some people assume that Scripture is always prescriptive. For such people, even narrative sections of Scripture prescribe (through example) exactly the kind of behavior God wants to see from his people regardless of the differences that may exist between the historical-cultural context of the biblical text being studied and the contemporary context of the reader/interpreter. For example, the book of Acts is a selective narrative account of the development of the early church. In the story told in the book of Acts, believers sell personal property in order to have funds to take care of poor believers. Church leaders performed amazing miracles including exorcising evil spirits. Believers were baptized as soon as they believed, believers worshipped each week in house churches, where they ate the Lord's Supper while enjoying a fellowship meal. They sang without the accompaniment of musical instruments. On and on the list could go. The point, however, is, what is our responsibility regarding this material? Are Christians today obliged to emulate the behavior of the first century believers? As we read an account of what they did, are we required to consider it an example to be followed, doing what they did they way they did it? Is Luke's narrative text a divine prescription for Christian worship and behavior for all people in all places for all time? Or is it merely a description of what those believers did in that time and place? Is it prescriptive or descriptive?

Is it possible that some parts of Scripture are prescriptive and some are descriptive? Can Scripture be both? If so, how would one go about deciding which sections are prescriptive and which are descriptive? For starters, it is probably safe to say that narrative sections that describe historical events may be descriptive rather than prescriptive. An exception may be if a descriptive text (such as the book of Acts) contains a specific statement that appears to be prescriptive. For instance, when the people of Jerusalem asked Peter what to do to be saved, he told them to repent and be baptized for the forgiveness of sins (Ac. 2:37-42). Within the generally descriptive narrative of what occurred on that day in Jerusalem in 30 AD, there is a section that may be prescriptive rather than merely descriptive. Scripture itself may be helpful in ascertaining the difference. If non-narrative sections of Scripture (such as

Romans 6:1-5, Galatians 3:26-27, Titus 3:3-5) seem to suggest a highly significant role for repentance and baptism, then perhaps Peter's comments about repentance and baptism in a narrative text can be considered prescriptive. Determining whether a text is descriptive or prescriptive may have to do with supporting evidence found in other non-narrative texts.

What about behaviors such as daily worship at the temple (Ac. 3:1-2) and the utilization of house churches? Should these be considered from a descriptive or a prescriptive point of view? Do Christians today have to worship daily at the temple or worship in a house church? Or was Luke merely telling us what those first believers in Jerusalem did?

If one takes the position that Scripture contains some sections that are descriptive and some that are prescriptive, as well as some descriptive texts which contain prescriptive passages, it becomes necessary to develop some basic guidelines for determining whether or not a text is prescribing a specific behavior or merely describing what someone else once did. Without guidelines, one is left with an arbitrary *pick-and-choose* kind of approach, which will often be applied inconsistently. Three basic guidelines or interpretive principles seem apparent.

First, one should not assume that a narrative or descriptive text contains prescriptive elements. Description can simply be description. *The Bible does not instruct us to follow the examples of ancient believers in the way they worshipped and lived out their faith in their historical-cultural context.* We are to imitate their faith, that is, we are to have the kind of genuine faith they had. But that does not necessitate that our faith be expressed in the same forms as was theirs. For instance, they worshipped in small groups in the homes of believers. That was the *form* of their worship. If that same form works for us, then we certainly may worship as they did. But is imitating or duplicating their worship form a requirement? There is nothing in the Bible to suggest that it is. Many would suggest that it may actually be preferable to worship in small groups in homes. And they may be right. But few would suggest that God will only accept worship that is offered in the informal context of a small group in someone's home.

Second, as already noted above, another factor in determining whether a text (the book of Acts for instance) is purely descriptive or also prescriptive is whether or not other non-narrative texts support the ideas one suspects may be prescriptive. Peter's comment (in Ac. 2:38) about repentance and baptism appears to be more than simple description, for numerous texts emphasize the importance of baptism in the lives of believers. However, when it comes to selling one's possessions to care for the poor (which is also part of the behavior described in the Acts narrative) there are few other texts that appear to make such behavior mandatory. Perhaps, then, those texts that describe believers selling their property to care for the poor are not prescribing behavior God requires of all believers.

Third, common sense must also be used in analyzing the prescriptive/descriptive nature of a given text. For instance, Acts 20:7-10 describes the church in Troas meeting for worship on a Sunday night in a third story room. The meeting lasted all night long. In addition to describing what those believers did on that occasion, is Luke's text also prescribing what contemporary believers must do—meet for worship on Sunday night in a third story room, worshipping all night long? Few Bible students would suggest that such a view of that text is warranted. The church in Troas met on Sunday, the Lord's Day, for worship. Their meeting together for worship included participating in the Lord's Supper, as did all Lord's Day worship assemblies in the first century. Where they met, what time they met, and how long they met appear to be irrelevant. How do we know those concerns are irrelevant? Ancient Christian documents inform us that first century believers sometimes met in the evening and sometimes very early in the morning. Often, perhaps even normally, they met in believers' homes. From those ancient accounts considerations such as time of day or specific location do not appear to have been crucial factors. That which appears to have been crucial was that they met in a weekly assembly to worship, which included participating in the Lord's Supper (Ferguson 1971:81-105).

There are sections in Scripture which prescribe how God's people ought to live. They are prescriptive. But much of Scripture is simply describing what occurred in previous places and times. They are descriptive. It is important that we not turn a descriptive text into a prescriptive text.

The Nature of Interpretation: Objective or Subjective

One's assumptions regarding the nature of Scripture—whether it is prescriptive or descriptive or both—makes an enormous difference in how one interprets and applies Scripture. Another crucial assumption has to do with one's view of the interpretive process, whether it is objective or subjective.

Part of the discussion in chapter one had to do with the inferential nature of the communication process. Ideas are encoded by a communicator into linguistic symbols and sent (spoken or written) to receptors who must attach meaning to the symbols being received. While people who speak the same language generally agree on the basic meaning of linguistic symbols, there is a great deal of individual "meaning" attached to linguistic symbols as they are heard or read by receptors. It is the receptor who attaches meaning to incoming messages and who is then impacted by or reacts to that meaning. If the meaning the receptor attaches to the incoming messages is similar to the intended meaning of the communicator, communication has occurred. If, however, the meaning attached by the receptor is not similar to the intended meaning of the communicator, miscommunication has occurs.

What this adds up to is quite simple: communication is a subjective process. The communicator may know exactly what he wants to say, but has no control over how a receptor will understand or react to the message he sends via linguistic symbols. One of the crucial points discussed in chapter one was that this is not only true of communication between humans, but is also true of communication between God and humans. God, as the communicator, does not control how receptors will interpret and react to his message. Communication between God and humans is just as subjective as communication between humans. This is true because of the nature of the communication process, not because of any inherent limitation on God's part. Communication is a subjective process, regardless of who is involved in the process.

Many people, however, fail to understand this reality, not only as it relates to communication but to life in general. They assume that it is possible to understand everything about the world around them in an absolutely objective manner. They assume that the way they see things is the way things really are. This way of thinking is known as *Naïve Realism*, because people who think this way naïvely assume that their perspective on life is not impacted (and skewed) by their culture, their education, their gender, their life experiences, their age, their religious beliefs (or lack thereof), and their sociopolitical and socioeconomic perspectives. This naïve way of thinking manifests itself in biblical interpretation when a person assumes that he or she is thinking about a biblical text in an objective manner, completely unaffected by his or her culture, education, gender, life experiences, age, existing religious beliefs, and so on (Hiebert 1999).

Naïve Realism is rooted in assumptions about the nature of life in this world that simply do not hold up against what we know to be true. . . that *perception is impacted by perspective.* A baseball game viewed from ground level behind home plate has a different look and feel than the same game viewed from the seats high above center field. The Pacific Ocean has a different look and feel to one flying over it in a jet at thirty thousand feet than it does to the person adrift in it in a small lifeboat. Perception is impacted by perspective. This is true in life and it is true in the interpretive process. The interpretive process is a subjective process. The interpretation of Scripture is part of the divine-human communication process. It is naïve to believe that we can step outside of our specific human cultural context and understand what God is trying to say to us in some objective way, unaffected by who we are.

An alternative to Naïve Realism is *Critical Realism.* Those who approach life from a Critical Realism perspective understand that only God sees everything exactly as it is, unaffected by perspective. People perceive the world through eyes that have been impacted by culture, education, gender, age, life experiences, and so forth. What they see has been filtered (and interpreted at the subconscious level) through their worldview—through the sum total of who they are. Critical Realism acknowledges that our perception is affected by our perspective (Hiebert 1999). We interpret life as it is filtered through all that makes us us. The eighteen year old woman with a high school education from a farming community in middle America has a different view of life than the fifty-year-old man with multiple graduate degrees who lives in Boston. The Anglo factory worker in Ohio thinks about and interprets the events of life very differently than does the African farmer, the Indian craftsman, or the Chinese college student.

As perspective manifests itself in the way we think about, interpret, and react to life, it also manifests itself in the way we think about, interpret, and react to God's communication to us. *The Ohio factory worker, the African*

184

farmer, the Indian craftsman, and the Chinese student may all be Christians, but they will read and interpret the Scriptures from their own unique cultural and personal perspective. It is imperative that we understand the subjective nature of the interpretive process.

Our basic assumptions about the nature of Scripture and the nature of the interpretive process will determine how we go about the task of interpretation. It is important that we understand what our assumptions are, how valid they may or may not be, and whether or not we may need to modify or change our assumptions so we can approach the interpretive task with a clearer understanding of what we are doing.

Finding the Interpretive Middle Ground

Knowing the dangers of extremist approaches to interpretation (literalist on the one hand and relativist on the other), and having considered the importance of hermeneutical assumptions, it is appropriate to discuss the need for finding the interpretive middle ground.

Moral absolutes exist and are communicated by God to his human children in the Holy Scriptures. But the Scriptures were produced in and impacted by a historical-cultural context. How does one acknowledge in a practical way the presence of supracultural moral absolutes in Scripture and at the same time acknowledge the presence of ancient cultural practices and perspectives intermingled with those supracultural moral absolutes? Or, more precisely, how does one distinguish between the cultural and the supracultural? How does one know where human culture ends and God's moral absolutes begin?

The Cultural and the Supracultural

Knowing where human culture ends and God's moral absolutes begin is not simple to ascertain. There is no step-by-step formula that identifies and separates the cultural from the supracultural. There are, however, several things for Bible students to remember and do while struggling with the cultural/supracultural question.

First, is simply being mindful that the tension between the cultural and the supracultural exists. When we remember that the text we are studying was written in and impacted by a specific historical-cultural context, and that elements, attitudes, perspectives and practices of ancient cultures are part of the material we are sifting through, we are better equipped to identify which features of the text may be cultural and which may be supracultural.

Second, when we encounter something in a text, a practice such as polygamy or slavery for instance, that we suspect may be a cultural practice rather than a moral absolute, we need to study that custom in more detail. Several questions need to be asked and answered. 1) When and where does the practice first appear in the Scriptures? 2) What historical information is available regarding the practice? 3) Does it exist in cultures beyond the biblical culture being studied? 4) If so, does its presence in other cultural contexts predate its presence in the biblical culture being studied? 5) How is the practice presented in the biblical text? Does it appear to be something being introduced by God, or is it simply presented in a matter-of-fact way as part of life that people understand and accept? Does God appear to approve of the practice? Does he condemn it? Or is it presented in something of a neutral manner, neither approved nor condemned? Does the practice appear to be accommodated or merely tolerated?

Answering these questions gives us some perspective on the subject being considered. Polygamy, for instance, is first encountered in the biblical text in the story about Abraham. Sarah suggests that he take (have relations with, marry) her handmaid in order to produce children. When ancient sources are considered, it is apparent that the practice

Sarah suggested was a long established custom in the ANE. It was not a new idea. It was not invented by Sarah or Abraham. Neither did God suggest it. However, a thorough study of polygamy in the biblical text reveals that while God did not suggest it, neither did he condemn it. In fact, he refers to having given David Saul's wives (2 Sam. 12:7-8). At the time God gave David Saul's wives, David already had four wives of his own. Does this mean, then, that God approved of polygamy? Why would God participate in something of which he disapproved? Was God accommodating or advocating the practice? It may be impossible to answer such questions with any certainty, but what does seem apparent is that God did not introduce the practice. It was a cultural reality with which Sarah and Abraham were familiar. And even if there seems to be no evidence to suggest that God advocated polygamy, it does seem clear that he accommodated it. Is polygamy something that ought to be practiced, or something that ought to be condemned? Polygamy does not appear to have been part of God's original vision for how males and females should interact. Yet God does not condemn it. He even participated in it. From the evidence in Scripture (which has absolutely nothing to do with our Western cultural perspective on the matter) it is difficult to suggest that polygamy rises to the level of a supracultural moral absolute. It is difficult to say that it is absolutely right or absolutely evil.

The practice of slavery provides an additional example of how to analyze a practice in light of the historical-cultural evidence. Again, the issue of slavery in the biblical text appears first in the story of Abraham (Gen. 15:2). Eliezer, referred to as a servant or steward, is Abraham's slave. References to slaves and slavery abound in the Old Testament. Historical sources reveal that the practice is much older than the cultural context of the biblical stories in which it appears. It is not a practice God introduces, but one which is presented in a matter-of-fact

187

manner. It is simply a part of life in that place and time. Never does God condemn the practice. He does participate in it, however, by allowing his people to become slaves and by making laws which allow for slavery among his people. God does not appear to oppose slavery. He does, however, expect his people who own slaves to treat them with kindness. Can it be said that God is advocating slavery, or merely that he accommodates it as a cultural practice of that time and place? God can accommodate a practice without advocating it. But since he did accommodate it, it would be difficult to suggest that he considered it absolutely evil, as he did murder, oppression of the powerless, adultery, and so forth—practices he would not tolerate or accommodate[13].

These kinds of questions should not be considered as means to generate iron clad answers to complex interpretive issues. They provide a framework for discussion rather than a formula for arriving at conclusions.

A third step in differentiating between a cultural practice and a moral absolute involves looking for principles behind actions. This step is especially meaningful if one suspects that a moral absolute may be present in a text. For instance, in the Bible it appears that God is willing to accommodate slavery and polygamy—regardless of what our contemporary Western attitudes toward those practices may be. However, he is not willing to tolerate murder. Even animals that shed the blood of a human being are dealt with harshly (Gen. 9:5-7). Why? Because human beings are created in God's image and life is a precious gift. Murder, therefore, is not to be tolerated. The heinousness of the physical act is understood in relation to the spiritual concept associated with life. The same is true for other moral absolutes that flow from God's nature. God is life, so murder is morally wrong. God is truth, so lying is morally

---

[13] Obviously, I'm not advocating either polygamy or slavery. Neither is acceptable in our cultural context. They serve as examples of practices God was willing to accommodate. Patriarchy is a similar practice.

wrong. God is love, so hate is morally wrong. God is just, so injustice is morally wrong. God is faithful, so unfaithfulness (of any kind) is morally wrong. It is the principle or concept behind the act that clarifies the nature of the act, determining whether it is morally right or wrong.

On the surface this seems simple enough. Yet an additional layer of difficulty develops when precise definitions are attempted. For instance, the statement that God is just, so injustice is morally wrong, requires a definition of injustice. Most contemporary Western people would consider slavery an injustice. Yet in ancient times God did not consider it an injustice. His own law provided for slavery. Oppression of widows and orphans, however, was an injustice he condemned vigorously (Isa. 10:1-3). The issue, therefore, is not how we would define injustice, but how God defines injustice. After all, it is God who determines supracultural moral absolutes, not human beings.

So what is the point of all this? The point has not been to overly complicate an already complicated matter, but to illustrate that there is no simple way to extract supracultural moral absolutes from the human historical-cultural context in which they were given. The task is not impossible, but it is challenging, requiring patience and humility. The suggestions offered above are suggestions, guidelines designed to jump-start the process of finding the interpretive middle ground. Perhaps others can refine or further articulate the process. The goal of the process is to avoid extremist reactions, recognizing that moral absolutes do exist, and that they were given in a historical-cultural context. While trying to differentiate between the cultural and the supracultural we must avoid extremes and remain in the interpretive middle ground.

Form and Meaning

Remaining in the interpretive middle ground requires an appreciation for the difference between form and meaning in the biblical text. To what does "form and meaning" refer?

In chapter one, culture was presented as a three-tiered phenomena (see figure 1), consisting of deep-level worldview assumptions (level 1), mid-level responses to those deep-level assumptions—values, feelings, thinking (level 2), and surface-level cultural structures and behaviors (level 3). The surface-level cultural structures and behaviors of level 3 are the forms of culture. A Western style wedding ceremony is a Western cultural form. A little league baseball game is a cultural form. Driving on the right-hand side of the road is a cultural form. The English language is a cultural form. Wearing shoes and socks is a cultural form. Sleeping in a bed is a cultural form—not all people sleep in beds. The food we eat, the clothes we wear, the kind of houses we live in, our educational system, our ways of worshipping, entertainment, sports, family traditions, the holidays we observe, the ways we do business—everything about how we live our lives, the things we do on a day-to-day basis are the forms of our culture. These level 3 structures and behaviors grow out of our level 2 values, feelings, and thinking, which, in turn, grow out of our level 1 worldview assumptions about how the world works.

Cultural forms are symbolic in that they are actions or behaviors that represent the way we feel or think about things. We believe that marriage is a committed relationship between a man and a woman, so we have a couple stand in front of an official in the presence of witnesses and make promises to each other. We believe that certain parts of our bodies should not be seen in public so we wear clothes to cover those parts of our bodies. We believe in efficiency, productivity, and punctuality, so we wear watches, carry calendar books, hurry from one place to another, and work long hours. We believe progress is good, so we constantly invent new, faster, better ways of doing things. The things we do represent the things we believe, think, and feel. They are representative, and are therefore symbolic, of our deepest worldview assumptions about life in this world. They are our cultural forms.

What is the relationship between the form (the surface-level behavior) and its meaning?[14] The relationship between form and meaning in society is complex. It is sometimes difficult to separate the two so they can be analyzed independently, but they are in fact two separate things and must be considered from that perspective. To answer the question, *what is the relationship between form and meaning*, several points need to be reiterated.

1. A form is a symbol used to convey meaning. The English word *chicken* (a linguistic symbol, a form) represents a specific kind of bird in the mind of an English speaking person. Neither the individual letters c/h/i/c/k/e/n used to create the word *chicken*, nor the word *chicken* is the actual bird. They are linguistic symbols that represent the actual bird. Forms are used to represent other things. They symbolize ideas. They convey meaning.

2. Different forms can be used to convey the same meaning: pig/swine, bucket/pail, fat/obese/overweight, thin/skinny.

3. In a different culture, the same meaning may require a different form. For a person who speaks (only) Spanish, the linguistic symbol *chicken* is not meaningful. The Spanish form for that rather unattractive bird that does not really fly, that clucks, lays eggs, and is quite good to eat is *pollo*. *Pollo* and *chicken* are two different forms used in two different cultures that mean the same thing.

4. From culture to culture the same form may have a different meaning. In America, raising one hand and while

---

[14]For a lengthier discussion of form and meaning, see Kraft 1996:132-147

touching the tip of your index finger to the tip of your thumb, creating an "O" means "OK." In some Middle Eastern countries that same gesture means, *I'm going to ring your neck.* In other cultures it is a rather crude anatomical reference. Same form. Very different meaning in different cultures.

5. Meaning can only be conveyed by the use of forms. All communication involves the use of symbolic representation. Ideas that are in our heads must be put in some symbolic form—a spoken or written word or some action performed—in order to convey the idea to another person.

6. The symbolic form is less significant than the idea it is designed to represent. A wedding ring is significant. But the love and commitment it represents is more significant. The linguistic symbol d/o/g is significant. But the living, affectionate animal it represents is more significant. Form is less significant than meaning.

What does this mean in the context of this discussion concerning the interpretive middle ground? Forms are used to convey meaning. God uses forms to convey meaning just as humans do. The words of Scripture are linguistic symbols designed to convey ideas. The ideas they convey are more significant than the forms used to convey them. That is, the ideas conveyed by the words are more important than the words themselves. We should not place so much emphasis on the forms used to express ideas that we lose sight of the concept behind the form. The form is simply the medium of expression. It is not the crucial factor. Perhaps this is why Paul told Timothy not to argue over the meaning of words (2 Tim. 2:14). Keeping this in mind will help interpreters maintain balance, avoiding an overly literal interpretation of that which, in reality, is a symbolic representation.

However, to say that the forms are less significant than the meanings they are intended to convey is not to say that forms are not important. Are wedding rings important? Are the words, *I love you* important? Of course they are.

192

They are concrete symbols of an abstract idea. Since life is lived on the basis of abstract ideas being communicated by means of symbolic representations, those symbols become highly significant. The words, *I love you*, are linguistic symbols. They are only representations. But they are representations that we need to hear. The importance of forms should not be minimized to the point that they do not matter. Forms do matter. To minimize them to the point of irrelevance is an extremist response just as elevating them to the point of losing sight of the meaning they are intended to convey is an extremist reaction in the opposite direction. Again, the point is to find the middle ground.

Form and meaning go hand in hand. Meaning can only be conveyed through forms, but the same meaning can be conveyed by different forms. If a perfect balance between the two cannot be maintained, meaning must take precedent. The form used to convey a particular meaning in an ancient society may not adequately convey that same meaning in contemporary societies. Understanding this is crucial in interpreting and applying the Scriptures effectively in various cultural contexts.

Implications

What implications emerge from the culture-related interpretive issues discussed in this chapter? There are many.
1. The fact that Jesus and his Jewish followers used interpretive methodologies that many Western interpreters would not be comfortable using ought to lead us to a re-evaluation of our attitudes toward hermeneutics. Since the Bible does not instruct us in how to interpret and apply it, *interpretive methodology is a matter of opinion*. Our rigorously scientific analysis of the biblical text is but one of many ways to approach the interpretation and application of Scripture. We must remember that it was not Jesus' chosen

methodology. To assume that our Western historical-grammatical approach is the only acceptable hermeneutical methodology smacks of ethnocentric arrogance.

2. The fact that interpretive methods changed as the cultural makeup of the church changed (from predominantly Jewish to predominantly Gentile) ought to suggest to us that one's interpretive methods are linked to one's cultural identity and perspective. In our ethnically diverse Western society, *ethnohermeneutics* (the study of how peoples of various ethnic backgrounds approach the process of interpreting and applying the Scriptures) must be given greater attention.

3. Since the historical-cultural context of the biblical author and the contemporary context of the reader/interpreter are equally important, we must give equal emphasis to both of those contexts when interpreting and applying the Scriptures. Traditionally, conservative readers/interpreters have been very concerned about the historical context of the author. They have not, however, given adequate attention to the author's cultural context in relation to the contemporary cultural context of the people for whom they wish to interpret and apply the Scriptures, especially if those people are of a different cultural group than the interpreter.

4. Given the prevalence of extremist responses in interpretation, and the theological dangers they pose, we must guard against literalist or relativist extremes.

5. Since most of the Bible is presented in narrative form, we should be careful about assuming that descriptive texts are also prescriptive. They may be simply descriptive. The Scriptures contain many texts that are prescriptive. As those texts are identified they should be taken seriously. But care must be taken not to nudge texts that are descriptive over into the prescriptive category.

6. Interpreters must be aware of the fact that communication (including God's communication to humans) is a subjective process. The individuals God selected to recommunicate his message to other humans selected the linguistic symbols they

believed would best recommunicate God's intended message in the cultural context in which they lived out their faith. Biblical readers and interpreters (receptors) throughout the world must attach meaning to those linguistic symbols as they read the Scriptures. Their deep-level worldview assumptions, their life experiences, their education, their gender, their age, and a host of other factors will impact how they understand and apply God's message. This does not mean that the Scriptures mean anything anyone wants them to mean. If that was the case the Scriptures would mean nothing at all. While acknowledging the subjective nature of the communication process, we must also acknowledge that God has an intended meaning and readers cannot ignore his intention or purpose.

7. While supracultural moral absolutes exist, they were given within the context of ancient human cultures. Extracting the supracultural from the cultural is neither an exact science nor a simple task. It is a complicated process of ongoing historical-cultural research and theological reflection.

8. Form and meaning issues must be given proper attention. God's message is delivered by means of linguistic forms (symbols). The forms are vehicles by which meaning is conveyed. Ultimately, meaning is more crucial than the form used to convey it. Meaning must be given top priority. But that does not mean that forms are unimportant. Without forms, meaning could not be expressed. So forms are important. Meaning is just more important.

Added together, what does all of this mean? It means that culture-related interpretive issues are numerous, multifaceted, and complex. It means that interpreting and applying an ancient book in any contemporary society will be challenging. It means that we must be thorough and careful in our historical and cultural research and humble in our interpretation and application of the Scriptures.

CHAPTER 8

CULTURE IN SCRIPTURE AND INTERPRETATION: TWO EXAMPLES

Interpreting and applying Scripture is a multifaceted, complex task. One goal of effective, appropriate interpretation is to separate the cultural from the supracultural. How does one accomplish this? Previous chapters have offered suggestions concerning different aspects of the process. At this point, rather than enumerate a step-by-step process, it may be more helpful to examine two issues which generate a great deal of discussion in contemporary Western culture, examining the role of human culture in the biblical presentation of those issues. The issues which we serve as examples in this chapter are patriarchy and homosexuality.

Patriarchy

Patriarchy refers to the social organization rooted in male dominance. In a patriarchal society the husband/father is the supreme authority in his family. Property rights, inheritance, and ancestry and descent are all reckoned through the male line. In patriarchal societies, women are, to varying degrees, subservient and have few rights or advantages. They are not considered equal to men— regardless of occasional rhetoric to the contrary.

There is no doubt whatsoever that patriarchy is presented as the common and excepted social organization in the societies represented in the Scriptures. The Scriptures were produced in, by and for societies that reflected patriarchal values and practices. The question is not whether patriarchy exists in the Scriptures. It does. The question is, *did God specifically and intentionally ordain patriarchy as his preference for how society ought to be organized, or is patriarchy a human cultural phenomenon with which God was willing to work?* Or, asked another way, do we find patriarchy in the Scriptures because God wanted it there, or because God selected Abraham as the one through whom he would accomplish his will and Abraham happened to be from a patriarchal society? This question can only be answered by a careful analysis of Scripture, as free of cultural and interpretive presuppositions as possible, combined with an awareness of extra biblical history and culture.

The controversy over the role of women in the church is rooted in the patriarchal assumptions present in Scripture. Patriarchal values permeate the sacred text and some readers/interpreters assume that they are there because God wanted them there, that male dominance and female subservience is God's preferred social organization. But are those good assumptions? That is what a careful textual analysis combined with an investigation of extra biblical history will clarify for us.

The place to begin a textual analysis of male/female relations is in the beginning, when God created human being in his image.

> *Then God said, 'Let us make people in our image, to be like*
> *ourselves. They will be masters over all life—the fish in the sea,*
> *the birds in the sky, and all the livestock, wild animals, and*
> *small animals.' So God created people in his own image; God*
> *patterned them after himself; male and female he created them*
> (Gen. 1:26-27 NLT).

Taking this text as it stands, as free of cultural and interpretive presuppositions as possible, one sees that both males and females were created in God's image and likeness. They appear to be equal in every way. They are both given the same responsibility—masters or caretakers of the rest of God's creation. Neither is dominant over or subservient to the other. Each is like God. Each is a spiritual being who will live forever. Each is an intellectual-emotional being who is capable of communication, relationship, and creativity. If there is any social structure or organization to be seen in Genesis 1, it is egalitarian, not patriarchal. The only way to get patriarchy into Genesis 1 is to read it into the text from other biblical contexts.

The creation story told in Genesis 2 is slightly different from the story told in Genesis 1. In Genesis 2, Adam is created first and is alone. His aloneness is not a good thing, so God brings the animals before Adam to see if he will select one of them as a companion. God knew Adam would not find a true companion among the animals, for none of the animals were *like* Adam. They had not been created in God's image, and were, therefore, fundamentally different from Adam. God was right. Adam did not find himself a companion among the animals, so God put Adam to sleep and from him created woman. Eve was like Adam. She was a human being created in God's image. Biologically she was a female while Adam was a male, but that difference is only biology. In essence, she was the same as Adam—human. She had been created in God's image. Like Adam, she was like God. Adam and Eve were two of a kind. Eve was a suitable companion for Adam because she "*corresponded*" to him (Mathews 1996:213). She was the female version of a human being while Adam was the male version, who corresponded to her.

Some interpreters have attempted make an argument for female subservience based on the idea that Eve was to be Adam's *helper*. Such arguments are based on a Western English understanding of the role of a helper rather than on the Hebrew idea behind the word helper. The Hebrew word translated helper in Genesis 2:18 is *ezer*. The word e*zer,* or a form of *ezer*, or a closely associated word which also means helper, is used ten times in the Old Testament to describe God as the helper of Israel[15]. Clearly, the Hebrew word *ezer* does not imply subservience in any way. To suggest that it does is to suggest that God as the helper of Israel was subservient to Israel. In fact, if one wishes to focus attention on the word *ezer* and discuss the female's existence as the male's helper, to be consistent with how the word is used in the biblical text, one would have to argue that female sustains the same relationship to the male as God sustained to Israel—Israel was incapable of getting along without God's help!

In the text of Genesis 2 (as with the text of Genesis 1) if there is a social structure present it is egalitarian not patriarchal. There is no patriarchy in Genesis 2. The only way to get patriarchy in the text of Genesis 2 is to read it into the text from another biblical context. There is plenty of patriarchy in the Bible, but not in Genesis 1 or 2. The creation stories of Genesis 1 and 2 present Adam and Eve as equals, both created in God's image, each given the same responsibility, and corresponding to one another. They are like each other and like God, the male having some of the characteristics of God built into his maleness, and the female having some other characteristics of God built into her

---

[15] See Ex. 18:4; Ps. 27:9, 40:17, 54:4, 70:5, 115:9, 10, 11, 146:5; and Hos. 13:9.

femaleness. Neither are a complete representation of God, but when male and female are united, when they become one, they are so much like God that they can even create human life—just as God can! In that creative collaboration they are equals. Neither is dominant nor subservient. Their maleness and femaleness, which are used to reflect different aspects of God's nature, combine to create a new entity (their relationship) which did not exist before. From that relationship, the children they create are created in their images and also in God's image.

To reiterate the point, there is nothing in Genesis 1 or 2 that can be described as patriarchal in nature. It is strictly egalitarian. Adam and Eve are equals in every sense of the word. Neither is dominant. Neither is subservient.

In Genesis 3, after Eve has eaten the fruit and persuaded Adam to eat also, God confronts them about their sin. God's comments to Eve have led many interpreters to assume that male dominance of females is a specific divinely ordained punishment for all women because of Eve's sin. We are familiar with the text. *"To the woman he said, 'I will greatly increase your pains in childbearing; with pain you will give birth to children. Your desire will be for your husband, and he will rule over you'"* (Gen. 3:16 NIV). God is specific in saying that he would increase Eve's pain in childbirth. But what God is not saying is that his desire, his intention, is that women be subservient to men. What he says is that even though childbirth will be painful for Eve (and thus for all women) she will still desire to have sexual relations with her husband. She will still want to have children. And her husband will rule over her. Is this last comment *"and he will rule over you,"* part of God's punishment for what Eve did? This is what many interpreters suggest. One wonders, however, if such a suggestion is not rooted deep in their patriarchal presuppositions. There is alternative interpretation that is just as viable and not rooted in patriarchal assumptions. It is that God's statement *"and he will rule over you,"* does not represent God's wishes in the matter, but is rather a comment about the inevitable consequences of what Eve has done—that is, brought sin into the world. There is a text in 1 Samuel that illustrates this point:

> *Finally, the leaders of Israel met at Ramah to discuss the matter with Samuel. "Look," they told him, "you are now old, and your sons are not like you. Give us a king like all the other nations have."*
>
> *Samuel was very upset with their request and went to the LORD for advice. "Do as they say," the LORD replied, "for it is me they are rejecting, not you. They don't want me to be their king any longer. Ever since I brought them from Egypt they have continually forsaken me and followed other gods. And now they are giving you the same treatment. Do as they ask, but solemnly warn them about how a king will treat them.*
>
> *So Samuel passed on the LORD's warning to the people. "This is how a king will treat you," Samuel said. "The king will draft your sons into his army and make them run before his chariots. Some will be commanders of his troops, while others will be slave laborers. Some will be forced to plow in his fields and harvest his crops, while others will make his weapons and chariot equipment. The king will take your daughters from you and force them to cook and bake and make perfumes for him. He will take away the best of your fields and vineyards and olive groves and give them to his own servants. He will take a tenth of your harvest and distribute it among his officers and attendants. He will want your male and female slaves and demand the finest of your cattle and donkeys for his own use. He will demand a tenth of your flocks, and you will be his slaves. When that day comes, you will beg for relief from this king you are demanding, but the LORD will not help you* (1 Sam. 8:4-18).

When Samuel told the people how the king would treat them, did those things represent God's wishes? Did God want the king to tax the people, draft their sons into the army, take their daughters from them to be his servants, and so forth? Or was he saying that those things (taxation, a military draft, and so forth) would be the inevitable results of having a king? This is obviously the sense of the passage. Samuel was not suggesting that God actually wanted the king to treat the people that way. He was saying that those are the kinds of things that kings do. They tax their subjects. They build an army. They require servants to do their bidding. God was telling the people that if they wanted a king they could have a king. But in having a king they would also experience all that goes with having a king—the negative as well as the positive.

In Genesis 3 we have a similar situation. Eve had believed the serpent's lie. She had sinned and then persuaded Adam to sin. In so doing, she had ushered sin and all that goes with it into God's perfect world. In a perfect world, people love each other, care for each other, treat one another with respect and courtesy. People created in God's image value one another. In a sinful world, people are selfish and cruel. The strong dominate the weak, the powerful oppress the powerless. Eve's punishment for bringing sin into God's perfect world was to experience great pain during childbirth. God specifically did that. One of the inevitable consequences, however, of what she had done was that the strong would dominant the weak. Men would dominant women. God did not specifically cause or desire that. It was the inevitable consequences of life in a sinful world.

Other similar consequences were slavery, polygamy and polythesim. Did God intend for one person or one group of people to enslave another? When God created Adam and Eve in his image, did he intend that as generations of their offspring populated the earth that the strong among them should dominate, mistreat, and enslave the weak among them? I think we can safely say that he did not. When God created Adam and Eve in his image, did he intend that one man should have many wives, or that one woman should have many husbands? Again, I believe the answer is, no. When God created his human children, giving them everlasting life, did he intend that they believe that there were many gods they should worship? No. God did not intend any of those things. He did not envision slavery as a preferred way for one person or one group of people to relate to each other. Neither did he intend for one man to have many wives, or for his people to believe in many gods. . . *or for males to dominate females.* God did not envision slavery, polytheism, polygamy or patriarchy as ways for people created in his image to relate to one another. Each of these things developed as a result of sinful human culture. But each of these behaviors was also something God was willing to tolerate.

God did not condemn slavery. As noted earlier, he built provisions for slavery into the Law of Moses. When God entered into a covenant with Israel he did not tell them that they could not or should not believe in other gods. They were, however, forbidden to worship other gods (Ex. 20:1-5). God did not condemn polygamy. He even participated it in by giving David Saul's wives (2 Sam.12:7-8). In a similar way, God did not condemn patriarchy, even though it involved the domination of one group of people created in his image by another group of people created in his image. But not condemning it is not the same as ordaining it. Accommodating is not the same as advocating. God has always tolerated behavior that was less than ideal from his sinful human children. We should understand the difference between God tolerating or accommodating something and God advocating it.

This explanation of Genesis 3:16 will not satisfy everyone. Some will continue to claim that Eve being dominated by Adam, and subsequently all women being dominated by men, was God's specific intention, his punishment for bringing sin into the world. Those individuals may be right. Perhaps God did intend such a punishment. Even if God decided to punish Eve that way, Paul's comments in Galatians 3:26-28 must be taken into consideration. *"So you are all children of God through faith in Christ Jesus. And all who have been united with Christ in baptism have been made like him. There is no longer Jew or Gentile, slave or free, male or female. For you are all Christians--you are one in Christ Jesus."* When believers are united with Jesus and sins are forgiven, the distinctions that divided and separated them ought to disappear.

In the body of Christ, whether one is a Jew or not should make no difference. Ethnicity does not matter because all people are created equal. Whether one is a slave or a free person (or a slave owner) should make no difference as to how they function in the body of Christ, because in Christ all people are equal. Social status should make no difference. Whether one is a male or a female should make no difference because in Christ all people are equal. Gender should make no difference. Even if patriarchy was a punishment from God for sin, when sin is forgiven reconciliation occurs, relationship is restored, and all things are as God intended for them to be from the beginning—everyone has equal status. Is there anything in the church that a Jewish person can do that a non-Jewish person cannot do? Is there anything in the church that a free person can do that a slave cannot do? If males and females are equal in Christ, if they share the same status before God, then patriarchy cannot be considered an appropriate social structure any more than slavery can be considered an appropriate social structure.

If God does not share a patriarchal perspective, why does patriarchy appear to be advocated in the Scriptures? Because the Scriptures are a product of the historical-cultural context in which they were produced. The Bible is a divine-human collaboration where humans selected by God to recommunicate his message to others spoke and wrote from the only perspective available to them—their own historical-cultural context. This is where the material from Part 1 of this study (about culture and the communication process) dovetails with the historical material from Part 2 of this study. God communicated with selected individuals, giving them *wisdom* (spiritual insight) regarding his will for humankind. With that divine wisdom guiding them (inspiring them) they recommunicated the divine message to others through speaking and writing. Enjoying the benefit of divine wisdom, they decided how best to recommunicate God's message to others.

The only way they could communicate the message that would make sense to the people to whom they wrote was to communicate it in normal cultural ways. They spoke and wrote in the language of the people. They used terms and concepts familiar to their audience. The message was cloaked in the cultural clothing of their time and place. And in those times and places, the cultural clothing included patriarchal values. The historical overviews of ANE cultures in Part 2 make it clear that all ancient cultures in that part of the world shared a patriarchal perspective.

What this amounts to is God allowing his recommunicators to make assumptions and recommunicate his message to others based on those human cultural assumptions and perspectives. They were allowed to cloak God's message in the cultural clothing of their day. Why would God allow them to do that? Because the only way humans can communicate effectively is from within the framework of their own cultural context—communication is culture-bound and culture-laden. There were some aspects of human culture that God was absolutely unwilling to tolerate, such as murder, oppression of widows and orphans, adultery, and idolatry. There were other aspects of human culture God was willing to tolerate, such as polytheism, slavery, polygamy, and patriarchy. The human cultural beliefs and practices that he was willing to tolerate became intertwined with those beliefs and behaviors that he specifically wanted his people to believe and practice.

The cultural became intertwined with the supracultural. It is the interpreter's job to untangle them, to separate the cultural from the supracultural so we can observe God's moral absolutes without being unnecessarily burdened by ancient human cultural assumptions and perspectives.

The biblical authors were products of their cultural environment. All people are products of the culture in which they were raised. Through the process of enculturation (the process of learning one's culture) individuals acquire their deep-level worldview assumptions, the values, feelings and thinking that go with those assumptions, and the surface-level behaviors that are appropriate for their culture. Gender roles are part of that enculturation process.

One's sex is a matter of biological inheritance. Genetics determines our sex, which involves certain basic biological realities: male or female sex organs, hormones, body mass and so forth. But how does one whose biological inheritance is male think and act? How do males think and act in relation to other males, or to females? How do they think about society and their place or role in their community and their family?

How does one whose biological inheritance is female think and act? How do females think and act in relation to other females and to males? How do they think about society and their place or role in their community and family? These thought patterns and behaviors are not entirely matters of biological inheritance. There may be some inclination toward basic male and female behavior associated with the hormonal differences between males and females. Males are often more aggressive while females are often more nurturing. But research indicates that those basic tendencies are reinforced and strengthened in the process of enculturation. Boys are taught to be boys and girls are taught to be girls. The "teaching" is not always overt and explicit. It is subtle, expressed in established patterns of male/female behavior witnessed by children in the home and in society. But whether it is explicit or implicit, the traditional gender expectations of a society are taught to children, who become the people they are expected to become.

Societies that have strong patriarchal values transmit those values to children in many subtle ways, producing young people and adults who share those values. They learn to see and interpret life from that point of view. At that point, thinking about life from a different point of view becomes very difficult. Only the most imaginative and creative thinkers can step outside the societal paradigms they have learned and think about what life would be like if it were lived from another point of view.

Because biblical writers had been enculturated with a patriarchal perspective, and because God was willing to tolerate patriarchy, he allowed biblical writers to recommunicate his message from a patriarchal perspective. Indeed, thinking about and expressing God's message from an egalitarian perspective would have been extremely difficult for ancient Near Eastern people. Such a thing would have turned their entire culture upside down. When it came to issues such as adultery, oppression of widows and orphans, murder, idolatry and the like, God was willing to demand change regardless of the social consequences. But some things, such as slavery, polygamy and patriarchy he was willing to tolerate.

This is why the New Testament includes passages such as Ephesians 5:22-33, where Paul discusses the husband-wife relationship from a patriarchal perspective. A patriarchal perspective was the only way Paul and the people of his day could think about male-female relationships. God's goal was not to have his representatives unnecessarily disrupt society, but to express Christianity in terms of the society's existing structures. This is why individuals who owned slaves were not instructed to free them, but to be kind to them. Slaves were not told to rebel in an attempt to gain their freedom, but to submit and to work hard and be good slaves. In a similar way, patriarchal values were reinforced. It is interesting that Paul's comments about masters and slaves occur in the same context as his comments about patriarchy. For a long time interpreters have been quite comfortable expressing the cultural realities related to the slavery issue. How is it that in the same text slavery is recognized as a cultural issue but patriarchy is not? Because deeply rooted unexamined assumptions and the unique perspectives they produce are not easily recognized and overcome.

It is essential that interpreters examine their own assumptions as well as those of the biblical writers so that they can begin to separate the cultural from the supracultural within Scripture. Charles Kraft's book, *Worldview for Christian Witness,* is an excellent resource for studying worldview and discovering one's own deep-level assumptions. Understanding one's own assumptions and the impact they have on life can help clarify the impact of assumptions held by the biblical writers[16].

One of the assumptions that many interpreters have is that the process of inspiration somehow eliminated the presence of cultural assumptions in the writings of the biblical authors. Such as assumption is unwarranted. It is also unnecessary. The Scriptures are a product of a divine-human communication collaboration. There is no need to eliminate the human side of the collaboration any more than there is a need to eliminate the divine side of the collaboration. Interpreters need to do their job in light of that collaboration. When they do, passages such as 1 Corinthians 11:1-16, 14:34-35, and 1 Timothy 2:8-15

---

[16] A helpful resource on biblical interpretation in regards to family structures is Lingenfelter 1996:97-120.

(passages that deal one way or another with the role of women in the church) will not be so troubling.

What each of these texts says is not difficult to ascertain. How they should be interpreted and applied is the issue. In 1 Corinthians 11:1-16, Paul is discussing why it is necessary for women to cover their heads when praying or prophesying. Verse 16 makes it clear that he is discussing *customs* or cultural issues. In patriarchal societies, women must be ever mindful and, as occasion demands, be able to demonstrate their submission to men. In the church, when women are praying or prophesying, they must cover their heads. In that time and place (first-century Corinth), such an action was a demonstration of patriarchal social order. Notice that Paul does not tell the women they cannot prophesy (teach). If they had the gift of prophesy they were allowed to use it. But they had to use it within the parameters of their social context, which was patriarchal.

Not many verses later, in 1 Corinthians 14:34, Paul suggested that in the assembly women who had questions should not speak up, interrupting the assembly with their questions. Is the issue that women were not allowed to speak, or that they should not interrupt the worship assembly with questions? Clearly, women were allowed to speak. How else could women who had the gift of prophecy utilize that gift? The issue that Paul is addressing in 1 Corinthians 14 is women interrupting the worship assembly to ask questions. Were men allowed to interrupt the assembly to ask a question? The text does not suggest an answer. Whether or not men were permitted to interrupt was not the issue being addressed. Women were interrupting the worship assembly to ask questions. Generally speaking (in my experience) women tend to ask more questions than men. Perhaps there were a number of recently converted women in the church in Corinth who had been priestesses in the pagan cults and who were accustomed to authority in a religious context. They were used to being able to speak up. In their new context, however, their speaking up, asking questions during the worship assembly, was disruptive. So they should be quiet. Questions could be asked in other contexts. The issue was not whether women could speak in the assembly, but that no one's behavior should disrupt the smooth flow of the worship.

The situation in Ephesus, where Paul had sent Timothy, was somewhat different. In Corinth, women who had been given the gift of prophecy (teaching) were allowed to use it as long as they covered their heads when doing so. In Ephesus, however, false teachers had targeted women and were creating serious problems within the Christian community by leading Christian women (perhaps new believers) into heretical beliefs and practices (2 Tim. 3:1-7). In light of the difficult situation in Ephesus, Paul's advice to Timothy is not to let any women teach. They should be submissive learners rather than assertive teachers. Why? Because there is something inherently wrong with women teaching men? No. Women in Corinth who had been given the gift of prophecy could use their gift to teach. There was no restriction placed on the women in Corinth as to who they could speak to—men or women—as long as they covered their heads when speaking. But there was something about the situation in Ephesus that concerned Paul so much that he decided the best approach there was to not let any of the women teach men—not because there was anything inherently wrong with women teaching men, but because of the unique situation (which we do not fully understand) there in Ephesus.

How does Paul justify what appears to be such an arbitrary decision on his part? He appeals first to creative order, then to Eve's sin. Adam was created first, then Eve. Here Paul follows the older creation story of Genesis 2 where Adam is created before Eve. However, the later creation story of Genesis 1 does not leave that impression. That account simply says that God created Adam and Eve in his image. Some interpreters suggest that Genesis 1 is a simplified creation overview and Genesis 2 is the more detailed creation account—at least of human creation. Other scholars would suggest that the older oral tradition of Genesis 2 cannot possibly be a more detailed explanation of Genesis 1, for it predates the tradition of Genesis 1. Regardless of what position one takes on the creation accounts of Genesis 1 and 2, the issue remains the same: the interpretive framework of the apostle Paul. It is clearly an interpretation that grows out of patriarchal assumptions. Since Adam was created first, he must hold a preeminent position. In Jewish culture, firstborn sons held a preeminent position, receiving a double inheritance upon the passing of their father. Since Adam was God's "firstborn" (figuratively speaking) he must hold a preeminent position over Eve, who was created later. This is the first part of Paul's argument.

Is this logic divine logic? Or is this human logic rooted in human cultural assumptions and practices? If one assumes that everything Paul said came directly from God, then the human side of the divine-human collaboration is eliminated. If that is the case, it is not Paul's argument, it is God's argument. However, I do not believe it is God's argument. Evidence within Scripture itself does not support the dictation theory of inspiration. The logic and the argument is Paul's. And it is rooted in a Jewish cultural patriarchal perspective—a perspective which God was willing to tolerate, even to accommodate, but which he did not specifically advocate. In Genesis 1, Adam is not given special treatment, privilege, or responsibility. He and Eve are treated equally because they are created as equals, both given the same responsibility as caretakers of God's creation.

The patriarchal argument of preeminence based on creative order was an argument rooted in Paul's Jewish patriarchal perspective. It was an explanation designed to provide biblical support for the rightness of Jewish patriarchal cultural practices. But unless one is prepared to

211

accept the entire premise of the preeminence of the firstborn (as they did in Jewish society, and which would have far-reaching implications for our own society) the argument collapses upon itself.

The second part of Paul's justification for disallowing the women in Ephesus to teach men had to do with Eve's sin. Her sin was rooted in her having been deceived by the serpent. The implication is that females are too naïve, too easily fooled to be in a position of authority. Therefore, the male dominance associate with a patriarchal perspective is justified—men are not as easily fooled as women. Given the research that exists today on the intellectual and emotional equality of males and females, it is simply unacceptable to suggest that females are more naïve than males. Naiveté and gullibility (the likelihood of being deceived) have nothing to do with sex or gender and everything to do with one's individual personality. Like Paul's previous argument, this one is also rooted in patriarchal assumptions regarding women and their role in society. Paul is making standard rabbinic-style arguments to justify his decision not to allow women in Ephesus to teach or exercise authority over men.

There are several things to consider in analyzing Paul's argument in this text. First, his limitation on women teaching men was specific to the churches in the region of Ephesus. He had not placed the same restrictions on women in Corinth or in other locations[17]. Second, it is simply unwarranted to suggest that females are inherently, genetically more gullible than males. A person's level of

---

[17] Corinth was not the only place where women prophesied—which included teaching. The evangelist Philip had four daughters, all of whom had the gift of prophesy (Ac. 21:8-9). To suggest that all the women in the Christian community who had the gift of prophecy only spoke to (taught) women is an unwarranted assumption. Only in Ephesus were women forbidden to teach men. One can only conclude that there were some very special circumstances in Ephesus that warranted such a restriction.

gullibility has nothing to do with his or her sex or gender. Males can be just as gullible as females. One wonders if Adam would have fared any better if he had been the target of the serpent's deceptive tactics. Has not Satan been deceiving, manipulating, tormenting, and tempting both males and females for millennia? Males are no less susceptible than females. Paul's argument that the first one to sin is more culpable is similar to his argument that the first one created is more worthy. In that culture such an argument may have been acceptable. Many contemporary Western thinkers, however, would question such logic. Again, the question is whether the argument is God's or Paul's?

If the argument was Paul's and not God's, and rooted in human cultural assumptions, why would God have allowed Paul to use it? Because in that time and place, for people with patriarchal assumptions, it was an argument that made sense. It worked. For people from a different time and place, with different cultural assumptions, it may not be an effective argument.

Consider some of Paul's statements to the believers in Corinth. In chapter seven of First Corinthians Paul actually told believers it was better not to get married but to remain single. Given God's basic plan and desire that his human children get married and have children Paul's admonition to remain single is amazing. How can he justify such advice? In verse 26 Paul explains that his advice to remain single is based on the "present crisis" facing believers, that is, the persecution they faced. In the face of life-threatening persecution, having only yourself to worry about simplified matters. Being married complicated matters. So, given the specific context of their lives, Paul's advice was to remain single—even though that was not the way God intended life to be lived. Their specific life context had to be factored into the general plan for how God intended for people to live.

In 1 Corinthians 7:6, 12, and 40, Paul makes it clear that he feels quite comfortable giving his personal advice and opinion to believers. Paul knew very well that he was not simply receiving dictation from the Holy Spirit, but was speaking out of his own spiritual wisdom as a trusted servant, an ambassador of the Lord. However, his wisdom was obtained and offered within the cultural context of first-century Jewish patriarchal perspectives.

On the surface, this may to some appear to be a denial of plain Bible teaching. It is not. What it is, is an untangling of the cultural from the supracultural. It is an acknowledgment that the Bible is the product of a divine-human communication collaboration. The Bible contains the message of God communicated to humans within the framework of their cultural context, recommunicated to other humans within the framework of their cultural context. The human cultural context cannot be eliminated from the Scriptures. Patriarchal perspectives were part of the human cultural context of the ANE. That is why a patriarchal perspective is present in Scripture. Its presence, however, is an accommodation by God, not a supracultural moral absolute.

Christians do not have to practice patriarchy. They may, but they do not have to.

Homosexuality

Another issue generating a great deal of discussion in both social and theological circles is homosexuality. Most conservative Christians consider homosexuality a sin. Most non-Christians consider it a legitimate alternative lifestyle. Is the Bible's condemnation of homosexuality rooted in God's moral absolutes or in human cultural assumptions about homosexuality? Most conservative Christians would say that the Bible's condemnation of homosexuality is rooted in God's supracultural moral absolutes. They would say that homosexuality is absolutely wrong and that God will not tolerate it. Most non-Christians (and even some Christians) would say that the Bible's condemnation of homosexuality is rooted in the cultural assumptions of ancient unenlightened people. Can the cultural and the supracultural be untangled when it comes to homosexuality in the Scriptures? I believe so. Before discussing textual considerations, however, it may be helpful to define terms and examine briefly the suspected causes of homosexuality, the inclinations resulting from one's sexual orientation, and the behaviors that often accompany those inclinations.

Causes and Inclinations

A great deal of scientific research has been focused on the development of sexual orientation. The American Psychological Association defines sexual orientation as "an enduring emotional, romantic, sexual or affectional attraction to another person." For most people, "sexual orientation emerges in early adolescence without prior sexual experience" (APA 2004). Sexual orientation develops at one stage in a person's life (or during different developmental stages), emerging later in life. While there are many theories about when and how sexual orientation develops, most research scientists, medical doctors and psychologists agree that one's sexual orientation is not a matter of choice. Factors such as biology and perhaps environment are involved in the development of sexual orientation—though exactly how or in what combination is not yet clear.

In a paper entitled *The Biology of Sexual Orientation*, Simon LeVay provides an overview of theories regarding the origins of sexual orientation (2003).

In the early twentieth century, Sigmund Freud suggested that family dynamics impacted sexual orientation. Subsequent studies have confirmed that "gay men tend to describe their relationships with their mothers as unusually close and with their fathers as distant or hostile." LeVay notes, however, that the attitudes of parents (a father's withdrawal, for instance) toward "pre-gay" children may be a reaction to the presence of gender-variant traits noticed by the parent. This would make family dynamics a response to rather than the cause of gender variation.

Researchers with an interest in behavioral approaches to socialization have suggested that "gender traits, including sexual orientation, emerge from a conscious or unconscious training regimen imposed by parents, teachers, peers, and society in general." In other words, sexual orientation is the result of enculturation. While enculturation, generally speaking, explains why people tend to conform to societal norms, it fails to explain why some individuals do not conform—especially when certain kinds of nonconformist behavior, such as homosexuality, can be so costly socially and relationally. If enculturation is a significant determinant in sexual orientation one would expect that children of homosexual parents, who may tend to foster gender variation in their children, would, for the most part, also be homosexual. Research however (as noted by LeVay), indicates that children of homosexual parents usually become heterosexual. While enculturation will impact how a person lives out his or her sexual orientation (based on what is acceptable or unacceptable in society), it is probably not a viable explanation as to the origin or cause of sexual orientation.

Another explanation for the development of sexual orientation is that early sexual experiences influence sexual orientation. For instance, a girl who is molested or raped by a man may develop a dislike for males and a subsequent attraction for females. Young boys who are seduced and molested by an older man, and who experience sexual arousal in the process may develop homosexual interests. However, as LeVay points out, this theory fails to explain why so many children who have sexual encounters early in life develop heterosexual preferences.

Another major area of research into sexual orientation has to do with biology. Most of the biological theories concerning the development of sexual orientation are related to genetic studies, hormonal studies, or brain studies. Genetic studies focus on finding a gene which impacts the development of sexual orientation. Some researches have postulated the existence of a "gay gene" which determines one's sexual orientation. They suggest that the gene can be passed on from parent to child. However, claims (in 1993) to have discovered such genetic links to sexual orientation were highly exaggerated. Genetic researchers have accomplished a great deal since 1993 (when the "gay gene" theory was first suggested), yet no gene determining sexual orientation has been discovered.

Hormonal research into sexual orientation has to do with prenatal hormonal levels (such as testosterone) that impact how the brain develops. Research indicates that in animals the sexual differences between males and females are associated with the presence of sex hormones during prenatal development. "High prenatal testosterone levels organize the brain in a male-specific fashion; low levels testosterone permits it to organize in a female-specific fashion." Based on this animal research, a number of scientists, including the German researcher, Dörner, have suggested the *prenatal hormonal theory of homosexuality*.

According to this theory, in a male fetus, the presence of sufficient amounts of testosterone would generate an appropriately male organized brain which will result in a heterosexual male. Low levels of testosterone would produce a brain organization that would result in a male with homosexual tendencies. In a female fetus, the presence of too much testosterone would produce a brain organization that would result in a lesbian female, while lower levels of

217

testosterone would produce a female organized brain that resulted in a heterosexual female.

Commenting on this theory, LeVay notes that, "Although the prenatal hormonal theory has not been proved or disproved in the decades since Dörner proposed it, a body of supportive evidence has accumulated, and it is probably the dominant idea among those who think about sexual orientation from a biological perspective." However, LeVay goes on to explain that hormonal theories still do not answer all the questions related to sexual orientation.

In brain studies related to sexual orientation, attention has been focused on the size of specific areas of the brain that appear to be connected to sexual functioning. In studies of deceased gay men, certain sections of their brains related to sexual behavior were smaller than corresponding sections of the brains of deceased straight men. The differences in the size of sections of the brain may explain differences in the functions regulated by those sections of the brain. What may account for the difference in the size of various sections of the brain? In animals, the prenatal and perinatal levels of testosterone impacted the development (the size) of specific sections of the brain.

In concluding his lengthy article, LeVay's general conclusion is that "biological processes, especially the prenatal, hormonally-controlled sexual differentiation of the brain, are likely to influence a person's ultimate sexual orientation."

Not all researchers would agree with LeVay. In a position paper produced by the Council for Responsible Genetics, LeVay's research is called into question. They point out (and LeVay would agree) that to date no definitive answer has been offered as to how sexual orientation develops.

Research into the development of sexual orientation will continue and one day scientists may discover exactly what is involved. But how sexual orientation develops is not the most important consideration. Based on what scientists have already discovered it seems clear (to many at least) that sexual orientation is not a choice. Its development is at least a biological process that may also be impacted by environmental factors.

More important than the causes of sexual orientation are the inclinations associated with it. A heterosexual orientation inclines one to be interested in and attracted to members of the opposite sex. A homosexual orientation inclines one to be interested in and attracted to members of one's own sexual group. A bi-sexual orientation inclines one to be interested in and attracted to members of both sexes. The basic reasoning among those who accept or embrace homosexuality and bi-sexuality as legitimate alternative lifestyles is that if one's sexual orientation is biologically determined (and perhaps environmentally reinforced) then choice has been removed from the equation and homosexual and bi-sexual people are simply being who they are—as are heterosexual people. Who can fault them for simply being who they are?—so the argument goes.

There is, however, a great deal of evidence that sexual orientation can be changed when individuals desire to change. Swartley notes that research experiments in the Britain in the 1970s resulted in a 71% change rate in homosexual men who entered therapy wanting to change their sexual orientation. Other studies on a smaller scale reveal changes rates of just below 50%. The National Association for Research and Therapy of Homosexuality (NARTH) has over one thousand members who are part of a growing "movement in psychoanalytic practice who believe that change [in sexual orientation] is possible for those who desire it" (2003:86-87).

For the sake of argument, however, let us assume that change is not possible. One's orientation is one's orientation. Therefore, the argument goes, people should be allowed to be who they are. They should be allowed to follow their inclinations. That argument sounds good on the surface. Upon closer examination, however, it is not an approach that society readily embraces. Legitimate arguments can be made that biological and environmental factors are at work in the development of all kinds of behavioral inclinations. Biological and/or environmental factors are at work behind the inclinations and behaviors of pedophiles, alcoholics and drug addicts, of those who engage in incest and bestiality, of those who are verbally or physically abusive, of those who lie, steal, and cheat. Do the biological and/or environmental factors associated with those behaviors (and perhaps dozens of others) make those behaviors socially or morally acceptable? No.

Some will respond that homosexual behavior should not be put in the same category as the behaviors noted above. After all, homosexual behavior between two consenting adults harms no one. The same argument is made concerning prostitution. Sex (for a price) between two consenting adults harms no one. Really? Is prostitution a victimless crime? Many people would say that it is not. Is homosexuality harmless? Many parents, spouses, siblings, and children can attest to the pain and agony homosexuality has generated in their lives.

Many people accept homosexuality as a legitimate alternative lifestyle. The same argument used to legitimize homosexual relationships can also be used to legitimize polygamous relationships. As long as polygamy is the choice of consensual adults, why should it not be considered a legitimate alternative lifestyle?

Human beings are, by nature, selfish and indulgent. We come into this world concerned only for our own needs. We want what we want when we want it and we do not care who we inconvenience by our demands. As we grow, we learn (hopefully) to monitor and govern our self-interests. We learn socially acceptable ways of expressing our self-interests and meeting our needs, or having them met, by others. And if our parents were good teachers and we were good students we became aware of the need to look beyond our own needs and desires to the needs and desires of others. Part of our humanness involves the struggle to grow beyond our inclinations toward self-involvement and self-indulgence. The argument, therefore, that people should simply be allowed to be who they are (as far as following their natural inclinations is concerned) is fundamentally fallacious. Life is about growth and change. It is about becoming the best person one can become. I need not become anyone else. But I must become the best version of myself that I can be. This means that my biologically and/or environmentally influenced inclinations, whatever they might be, must be monitored and controlled. Simply being who I am (in every respect) is not acceptable. It never has been and never will be.

All of this is considered within the context of that which is *socially* acceptable. Societies are given a great deal of latitude in determining for themselves that which is acceptable or unacceptable. For a number of societies, especially those in subtropical or tropical climates, it is acceptable to live life without the benefit of much in the way of clothing. In other societies, nudity is simply not an option. In some societies, nudity or partial nudity is an option in some circumstances. For instance, some European societies consider it acceptable to be nude or partially nude at the beach. All other social contexts, however, require clothing. In some societies, polygamy is acceptable. In others, it is not. In some societies marriages of young people are arranged by parents. In others, individuals select marriage partners themselves.

Who gives societies the right to determine for themselves social customs such as these? People have the inalienable right to determine for themselves how to live. God has created human beings in his image, and as self-aware beings all people enjoy free will. People have the

God-given right to live as they choose. Yet God hopes that with their freedom people will choose to acknowledge his sovereignty. At some point in the future, God will exercise his free will and invite those who have acknowledged his sovereignty in their lives to spend eternity with him. Those who have refused to acknowledge his sovereignty in their lives will not be invited to join him.

The Bible's Condemnation of Homosexuality: Cultural or Supracultural

While societies enjoy the right of self-determination, God hopes they will use their rights responsibly, acknowledging his sovereignty, adopting his supracultural moral standards as a framework for life in their societies. If a society decided to scrutinize their thinking regarding homosexuality in light of the Scriptures, what might they find? Would they find that attitudes expressed in Scripture toward homosexuality are rooted in human sociocultural attitudes, or in God's supracultural moral absolutes? As with our analysis of patriarchy, the place to begin in an attempt to distinguish the cultural from the supracultural as far as homosexuality is concerned is *"in the beginning."*

God created human beings in the divine image, infusing into the male and female aspects of his divine nature, character and personality[18]. Characteristics that we generally consider male are part of God's nature and character. Characteristics we generally consider female are also part of God's nature and character. Males are not more like God than females. Each is equally created in God's image. Human beings are rational, emotive beings,

---

[18] Perhaps in light of this particular discussion it is helpful to remember that God, as a spiritual being, is neither male nor female. Sex and gender are considerations linked to physical existence. I use masculine pronouns to refer to God not because he is male but simply out of tradition and convenience.

communicative, relational, communal, creative, spiritual (and therefore everlasting), free to choose, and so forth. Individually, human beings, because we are created in God's image, are pretty impressive. But humans demonstrate their link to divinity most clearly and powerfully in their creativity, especially when male and female in combination create human life. It is when human beings enjoy and use their sexuality to create life that they most clearly reflect God's image and likeness.

It is clear from the creation accounts that God intended for human pairing and companionship to be rooted in male-female relationships. God knew that Adam's aloneness was not good. The male needed a companion, a counterpart, someone who corresponded to him (Mathews 1996:213). To fill the void in Adam's life, God created Eve. She was his counterpart. Her femaleness corresponded to his maleness. The combination of the two in close relationship with each other (in oneness) provided the most complete human representation of God. This was God's intent. To ignore his desire for males and females to pair with one another in a reflection of his image is to defy God's basic design for human life. That basic design for how people ought to live is not a cultural consideration. It is rooted in God having put some of his characteristics in males and some other of his characteristics in females so that in an intimate union of their physical bodies they could create life, which is the grandest reflection of his glory[19].

This is the picture painted for us in Genesis 1 and 2. The rest of what we see in Scripture related to sexuality grows out of this divine male-female design and intent. With the introduction of sin into God's perfect world came a

---

[19] This is not to say that the *individual* is not created fully in the image of God or that the couple who do not have children are not whole or complete. Each individual is created in God's image. However, the sexual union of male and female that creates life is a further representation of the divine image and reflects God's creative intent.

perversion of God's plan for human sexual interaction. Some people abandoned God's *opposite-sex* approach to relationships in favor of a *same-sex* approach to relationships. How did God react to that change? God's unwillingness to tolerate homosexual activity is clearly demonstrated in his response to the cities of Sodom and Gomorrah (Gen. 19)[20].

A few interpreters have attempted to demonstrate that where the biblical text appears to be discussing homosexual activity the real issue is a lack of hospitality. Others have suggested that the homosexual practices condemned in Scripture (Lev. 18:22, 20:13; and Rom. 1:24-27 for example) do not address the same kind of activity that exists in most contemporary homosexual relationships, that is, a loving, committed, caring, monogamous relationship. Willard Swartley, in his book, *Homosexuality: Biblical Interpretation and Moral Discernment*, has responded appropriately to these suggestions and duplicating the content of his discussion is not necessary (2003:30-37). The majority of scholars, including the hundreds of scholars who have worked together in teams to produce the various translations of Scriptures, concur that the behaviors condemned in the passages mentioned above refer to homosexuality, that is, to gay or lesbian sexual relationships. The Bible condemns homosexual behavior. Its condemnation is not merely culturally motivated, but grows out of God's creative intent and his supracultural moral absolutes.

How does one arrive at this conclusion? Why is patriarchy a cultural issue and the condemnation of homosexuality not a cultural issue? Sexuality, expressed in the male-female relationship, and the life created from that

---

[20] Richard Hays (1996:379-406) provides a thorough treatment of homosexuality. His interpretation of events in Gen. 19 differs from my own, but his handling of the subject is excellent. Even if Hays is right about Gen. 19, the texts in Leviticus and Romans are clear.

sexual relationship, was intended by God to be one of the ways humans would reflect his divine image. That creative design has nothing to do with culture. It originated in God's creative action when he created male and female and asked them to reproduce. Patriarchy was not part of God's creative design. Patriarchy appeared after the introduction of sin and was part of human culture.

It is also apparent that God did not approve of homosexual behavior since he destroyed two cities and their inhabitants because of their immoral practices. There were a number of cultural developments that God was willing to tolerate: polygamy, slavery, polytheism, even prostitution[21]. But homosexuality was not one of the practices God could tolerate. It is condemned as an abomination. Why? Because homosexuality is a perversion of God's intention for male-female oneness as a representation of the divine image. Anything that minimized or diminished the presentation of God's glory in his world was forbidden. That is why God has forbidden the making of images that are supposed to represent him. Nothing humans can make can represent God's nature. The only *image* that can adequately represent God is a human being. And the fullest human representation of God's image, the most complete expression of divinity, is the male-female relationship.

Patriarchy was tolerated, homosexuality was not. The fact that God reacted so negatively toward homosexual behavior demonstrates that it is not simply a cultural issue. The condemnation of homosexual behavior is a supracultural matter. How should the church react to homosexual people? Christians need to realize that one's inclinations do not make one unacceptable to God. Behaviors, not inclinations, are the issue. Some people are inclined to lie. Others are inclined to steal. Others are inclined to be immoral. People

---

[21] While prostitution is condemned in the New Testament, no such condemnation exists in the Old Testament Scriptures.

are inclined to lots of behaviors that are sinful: greed, hate, jealousy, spite, racism, arrogance, unkindness and so forth. Satan preys on the specific vulnerabilities of individuals, tempting them to do that which they are inclined to do. But being vulnerable, being inclined toward a specific sinful behavior, is not sinful. It is committing the act that is sinful. One may be tempted to lie. But if one resists the temptation and does not lie, no sin has been committed. One may be inclined toward same-sex erotic activity. But if one does not act on the inclination, if one resists the temptation, no sin is committed. What this amounts to is that people with a same-sex sexual orientation may be penitent believers who continue to struggle with personal holiness just as people who have an inclination toward greed may be penitent believers who continue to struggle with personal holiness.

Paul's reminder to the believers in Corinth as to the spiritual change that had occurred in them is appropriate in this context:

> *Don't you know that those who do wrong will have no share in the Kingdom of God? Don't fool yourselves. Those who indulge in sexual sin, who are idol worshipers, adulterers, male prostitutes, homosexuals, thieves, greedy people, drunkards, abusers, and swindlers--none of these will have a share in the Kingdom of God. There was a time when some of you were just like that, but now your sins have been washed away, and you have been set apart for God. You have been made right with God because of what the Lord Jesus Christ and the Spirit of our God have done for you (1 Cor 6:9-11).*

Inclinations and orientations are not condemned in Scripture. Certain unacceptable behaviors are condemned. Change and growth are desirable and possible, especially in a context where spiritual power is available to assist people who want to change. The church, then, should accept people with a same-sex orientation, encouraging inner healing, change, and holy living.

226

Summary

Inquiries in this chapter have been concerned with attempts to distinguish the cultural from the supracultural as they relate to patriarchy and homosexuality. Based on the text of Genesis 1 and 2, my conclusion is that patriarchy is a cultural phenomenon. In Genesis 1 and 2 the male and female were created equal. There is no patriarchy in the creation narrative. Male dominance of society arose as a natural result of sin entering the world. The strong dominated and oppressed the weak. Having no alternative, the weak submitted.

God was willing to tolerate and even accommodate patriarchy. Because humans can only communicate within the framework of their cultural perspectives, and because ancient Near Eastern societies were patriarchal, patriarchy is present in the Bible. So are slavery, polytheism and polygamy. But few people advocate that God's original creative intention for how people should interact with one another and with him ought to include slavery, polytheism, and polygamy.

Male and female were created as equals and given the same responsibility—to care for the rest of God's creation. That equality does not allow for one to dominate the other. The suggestion that God stripped Eve's equality from her, subjecting her to Adam because she was deceived by the serpent rather than simply defying God as Adam did, is an interpretation rooted in patriarchal assumptions and unwarranted by the text in Genesis 3. Eve being dominated by Adam was one of the inevitable results of sin becoming a part of the human experience. It is not what God wanted, it is what happened because of sin.

Patriarchal behavior is a product of human culture and is not representative of God's supracultural moral absolutes. The Bible's condemnation of homosexual behavior, however, is rooted in God's creative purpose and is

227

not simply a matter of societal attitudes. Just as God created males and females as equals, he created them as sexual opposites to compliment and correspond to one another, with the ability to reflect the divine image most completely in the creation of life. The fact that some individuals may be inclined toward homosexuality does not justify homosexual behavior anymore than inclinations (which are biologically and/or environmentally rooted) toward drug addiction, pedophilia, lying, or stealing justify those behaviors. Research indicates that in many cases individuals who desire to change their sexual orientation can do so. Change and growth are possible, especially in a Christian context where spiritual power is available to help people change.

The creation narrative of Genesis 1 and 2 provides the foundation for understanding patriarchy and homosexuality in light of human culture and God's supracultural moral absolutes. The presence of patriarchy in Scripture is of human origin. It is a cultural phenomenon. The Bible's condemnation of homosexual behavior is not rooted in cultural attitudes but is a reflection of God's supracultural moral absolutes.

CHAPTER 9

INTERPRETATION IN CROSS-CULTURAL OR MULTIETHNIC CONTEXTS

Historically, God's communication with his human children occurred within the framework of their cultural context. That is, in the past, when God spoke with individuals who were to recommunicate his message to others, he did so using standard forms and conventions of human communication. He spoke their language, encoding his messages as clearly as possible, knowing that those to whom he spoke would attach their own meanings to the linguistic symbols he used to send his messages. Part of the interpretive task is to understand and consider the historical-cultural context in which that original divine-human communication occurred.

In addition to the historical-cultural context, interpretation and application must also be accomplished in and for a contemporary cultural context. What the biblical text meant in the past is *part one* of the interpretive equation. What it means today is *part two* of the interpretive task. What the biblical text means *today* depends on whose *today* is under consideration. What it means to me as a Western, conservative, Anglo-Saxon, Christian male college professor enculturated and educated in America in the second half of the twentieth century will be quite different from what it means to a thirty year old Nigerian widow with three children whose husband died of AIDS and who has just learned that she is HIV positive. One's origin and circumstances combine to define one's interpretive *today*. Interpreters must keep this in mind when they engage in cross-cultural and multiethnic interpretation and application.

What is the difference between cross-cultural and multiethnic? In this study the difference has to do with geography. I use the term *cross-cultural* to describe interpretation and application that may occur in a foreign missions context. A missionary in Nigeria must take into account the worldview and cultural perspectives of the people among whom he is working if what he attempts to teach them from Scripture is to make any sense or have any relevance for them. I use the term *multiethnic* to describe interpretation and application that may occur in a contemporary Western context, but which, because of the multiethnic nature of contemporary Western society, will involve people of varied ethnic backgrounds. When people from non-Western societies come to the West, they do not leave their home culture behind. They bring with them their worldview and cultural practices and perspectives. Any interpretation and application offered in such a context must take the cultural perspectives of the different groups involved into consideration.

These explanations of cross-cultural and multiethnic interpretation and application assume the interpreter's perspective—a theologian interpreting the biblical text for individuals in a Bible class, worship assembly, counseling setting or some other context. Another perspective is that of the individual reader seeking God's will for his or her life. The interpretive process is the same: 1) what the text meant in its historical-cultural context, and 2) what it means today.

The difference may be that an individual reader making a personal application may not be as aware of the hermeneutical process as the theologian. This may not be as much of a disadvantage as one might at first imagine. If the theologian is accustomed to the typical Western hermeneutical approach but unfamiliar with *ethnohermeneutics*[22] or the culture of the people for whom he is interpreting the text, the individual reader interpreting the text from his or her cultural perspective may come closer than the theologian to arriving at an appropriate application of the biblical text for his or her cultural context.

What crucial factors must be kept in mind as interpretation and application is accomplished in cross-cultural and multiethnic contexts? These factors will be discussed from the perspective of an interpreter (theologian, teacher, minister) assisting others in understanding and applying the Scriptures rather than an individual reader engaging in personal interpretation and application.

Interpretation In Cross-cultural Contexts

While there may be many factors interpreters engaging in cross-cultural hermeneutics must keep in mind, I will discuss five. Interpreters in a cross-cultural context must remember that:

---

[22] Space does not permit a thorough discussion of the relatively new hermeneutical discipline known as *ethnohermeneutics*. In explaining the significance of ethnohermeneutics, Larry W. Caldwell says: "While the concepts of contextualization and ethnotheology have been very helpful to the cross-cultural communication of the gospel, they have not gone deep enough into the receptor culture. For those attempting to interpret the Bible in cross-cultural situations, ethnohermeneutics is needed. . . .With ethnotheology, one seeks dynamically equivalent theologies. With ethnohermeneutics, one looks for dynamically equivalent hermeneutical methodologies already contained in the receptor culture" (1996).

1. While God's supracultural absolute truth exists, it is culturally perceived, interpreted, and applied. Chapter 7 included a discussion of the difference between Naïve Realism and Critical Realism. Naïve Realism is the belief that absolute truth exists and that an individual can know it absolutely, completely, in its pure form. A naïve realist believes that he knows exactly how things really are. A biblical interpreter who operates out of a naïve realist perspective believes the Bible is God's communication to humans, that it contains absolute truth, and that he or she can understand and apply those absolute truths in the one absolute way they can be understood and applied. The naïve realist does not acknowledge that his perspective on life (and therefore on the Scriptures) is in any way impacted by his cultural perspective. As far as he is concerned, he sees what there is to see, and the way he sees it is the only way to see it.

Critical Realism is the belief that absolute truth exists but that it is culturally perceived, interpreted and applied. One's worldview (or cultural perspective) acts as a reality filter. Everything a person experiences in life (that which is seen, heard, felt, or in any other way experienced) is interpreted on the basis of our worldview. It is filtered through our cultural perspective so we can make sense of it. Our cultural perspective is the only way we can make sense of anything. The critical realist understands this. He knows that his perspective on any experience is colored by his cultural perspective. The biblical interpreter who operates out of a critical realist perspective understands that the Bible is God's communication to humans, that it contains absolute truth, and that his understanding and application of those absolute truths is a product of his enculturation.

Many years ago, the anthropologist and missionary, Jacob Loewen, conducted an experiment which illustrates how one's cultural perspective impacts the way he or she understands and applies the truths revealed to us in Scripture.

While in Africa, Loewen asked a group that consisted of Western missionaries and Africans to write down what they believed to be the main message in the biblical story of Joseph. The response from the Anglos was basically that no matter what happened to Joseph, he always remained faithful to God. The response from the Africans was that no matter how far Joseph traveled, he never forgot his family (Kraft 1996:27). Both answers are right. But why did the Anglos focus on one aspect of the story and the Africans on another? Because of different worldview and cultural perspectives.

One day, while I was teaching a Bible class in Nigeria, I asked the students (about 40 men) what they considered to be the main difference between themselves and me. Their response was immediate and unanimous. "The main difference between us and you," their spokesman said, "is that you are first and foremost an individual while we are part and parcel of our family." Africans are so family oriented that they do not think of themselves as individuals, but as a member of a family. This group orientation impacts every aspect of their lives in ways that Westerners do not understand. They see family issues in the story of Joseph, and throughout the Bible, that we do not see. Their group orientation impacts how they understand and interpret life experiences, how they act and react.

It is vital that interpreters understand that everything they experience in life, including the experience of reading the Scriptures, is impacted by their worldview and culture. The same biblical text, read by people from different cultures, can appear to be teaching something different. This does not mean that everything is culturally relative. Absolute truth exists. But absolute truth is culturally perceived, interpreted and applied.

In another conversation I had one day in class in Nigeria the subject of killing came up. The men in class asked me if in America killing was ever justified. I replied that in America we have the right to defend ourselves. If

233

someone breaks into our home, for instance, intending to harm us, we have the right to defend ourselves, including using deadly force if necessary. As an American, I have the right to kill someone to keep him from killing me, or my loved ones. Americans do not consider this in any way to be contrary to the biblical mandate against murder. To Americans, taking the life of an attacker in self-defense and murder are two completely different things. My students in Nigeria, however, were shocked to discover that a Christian could even consider taking the life of another person. For them, the biblical mandate against murder forbids any kind of personal killing—even in self-defense. Americans differentiate between "killing" and "murder." This distinction is clear and sensible to us. It was not so clear and sensible to my Nigerian students. To them, taking a life is taking a life and to claim self-defense as a justification is to engage in a form of rationalization that is inexcusable. God's absolute truth that murder is unacceptable is recognized by American and Nigerian Christians. But how that absolute truth is to be understood and applied is different for them than it is for us.

Absolute truth exists but it is culturally perceived, interpreted, and applied.

2. Interpreters cannot interpret and apply God's message to the people of another culture without a thorough understanding of that people's worldview and culture[23]. Worldview and culture impact everything a person experiences just as the wearing of colored glasses colors everything a person sees. To be effective, biblical interpreters must put on the colored cultural glasses of the people with whom they are working so they will know what the world looks like through the eyes of those people.

---

[23] Another book I have written, *The Role of Worldview in Mission and Multiethnic Ministry*, deals with this point in detail (Rogers 2002).

I had been in Nigeria about six weeks. I had already noticed that questions related to difficulties in life seemed to focus on *who* caused them to happen rather than the less personal Western question related to *why* bad things happen. A question like this came up in class one day. *Who causes bad things to happen?* I decided to take the opportunity to explain that many things simply happen and that often there was not a *who* to blame or to identify as the cause.

To illustrate my point I asked how many of them had ridden a bicycle down a dirt road or path. Nearly every hand in a class of eighty went up. "Now," I said, "how many of you have hit a soft, sandy spot in the road, lost your balance and fallen over?" Again nearly eighty hands went up. "All right," I said, "why did that happen?" You could have heard a pin drop in the large tin roofed open air chapel. Eighty sets of eyes were riveted on me in anticipation. I wanted to set up the situation again so no one would miss my point. I said, "Okay, you are riding down the road, peddling fast and everything is fine. Then suddenly you hit a spot of soft sand. The bicycle slows immediately. You are thrown forward. The front wheel begins to wobble. You lose your balance and fall down. Now why did that happen?" They waited. I hesitated. "Physics," I said triumphantly. And all eighty of them broke into laughter as if it was the funniest thing they had ever heard.

Their response caught me off guard. Why were they laughing? I must not have explained it properly. I had not given them enough information. Surely, with enough scientific information they would see my point. So when the laughter died down, I began again. This time I explained in more detail. I explained about the forward momentum, the weight of the rider, the rotation of the wheels, the speed, the sudden slowing due to the impaired rotation of the front tire mired in the soft sand. Inertia, balance, gravity. I explained it all. Then I asked again, "Why did you fall?" Again they waited with anxious anticipation. I was going to explain a mystery to them. The answer was so clear. Surely they would understand. Again I said, "Physics." And again all eighty of them burst into laughter. I was shocked. What was going on here? When the laughter died down I asked, "Why are you laughing?" From the back of the chapel, a confident, dignified older man asked simply, "Why are you telling us physics did it?" I had no answer.

I realized that day that I was in a very different place. Many of the differences between America and Nigeria had been immediately apparent: food, dress, climate, and other surface-level realities. But these, I was beginning to understand, were merely surface-level realities and were not fundamentally important. That which was becoming clear to me was that these people saw the world differently than I did. They were asking different questions than I asked, out of a framework that was completely unfamiliar to me. I was supposed to be their teacher. Yet it was becoming clear to me that I was first going to have to become the student of their worldview and culture (of them as a people) before I could be effective as their teacher.

Judith and Sherwood Lingenfelter discuss the importance of cross-cultural teachers understanding the *hidden curriculum* that exists in each culture. Whether a curriculum includes English, History, Math and Science, or the Bible, that particular curriculum exists within a larger cultural framework related to teaching, learning, relationships, and a host of other issues that impact the teaching-learning process. The cultural agenda or assumptions about how teaching and learning occur in that culture is the *hidden curriculum*. School teachers in cross-cultural contexts need to understand the cultural dynamics of teaching and learning in their cultural context. Cross-cultural Bible interpreters also need to understand the hidden curriculum of the culture in which they work. Learning how teaching and learning are expected to occur in a given society is part of learning the worldview and culture of a people and is necessary for successful teaching and learning to occur (2003:28-29).

Anyone who finds himself or herself needing to interpret the Scriptures in a cross-cultural context needs to step back and become a student of culture before attempting to be a teacher of Scripture. Interpreting and applying the Scriptures in one's own culture is difficult enough. The difficulty is compounded when cultural boundaries are crossed. If we want to work effectively in cross-cultural contexts we must understand the worldview and culture of the people among whom we are working.

3. Cultural outsiders, regardless of how well-informed they may be, will never understand the culture of another people as well as those people understand their own culture. Cross-cultural interpreters, therefore, must learn to trust and depend on local Christians (even if they are new believers) to instruct them in culturally appropriate applications of biblical truths.

In anthropological terms, a cultural insider, that is, a member of a local society, has an *emic* perspective. A cultural outsider has an *etic* perspective. Cultural outsiders can see some things about a culture that a person of that culture may not be able to see. African Christians, for instance, see how very materialistic American Christians are. Most American Christians, however, do not consider themselves to be materialistic. We don't see it. But people who are extremely poor, but happy, can see how focused American believers are on their material possessions. The perspective of a cultural outsider can be valuable. However, for understanding the culture of another people there is no substitute for the perspective of a cultural insider. People who are native to a particular culture, who have lived in it all their lives, will understand that culture better than people who study that culture later in life.

Biblical interpreters who find themselves working in a culture different from their own need to develop trusting relationships with local people who will be willing to teach them about life in that culture. These trusted teachers, sometimes called *informers*, explain, identify and interpret the surface-level cultural structures and behaviors of their society. They may also be able to identify and explain deeper level values, feelings, and thinking, as well as the underlying worldview assumptions upon which their culture is built.

It is unlikely that an interpreter could ask an informer to explain the deep-level worldview assumptions of his people and expect to get anything beyond a confused or uncertain look. Try asking a person on the street to explain the deep-level worldview assumptions of the typical American and see what kind of a response you get. Most people don't even know they have a worldview, let alone what it is. But if the Christian cross-cultural worker asks enough of the right kinds of questions[24], worldview assumptions as well as cultural values, feelings and thinking will emerge. As a clear picture of the worldview of a people begins to form in the mind's of cross-cultural interpreters, they will be able interpret and apply (contextualize) the biblical text in an appropriate, relevant way for the people with whom they are working.

In addition to depending on a local informer who can identify, explain and interpret local culture for them, cross-culture interpreters need to depend on the Holy Spirit to: 1) assist them in understanding the culture in which they are working, and 2) enlighten them as to how to interpret and apply the Scriptures in a meaningful way in that culture. The Holy Spirit inspired the Scriptures. Who better to help cross-cultural workers interpret and apply the message contained in them? We should not necessarily expect the Holy Spirit to inspire us with specific methodologies or dictate specific

---

[24] See Spradley, *The Ethnographic Interview* (1979) and *Participant Observation* (1980).

wording to be used in contextualizing the gospel. But wisdom and insight from the same Spirit who assisted the biblical authors in recommunicating God's message to others is available to those who must interpret and apply God's message to a new generation of believers. Not to depend on him is a dreadful mistake.

4. The best way to accomplish meaningful contextualization is to engage in the 4-step process of critical contextualization as explained by Hiebert, Shaw, and Tiénou in their book, *Understanding Folk Religion* (1999:21-29)[25].

Contextualization occurs at two levels, at the *proclamation* level and at the *application* level. Cross-cultural interpreters must understand enough about the receptor culture to contextualize the proclamation of the gospel. Contextualizing the gospel involves presenting the message in a culturally appropriate, relevant way. The content of the core message is not altered in any way, but the presentation of the message is adjusted to fit the audience. Paul's sermon to the Greek philosophers in Acts 17 is quite different from his synagogue sermon of Acts 13. But both sermons are rooted in the need to acknowledge God and turn from one's sin. Paul's synagogue sermon is laced with Jewish history, messianic expectations, and specific references to Jesus. His Athens sermon has none of those elements. It is rooted in God's creative activity, his connection with all human beings, the need for repentance, and the reality and implications of the future resurrection.

Paul contextualized his presentation of the gospel and so must we. But it is also necessary to contextualize the *application* of the gospel. While there will be similarities between Christian behaviors from culture to culture (kindness, hope, moral purity, and so forth), there will also be differences. The way Christian beliefs are expressed and practiced will vary from culture to culture. For instance, in

---

[25] Also see Hiebert 1985:186-189, and 1994:88-91.

southern Nigeria, when a believer dies, the members of the church will go to that person's home to spend the night with his or her family. They will spend all night in prayer, song, Bible readings, and other forms of comfort and encouragement for the grieving family. The practice is called *vigil night*. American Anglo Christians have nothing akin to vigil night in their way of living out their Christian faith. Their comfort and encouragement at the loss of a loved one may include a phone call or a brief visit, perhaps preparing some food for the grieving family so they do not have to cook. But typical Anglo believers do not spend the entire night in the bereaved family's home singing and praying together. That is simply not the Anglo way. It is not a matter of there being *a right way* to comfort the grieving family. It is a matter of there being *a culturally appropriate way* to comfort the grieving family. One's Christian faith must be expressed in ways that are appropriate for the culture in which one lives.

How can cross-cultural interpreters learn culturally appropriate ways for believers to express their faith? How can a cultural outsider know if a particular cultural practice is really appropriate or not? The 4-step process of critical contextualization allows cross-cultural interpreters to work with local believers in analyzing their culture in light of the Scriptures to determine appropriate cultural expressions of the Christian faith. The process is explained by Hiebert, Shaw and Tiénou (1999:21-29).

The first step in the process is *phenomenological analysis*. What kinds of things actually happen in the culture under consideration? Studying the phenomena of a culture is a time-consuming process that must be broken down into small incremental steps. The cross-cultural interpreter must select various behaviors and activities, investigating them in an effort to understand the role they play (their function) in that culture. The point here is not to simply observe and assume. The point is to investigate, to ask questions of

240

trusted informers who will explain the purpose and intention of specific behaviors. What are the assumptions behind the behaviors or customs? What is the logic behind the behaviors?

While cross-cultural interpreters engage in learning and analyzing the culture of another people, they must also engage in analyzing their own cultural structures and assumptions. How are the interpreters' assumptions similar to or different from those of the people among whom they are working? Understanding of others and of oneself develops as one engages in contrasts and comparisons of cultural assumptions and practices. A journal can be used to keep notes about the cultural phenomena investigated.

The second step of the critical contextualization process is an *ontological critique*. The phenomenological analysis has to do with *what happens*. The ontological critique has to do with the *rightness or wrongness* of what happens. At this point the cross-cultural interpreter must study the Scriptures to see how the cultural practices of the people among whom he is working may or may not conform to God's expectations for godly living as expressed in the Scriptures. This is a difficult step because at this point in the process cross-cultural interpreters are working with three cultures: 1) the ancient cultural perspective in the Scriptures, 2) their own cultural perspective, and 3) the cultural perspective of the people among whom they are working.

One day while teaching in Nigeria, I became aware of how difficult this step can be for many interpreters. A number of Ibo men were wrestling with a serious problem that was occurring among Ibo believers. Years before, as conservative American missionaries worked among the Ibo, translating the Scriptures into Ibo, they translated the old English term *revellings* (in the KJV of Gal. 5:21) as *all dancing*. The passage is, of course, condemning revellings as unacceptable behavior. The Greek word in Gal. 5:21, *komos*, has to do with carousing, riotous and revellous

241

behavior often associated with drunkenness. It has nothing to do with dancing *per se*, unless the dancing is part of the carousing, riotous, revellous behavior. The missionaries, however, believed dancing was wrong. As they translated Galatians 5:21 into Ibo, they translated *komos* as *all dancing* because it appeared to them that the Ibo folk dances were sexually suggestive and therefore improper. As far as the missionaries were concerned, Ibo folk dances were revellous in nature. There are two major problems with what those missionaries did long ago: 1) they evaluated Ibo folk dancing from their conservative American cultural perspective rather than from an Ibo cultural perspective, and 2) they imposed their culturally rooted interpretation on a group of people who decades later still struggle with a translation of the Scriptures that tells them that all dancing is wrong when, in their culture, tribal folk dancing is an extremely important medium of expression.

The mistake those missionaries made was in assuming that they understood the purpose and intent of the Ibo folk dances. They did not do a proper phenomenological analysis and then base their ontological critique on that analysis. Their ontological critique was not done from an Ibo perspective, but from a conservative American perspective. They failed to differentiate between the cultural perspective involved in the writing of Galatians 5, their own cultural perspective, and the cultural perspective of the Ibo people. The consequences of their failure have been troubling for the Ibo people for decades.

Cross-cultural interpreters must avoid such mistakes, differentiating between the three cultures involved, interpreting the Scriptures (as much as possible) from the perspective of the people among whom they are working. To be sure they do this, interpreters must: 1) be cognizant of the need to be culturally aware, 2) ask the Holy Spirit for help in understanding the text from a new cultural perspective, and 3) invite local believers to explain how they understand passages being studied. Only when interpreters take steps to root their ontological critique in the local cultural perspective will their critique be helpful to local people.

The third step in the process of critical contextualization is an *evaluative response*. An evaluative response involves the local church evaluating their cultural practices in light of the Scriptures. This is not the cross-cultural interpreter telling the people what is right and what is wrong. This is the local people doing their own evaluation. Cross-cultural interpreters can be part of the process, but they should not dominate it. Local people understand their culture better than any outsider ever will. They understand the assumptions behind and logic of their customs and behaviors. With the help of the Holy Spirit, they are capable of deciding—in light of what the Scriptures teach—whether or not a custom or behavior is acceptable to God.

The fourth step in the critical contextualization process is a *transformative ministry*. A transformative ministry involves a movement from where new believers may be to where God wants them to be. All cultures involve some practices which are unacceptable to God. People need to eliminate unacceptable practices from their lives and incorporate behaviors that will benefit themselves and others. This fourth step is about the transformation that occurs as people begin to make the changes that God asks and assists them to make.

Cross-cultural interpreters need to utilize this 4-step process in order to interpret and apply the Scriptures appropriately in cross-cultural contexts.

5. Cross-cultural interpreters must develop the ability to embrace and even think in cultural forms that may be different from their own cultural forms. The obvious comes to mind first. Cross-cultural interpreters need to speak the language of the people among whom they are working.

243

Learning to speak and eventually to think in the language of a people provides one with a solid foundation for understanding their culture. But language is only one cultural form. Cross-cultural interpreters need to understand and embrace cultural forms that may be subtly or dramatically different from their own cultural forms.

Americans, for instance, are very focused on punctuality, productivity, and efficiency. These are hallmarks of our cultural heritage and perspective, foundational to American technological superiority. In mainstream American culture they are practically priceless. In Africa they are practically useless. Generally speaking, Africans are not interested in punctuality, productivity, and efficiency. They are interested in the quality of relationships and events.

Americans are busy people. We hurry here and there. If we need to see someone about a business matter, the quicker we can conduct our business and be on our way, the better. If someone comes to see me, at home or at my office, about a business matter, they are usually discussing the matter about which they came within one or two minutes. After a brief greeting and an innocuous comment it is on to business. An African, however, may spend forty-five minutes to an hour visiting about other unimportant matters before getting down to business. There are two reasons for this: 1) to get right down to business is considered rude, and 2) visiting about non-business matters is relationship building. When an African comes to see you he does not usually come to see you just to get a business matter taken care of. He comes to see you because you and he have a relationship that is important to him. While he is there a small business matter can be taken care of, but business is secondary to the relationship. And even if the visit is purely a business matter, it would be rude to get right down to business. Socializing must come before business. This custom is a social form. It is the way things are done.

Bartering in the market place is another example of a social form. The relationship between buyer and seller is important. The process of the seller beginning with an unreasonably high price, and the buyer beginning with an unreasonably low price, when both know ahead of time that they are going to meet in the middle, is a social ritual rooted in a relational process. It highlights the importance of both seller and buyer in the economic system. Americans think in terms of a transaction. Keeping it simple and less complicated is preferable. Africans think in terms of the buyer-seller relationship. The barter system is a social form.

Cross-cultural interpreters may encounter forms of Christian expression that are unfamiliar. For instance, some aborigine believers may have their weekly worship on Sunday night, outside around a fire. Why? Because in their culture, important meetings are held outside at night around a fire. A cross-cultural interpreter working in China may have to adapt to a small informal house church format. Depending on the particular fellowship that church is part of, singing may be *a cappella* and the Lord's Supper may be observed each week. Or, there could be procedural differences. I remember how unsettling it was the first few times we worshipped in villages churches in Nigeria where a "church secretary" sat in front of the assembly and acted as a moderator. At the beginning of the service he actually took role, calling people's names and waiting for them to respond!

It is important to remember that the *form* a form takes is not as important as the meaning it is intended to convey. Whether the form under consideration is a word (the English word spirit or the Greek word *pneuma*), a gesture (lifting hands during a prayer or song), or a ritual observance (eating the bread and wine of the Lord's Supper), the meaning behind the form is more important than the form itself. Moving from one culture to another requires a willingness to accept and embrace new cultural forms.

245

These considerations are offered as factors that must be kept in mind as one engages in cross-cultural hermeneutics. It is certainly not an exhaustive list. It is intended to help cross-cultural interpreters begin to think in the right direction as they engage in one of the most challenging tasks God has given his people—sharing the story of Jesus with all people.

Interpretation in Multiethnic Contexts

What is the difference between a multiethnic context and a cross-cultural context? In the final analysis there may not be much difference. However, as noted earlier, for sake of clarity, cross-cultural (as I am using it) has to do with interpreters living and working in a culture other than their own while multiethnic refers to encounters one has with people of differing ethnic backgrounds while living and working in one's own culture. Cross-cultural mission occurs "over there" while multiethnic ministry occurs right here at home.

Obviously someone living and working in another culture has to pay attention to cultural considerations when interpreting and applying the Scriptures. But why would *ethnohermeneutics* be a consideration for interpreters working in their own Western culture? Because not everyone living in America is a *Western* person—in the worldview sense of being Western. The world has come to the West. People from just about every ethnic group on earth now live and work in the America. We encounter them in the workplace. Our children go to school with their children. We live in the same neighborhoods. Sometimes we worship in the same churches. And if we don't, we should. Jesus died so individuals from every nation, tribe and people could assemble together in worship. Ministers find themselves interpreting and applying the Scriptures to ethnically diverse groups of people whether they have been trained to do so or not. Whether or not they interpret them well will depend on several factors.

Interpretation and application of Scripture in a multiethnic context is essentially the same process as described in the previous section. However, there is a slightly different feel to the process. Subtle cultural assumptions and expectations come into play, coloring the process of multiethnic hermeneutics. One of those assumptions has to do with expectations regarding social assimilation. As Americans, proud of our country, proud of our freedoms, knowing that people from every other country on earth want to come here and enjoy what America has to offer, we assume that when they arrive they want to become "Americans" in every sense of the word. Why else would they come? We assume that they will (or at least should want to) look like Americans, dress like Americans, talk like Americans, eat like Americans, live like Americans, and think like Americans, adopting American values and perspectives. In making these assumptions we forget that in reality "Americans" do not look, dress, talk, eat, live, and think alike. America is a mosaic of ethnic diversity. And while America has much to offer, it is quite ethnocentric to assume that when people leave their beloved homeland to come to America to take advantage of all it has to offer that they wish to stop being who they are, that they no longer love their home culture or have no pride in their ethnic heritage. As incomprehensible as it may be for some Anglos to imagine, not everyone who comes to America wants to be assimilated into mainstream American (Anglo) society.

Acculturation is the process of learning a new culture in which one now lives: learning the language, habits and values of the new culture, being able to function in it. Assimilation (the next step beyond acculturation) is the process by which people enter the social structure of a new culture, participating in the educational, economic, political, and religious structures of a society (Thompson 1996:Vol. 1,

112-116). For many immigrants to America, acculturation and assimilation is the desired goal. They work hard to learn the language and fit in. They want to be Americans. They are willing to relinquish the cultural patterns of their home culture, replacing them with new ways of thinking and doing. Others, however, want to enjoy selected benefits of life in America without relinquishing the cultural patterns of their home culture.

Those who wish to retain the patterns of the culture in which they were raised cannot be faulted for this. As one who has lived for an extended period of time in another culture, I can testify to the importance of holding on to cultural patterns which have deep significance in your life. The missionary group of which my family and I were a part in Nigeria felt it was important for us to observe Thanksgiving. We were teachers in a college and made up a significant percentage of the faculty. Thanksgiving is not a holiday in Nigeria. We petitioned the administration to cancel classes that day so we could observe our American holiday. They were gracious and gave us the day off. Why was it important for us to celebrate Thanksgiving? As Christians we were thankful everyday. Why have a special day to be thankful—especially when it required a special consideration and change in the normal school schedule? Because as Americans Thanksgiving was an important event for us. We had grown up celebrating the holiday. It was one of the two or three most important holidays of the American year. How could we not observe Thanksgiving? It just wouldn't have seemed right. Even if we couldn't duplicate an American Thanksgiving meal exactly (and believe me, we couldn't) and even if there was no Macy's parade and no NFL game to watch on T.V. (there was no T.V. of any kind!) we still got together and enjoyed a big meal and each other's company in a relaxed atmosphere as reminiscent of "home" as we could make it. Why? Because even though we were where we wanted to be (teaching in Nigeria), we were still

248

Americans, proud of our cultural heritage. We also managed to find some fireworks to shoot off on the 4th of July. One's cultural heritage is important.

Acculturation and assimilation do not happen automatically. Desire and determination are involved. Children learn language easily. The older one gets the more difficult it is to learn a new language. Since acculturation for many immigrants involves learning a new language, and language learning is one of the key factors in the acculturation process, if language learning does not occur, or occurs at a very slow rate, acculturation is impeded or blocked.

One can easily observe that this is the case by visiting parts of ethnic communities where signs and billboards are in a language other than English, and where specialty stores cater to the members of a given ethnic community. Newspapers and magazines exist for non-English speaking groups, as do radio and television broadcasts. It is possible for immigrants from a number of different ethnic groups to come to America and not learn English. These communities exist because many immigrants have not been acculturated and assimilated. Such communities make it easier for new immigrants to avoid acculturation and assimilation.

Why would immigrants want to avoid acculturation and assimilation into mainstream American society? Because acculturation can be quite difficult and frustrating. Aside from the challenge of learning a new language, the worldview of mainstream American society (naturalistic, scientific, materialistic), the values, thinking, and feelings of middle class Americans, and the cultural patterns of a highly advanced, fast paced technological society leave many immigrants feeling disoriented and unable to compete and cope. It is easier and safer to simply avoid it, remaining part of a small community with whom they share a familiar life.

Another reason for slow or limited acculturation and assimilation is desire. Some people simply do not want to be

249

acculturated and assimilated into American society. Their attitude may involve some level of resentment toward middle class American values, disagreement with American foreign policy, or basic ideological differences. They want to enjoy the freedom and opportunity that America offers but may not want to fully embrace mainstream American culture[26]. For others, the desire to accomplish acculturation and assimilation is absent because as they see it they simply do not want to stop being who they are and become someone else.

It is interesting to note that a willingness to acculturate and assimilate (or an unwillingness to do so) can be linked to specific groups. Immigrants from some Asian countries, Korea and China for instance, are anxious to assimilate—to a degree. So are many Latin American immigrants. Immigrants from Mexico, however, are often not anxious to assimilate. On the surface, the desire to assimilate may be linked to educational levels, with better educated people exhibiting a greater willingness to be assimilated. However, surface impressions are often mistaken and more research needs to be done. Also, generalizations about groups of people are often inaccurate when compared to individual behavior.

Generational factors must also be considered in the larger picture of immigrant acculturation and assimilation. People who come to America as adults or nearly adults are referred to as generation 1. Individuals who are brought here as children are referred to as generation 1.5. Children of immigrants, whether generation 1 or 1.5s, who are born in America are referred to as generation 2; their children are generation 3. The older a generation 1 person is when he or she arrives in America the harder it is to become acculturated and assimilated. Conversely, the younger a generation 1.5 is

---

[26] For basic overviews of American culture, see Nussbaum 1998, and Stewart and Bennet 1991.

when he or she arrives in America the easier it is to acculturate and assimilate.

Difficulties often arise in families when generation 1.5s or generation 2s accomplish acculturation and assimilation while generation 1s in the same family have not or have not as thoroughly. While working in a community with a significant Hispanic presence in Southern California, I have encountered generation 1 immigrants who had accomplished significant acculturation but who complained that their children (generation 2s) were not [culturally] Mexicans, but were very much Americans. Generation 2 Hispanics often do not (or do not like to) speak Spanish and often do not enjoy visits to see family in Mexico. Some generation 2s become bi-cultural, equally at home in American culture and in the culture of their parents. Some, however, are "uncomfortably" bi-cultural. They can "get along" in their parents culture, but are not completely at home in it. They prefer American culture. Others are just the opposite. They can get along in American culture, but are not completely comfortable in it. They consider their parent's culture their real culture. Then there are the unfortunate bi-cultural individuals who do not feel completely comfortable in either American culture or their parent's culture. They feel culturally adrift, isolated, able to identify only with others who share their feelings of cultural isolation.

Individuals in these categories may be acculturated (speaking the language and understanding the values and customs) but have not been assimilated. They have not fully embraced the educational, political, social and religious systems of America. They do not participate in any of them in any meaningful way.

The greatest rate of assimilation usually occurs in generation 3. A higher rate of generation 3 children will graduate from college (compared to lower rates for generation 2s) becoming full participants in mainstream society.

Biblical interpreters in our multiethnic society must understand the complex issues related to acculturation and assimilation. They must not assume that everyone who comes to America thinks like an Anglo, shares Anglo values, or lives life based on Anglo worldview assumptions. Even if a recent immigrant is in the process of being acculturated and assimilated, they will still be thinking and living life based on the worldview assumptions and cultural patterns of their home culture. It is essential, therefore, for local ministers to study the cultures present in their communities, becoming as familiar with them as possible, so he can interpret and apply the Scriptures in a way that will be culturally relevant and appropriate for them.

Local ministers engaging in multiethnic ministry must remember the same five factors discussed in the previous section:

1. While God's supracultural absolute truth exists, it is culturally perceived, interpreted, and applied.

2. Multiethnic interpreters cannot interpret and apply God's message to the people of another culture without a thorough understanding of their worldview and culture.

3. Cultural outsiders, regardless of how well-informed they may be, will never understand the culture of another people as well as those people understand their own culture. Multiethnic interpreters, therefore, must learn to trust and depend on "culturally other" Christians (even if they are new believers) to instruct them in culturally appropriate applications of biblical truths.

4. The best way to accomplish meaningful contextualization is to engage in the 4-step process of critical contextualization.

5. Multiethnic interpreters must develop the ability to embrace and even think in cultural forms that may be different from their own cultural forms.

252

Those who interpret and apply the Bible in multiethnic contexts must remember the cultural diversity that permeates the biblical text. They must remain aware of those diverse cultural contexts, of their own cultural context, and of the cultural contexts of the people with whom they are working. Only from this multicultural perspective can the Bible be effectively interpreted and applied.

CONCLUSION

There are three basic points that need to be reiterated: the cultural context of God's communication to human beings, the need for hermeneutical humility, and being careful not to throw out the baby with the bath water.

The Cultural Context of God's Communication to Human Beings

Humans were created in God's image and likeness. They are so much like God that they and he can enjoy a mutually satisfying relationship with one another. The Bible is God's divine storybook, telling the story of God's desire for a relationship with all people. It is his communication to us, the product of a divine-human communication collaboration. God understood that his human children could only communicate meaningfully within the context of their culture. So God communicated within that historical-cultural framework. He spoke human languages within the context of human cultures so his message would be meaningful and relevant. He communicated with individuals with whom he enjoyed a relationship, and who gained wisdom and spiritual insight because of that relationship with God. Those people then recommunicated God's message to others. Exactly how they recommunicated the message was left up to them. God did not put words in their mouths, but allowed them, as individuals who had received a measure of divine wisdom, to select the words and images they knew were appropriate for the people with whom they wished to communicate. Occasionally, as they recommunicated God's message they would quote verbatim that which God had said to them. Trustworthy messengers will often do that. But whether they quoted him or not was up to them. The Holy Spirit was with them to assist them in the process.

That God communicated with his original recipients within their cultural context indicates that he understood the role of culture in the communication process. He did not ask them to step outside their culture and imagine what he was trying to say to them. Instead, he found a way to say what he wanted to say within the context of their human culture, allowing their culture to serve as a concrete reference point for meaningful communication. His divine message was clothed in human cultural concepts—the only concepts humans are capable of comprehending.

That reality leaves interpreters with limited hermeneutical choices: 1) a simplistic literal interpretation which ignores the historical-cultural realities of the text and the many contemporary cultural contexts into which the Scriptures must be interpreted, 2) an acceptance of the challenge and a relentless dedication to the differentiation between the cultural and the supracultural in Scripture, or 3) slipping inconsistently back and forth between a simplistic literal approach and a selective cultural approach. Obviously, I would suggest that numbers 1 and 3 be immediately eliminated, leaving number 2, the challenge of and relentless dedication to the differentiation between the cultural and the supracultural in Scripture, as the only acceptable choice. This is the only way to allow God to speak to each society throughout time without encumbering those people with the cultural baggage of ANE cultures.

The Need for Hermeneutical Humility

Our contemporary Western theological hermeneutic[27] is a reflection of our basic Western assumptions about how to read, interpret and apply a written text. Our interpretive methodology works well for us because of who we are and the way we think. But just because our methods work so well for most of us, we should not assume that they work equally well for everyone else in the world. Western ways of thinking and doing are of and for Western people. But all people are not Western people.

It is important to remember that hermeneutics is an extra-biblical subject. The Bible does not tell us how to interpret and apply it. Contemporary Western hermeneutics can be traced to the fourth century. How were the Scriptures interpreted before the fourth century? Should interpretation and application before the development of the Antiochene school of interpretation, which emphasized the historical-grammatical context, be automatically suspect? Should *pesher* methodology, used so effectively by Jesus and his Jewish followers, be considered inappropriate for use in contemporary cultural contexts? Is Western interpretive methodology correct simply because it is Western?

If God does not tell us how to interpret and apply his communication to us, we must allow for differences of opinion as to how the task is to be accomplished. As a Western person, it is hard for me to conceive of understanding God's communication intent without

---

[27] I recognize that Western theological hermeneutics is in a state of flux. Liberation theology, feminist theology, postmodernism, and pluralism are only a few of the influences that have, to a degree, reshaped Western hermeneutics, making it difficult to refer to a single Western hermeneutic. Postmodernism, especially, has impacted how a written text is interpreted. However, I believe that for the majority of serious textual scholars, basic Western hermeneutical assumptions regarding the importance of historical context and authorial intent continue to be crucial.

considering the subjective, inferential nature of the communication process and the historical-cultural context in which that communication occurred. I realize, however, that non-Western people may approach the task somewhat differently than I do. Hermeneutical humility demands that I acknowledge their way of allowing God to speak to them.

Being Careful Not to Throw Out the Baby with the Bath Water

My mother used to talk about *throwing out the baby with the bath water*. I was just a kid the first time I heard that phrase and was confused as to what it meant. I would wonder, why would anyone throw out a baby? I had seen children bathed in small washtubs. My mother told me that I had been bathed like that myself. I finally decided that it was probably not an intentional act, but a failure to pay attention to what one was doing. The dirty bath water needed to be discarded, but only after the baby had been removed from the washtub!

Over the years, I learned that the metaphor could be used effectively in a variety of contexts. It seems especially appropriate in this theological context. Why would anyone throw out the baby? Yet theological extremists on both ends of the spectrum do so regularly. Each time a fundamentalist denies the role of culture in the production and interpretation of the biblical text, claiming that to acknowledge the role of culture in biblical interpretation makes everything culturally relative, he is throwing out the baby with the bath water. And each time a liberal denies the divine part of the divine-human collaboration that resulted in the Scriptures, claiming that because culture played a role in the production of the biblical text that the Bible contains no supracultural moral absolutes, he, too, is guilty of throwing out the baby with the bath water.

The baby in this case is an appropriate appreciation of the role of culture in the production and interpretation of the biblical text. By *appropriate appreciation* I mean a recognition of the presence of supracultural moral absolutes in the text, supracultural absolutes that need to be identified and untangled from the historical-cultural context in which they were delivered. It means recognizing that the presence of cultural considerations in the biblical text does not make everything culturally relative. Appropriate appreciation for the role of culture in the production of the biblical text means acknowledging and maintaining the proper balance between the divine and the human aspects of Scripture.

To make everything in Scripture culturally relative is foolish. If everything in Scripture is subject to cultural critique then the Scriptures really mean nothing at all outside the bounds of the original culture in which they were produced. If everything in the Scriptures is culturally relative then the Scriptures do not really speak to our culture at all. If that is the case, why did God bother? At the same time, to suggest that culture has nothing to do with the interpretation and application of the text is just as foolish. If culture has nothing to do with the interpretation and application of the text, why are we not doing everything just as the ancients did? Why do we not live out our Christian faith in the same cultural context as first century believers, living our lives according to the same cultural norms as they did? Because whether or not we want to admit it, we simply know better than that. God's communication with ancient people was not a divine validation of their culture.

While many biblical interpreters would claim to recognize the need for an appropriate appreciation of the role of culture in the production and interpretation of the biblical text, the apparently inconsistent pick-and-choose method for differentiating between the cultural and the supracultural calls the claim into question. In many cases it would appear that cherished cultural forms, such as patriarchy, are simply

258

assumed to be supracultural. Such assumptions need to be replaced by a thoroughgoing analysis of the biblical text, an analysis rooted in a clear understanding of the subjective, inferential nature of the communication process and the historical-cultural context in which the divine-human communication collaboration we call Scripture occurred.

WORKS CITED

Adams, R. F. G., Etim Akaduh, and Okon Abia-Bassey
    1981 *English-Efik Dictionary*. Oron: Manson
    Bookshop.

Adkins, Lesley and Roy A. Adkins
    1994 *Handbook to Life in Ancient Rome*. New
    York: Oxford.

American Psychological Association
    2004 *Answers to Your Questions About Sexual
    Orientation and Homosexuality*.
    http://www.apa.org/pubinfo/answers.html

Bahn, Paul G.
    1996 *The Cambridge Illustrated History of
    Archeology*. Paul G. Bahn, ed. Cambridge:
    Cambridge University Press.

Baines, John and Jaromir Malek
    2000 *Cultural Atlas of Ancient Egypt*. New York:
    Checkmark Books.

Bauckham, Richard J.
    1983 *Word Biblical Commentary: Jude, 2 Peter*.
    Waco: Word.

Beamer, Linda and Iris Varner
    2001 *Intercultural Communication in the Global
    Workplace*. Boston: McGraw-Hill Irwin.

Berlo, David, K.
    1960 *The Process of Communication: An
    Introduction to Theory and Practice*. New York:
    Holt, Rinehart and Winston.

Bickerman, Elias J.
    1972 *The Columbia History of the World*. John A. Garraty and Peter Gay, eds. New York: Harper and Row.

Blenkinsopp, Joseph
    1997 "The Family in First Temple Israel," in *Families in Ancient Israel*. Leo G. Perdue, Joseph Blenkinsopp, John J. Collins, Carol Meyers. Louisville: Westminster.

Boyce, Mary
    1997 "Zoroastrianism," in *A New Handbook of Living Religions*. John Hinnells, ed. London: Penguin.

Bowra, C. M.
    1965 *Classical Greece*. Alexandria: Time-Life.

Bray, Gerald
    1996 *Biblical Interpretation: Past and Present*. Downers Grove: InterVarsity.

Bright, John
    1972 *A History of Israel*. Philadelphia: Westminster.

Bruce, F. F.
    1954 *Commentary on the Book of Acts*. Grand Rapids: Eerdmans.

Caird, G. B.
    1980 *The Language and Imagery of the Bible*. Grand Rapids: Eerdmans.

Caldwell, Larry W.
1996   Cross-Cultural Bible Interpretation: A View from the Field. *Phronesis* 3 (1) 1996:13-35.

Casson, Lionel
1965   *Ancient Egypt.* Alexandria: Time-Life.

1975   *Everyday Life in Ancient Egypt.* Baltimore: Johns Hopkins University.

Collins, John J.
1997   "Marriage, Divorce and Family in Second Temple Judaism," in *Families in Ancient Israel.* Leo G. Perdue, Joseph Blenkinsopp, John J. Collins, Carol Meyers. Louisville: Westminster.

Council For Responsible Genetics
2004   *Do Genes Determine Whether We Are Lesbian, Gay, Bisexual, or Straight?* http://www.gene-watch.org/programs/privacy/gene-sexuality.html

Day, John
1992   "Canaan, Religion of," in *The Anchor Bible Dictionary.* David Freedman, ed. New York: Doubleday.

Dearman, J. Andrew
1992   *Religion and Culture in Ancient Israel.* Peabody: Hendrickson.

De Blois, Lukas and Robertus J. Van Der Spek
1997   *An Introduction to the Ancient World.* Londen: Rounledge.

De Vaux, Roland
    1961 *Ancient Israel: Its Life and Institutions*. Grand Rapids: Eerdmans.

Dresden, Mark J.
    1962 "Persia," in *The Interpreter's Dictionary of the Bible*. George Buttrick, ed. Nashville: Abingdon.

Durant, Will
    1963 *The Story of Civilization: Our Oriental Heritage*. New York: Simon and Schuster.

Eliade, Mircea
    1978 *A History of Religions Ideas: From the Stone Age to the Eleusinian Mysteries*. Chicago: University of Chicago.

Ferguson, Everett
    1971 *Early Christians Speak*. Austin: Sweet.

    1993 *Background of Early Christianity*. Grand Rapids: Eerdmans.

Freeman, Charles
    1996 *Egypt, Greece and Rome: Civilizations of the Ancient Mediterranean*. Oxford: Oxford.

Garrett, Duane A.
    1996 *The New American Commentary: Proverbs, Ecclesiastes, Song of Solomon*. Nashville: Broadman.

Goldingay, John
    1995 *Models for Interpretation of Scripture*. Grand Rapids: Eerdmans.

Gray, John
1964 *The Canaanites.* New York: Frederick Praeger.

Grayson, A. Kirk
1992 "Mesopotamia, History of (Babylonia)," in *The Anchor Bible Dictionary.* David Freedman, ed. New York: Doubleday.

Haldar, Alfred
1962 "Canaanites," in *The Interpreter's Dictionary of the Bible.* George Buttrick, ed. Nashville: Abingdon.

1962 "Amorites," in *The Interpreter's Dictionary of the Bible.* George Buttrick, ed. Nashville: Abingdon.

Hadas, Moses
1965 *Imperial Rome.* Alexandria: Time-Life.

Harrison, R. K.
1970 *Old Testament Times.* Peabody: Hendrickson.

Hesselgrave, David J.
1991 *Communicating Christ Cross-Culturally: An Introduction to Missionary Communication.* Grand Rapids: Zondervan.

Hiebert, Paul G.
1983 *Cultural Anthropology.* Grand Rapids: Baker.

1985 *Anthropological Insights for Missionaries.* Grand Rapids: Baker.

1994 *Anthropological Reflections on Missiological Issues.* Grand Rapids: Baker.

1996 "The Gospel in Our Culture: Methods of Social and Cultural Analysis," in *The Church Between Gospel and Culture: The Emerging Mission in North America.* George Hunsberger and Craig Van Gelder, eds. Grand Rapids: Eerdmans.

1999 *Missiological Implications of Epistemological Shifts: Affirming Truth in a Modern/Postmodern World.* Harrisburg: Trinity.

Hiebert, Paul G., R. Daniel Shaw, and Tite Tiénou
1999 *Understanding Folk Religion: A Christian Response to Popular Beliefs and Practices.* Grand Rapids: Baker.

Hoehner, Harold W.
1993 "Herodian Dynasty," in *The Oxford Companion to the Bible.* Bruce Metzger and Michael Coogan, eds. New York: Oxford.

Holland T. A. and Ehud Netzer
1992 "Jericho," in *The Anchor Bible Dictionary.* David Freedman, ed. New York: Doubleday.

Kadish, Gerald E.
1992 "Egypt, History of (Neolithic), Early Dynastic—1ˢᵗ Intermediate Period," in *The Anchor Bible Dictionary.* David Freedman, ed. New York: Doubleday.

Kearney, Michael
1984 *World View.* Novato: Chandler and Sharp.

Kelcy, Raymond C.
1971 *The Living Word Commentary: The Letters of Peter and Jude.* Austin: Sweet.

Klein, William W., Craig L. Blomberg and Robert L.
    Hubbard
    1993   *Introduction to Biblical Interpretation.*
    Dallas: Word.

Kraft, Charles H.
    1979   *Christianity in Culture: A Study in Dynamic
    Biblical Theologizing in Cross-Cultural Perspective.*
    Maryknoll: Orbis.

    1991   *Communication Theory for Christian Witness.*
    Maryknoll: Orbis.

    1996   *Anthropology For Christian Witness.*
    Maryknoll: Orbis.

    2004   *Worldview for Christian Witness.* Pasadena:
    William Carey Library.

Kramer, Samuel Noah
    1963   *The Sumerians: Their History, Culture, and
    Character.* Chicago: University of Chicago.

    1978   Cradle of Civilization. Alexandria: Time-Life

    1981   *History Begins At Sumer: Thirty-nine First in
    Recorded History.* Philadelphia: University of
    Pennsylvania.

LeVay, Simon
    2003   *The Biology of Sexual Orientation.*
    http://members.aol.com/slevay/page22.html

Levine, Amy-Jill
1998 "Visions of Kingdoms: From Pompey to the First Jewish Revolt," in *The Oxford History of the Biblical World.* Michael Coogan, ed. Oxford: Oxford.

Lingenfelter, Judith E., and Sherwood G. Lingenfelter
2003 *Teaching Cross-culturally: An Incarnational Model for Learning and Teaching.* Grand Rapids: Baker.

Lingenfelter, Sherwood
1996 *Agents of Transformation: A Guide for Effective Cross-cultural Ministry.* Grand Rapids: Baker.

Littlejohn, Stephen W.
1999 *Theories of Human Communication.* Belmont: Wadsworth.

Livingston, G. Herbert
1974 *The Pentateuch in its Cultural Environment.* Grand Rapids: Baker.

Longenecker, Richard N.
1999 *Biblical Exegesis in the Apostolic Period.* Grand Rapids: Eerdmans.

Mathews Kenneth A.
1996 *The New American Commentary: An Exegetical and Theological Exposition of Holy Scripture, Genesis 1-11:26.* Broadman and Holman.

McCarter, P. Kyle
    1993 "Canaan," in *The Oxford Companion to the Bible*. Bruce Metzger and Michael Coogan, eds. New York: Oxford.

Meyers, Carol,
    1997 "The Family in Early Israel," *Families in Ancient Israel*. Leo G. Perdue, Joseph Blenkinsopp, John J. Collins, Carol Meyers. Louisville: Westminster.

Meyers, Eric M.
    1992 "Synagogue," in *The Anchor Bible Dictionary*. David Freedman, ed. New York: Doubleday.

Niebuhr, Richard H.
    1951 *Christ and Culture*. New York: Harper and Row.

Nussbaum, Stan
    1998 *The ABCs of American Culture: Understanding the American People Through Their Common Sayings*. Colorado Springs: Global Mapping.

Oppenheim, Leo A.
    1962 "Assyria and Babylonia," in *The Interpreter's Dictionary of the Bible*. George Buttrick, ed. Nashville: Abingdon.
    1977 *Ancient Mesopotamia: Portrait of a Dead Civilization*. Chicago: University of Chicago.

Orlinsky, H. M.
    1962 "Maccabees, Maccabean Revolt," in *The Interpreter's Dictionary of the Bible*. George Buttrick, ed. Nashville: Abingdon.

Osborne, Grant R.
1991 *The Hermeneutical Spiral: A Comprehensive Introduction to Biblical Interpretation.* Downers Grove: InterVarsity.

Perdue, Leo G,
1997 "The Israelite and Early Jewish Family: Summary and Conclusion," *Families in Ancient Israel.* Leo G. Joseph Blenkinsopp, John J. Collins, Carol Meyers. Louisville: Westminster.

Pfeiffer, Charles F.
1973 *Old Testament History.* Grand Rapids: Baker.

Rappaport, Uriel
1992 "Maccabean Revolt," in *The Anchor Bible Dictionary.* David Freedman, ed. New York: Doubleday.
Roberts, J. M.
1993 *A Short History of the World.* New York: Oxford.

Rogers, Everett M.
1995 Diffusion of Innovations. The Free Press: New York.

Rogers, Glenn
2002 *The Role of Worldview in Missions and Multiethnic Ministry.* Bedford: Mission and Ministry Resources

Rosenau, Pauline Marie
1992 *Post-modernism and the Social Sciences: Insights, Inroads, and Intrusions.* Princeton: Princeton University Press.

Schmitz, Philip C.
    1992 "Languages (Hebrew), Linguistic Affiliation,"
    in *The Anchor Bible Dictionary.* David Noel
    Freedman, ed. New York: Doubleday.

    1992 "Canaan (Place)," in *The Anchor Bible
    Dictionary.* David Noel Freedman, ed. New York:
    Doubleday.

Shaw, R. Daniel
    1990 *Kandila: Samo Ceremonialism and
    Interpersonal Relationships.* Ann Arbor: University
    of Michigan.

Shaw, R. Daniel and Charles E. Van Engen
    2003 *Communicating God's Word in a Complex
    World: God's Truth or Hocus Pocus?* Lanham:
    Rowman & Littlefield.

Silverman, David Peter
    2000 "Ancient Egypt," in *Encarta Encyclopedia.*
    Microsoft.

Snell, Daniel C.
    1997 *Life in the Ancient Near East.* New Haven:
    Yale University Press.

Sperber, Dan and Deirdre Wilson
    1995 *Relevance: Communication and Cognition.*
    Oxford: Blackwell.

Spradley, James P.
    1979 *The Ethnographic Interview.* Fort Worth:
    Harcourt Brace Jovanovich.
    1980 *Participant Observation.* Fort Worth:
    Harcourt Brace Jovanovich.

Starr, Chester G.
    1991   *A History of the Ancient World.* New York:
    Oxford.

Stewart, Edward C. and Milton J. Bennet
    1991   *American Cultural Patterns: A Cross-Cultural
    Perspective.* Yarmouth: Intercultural Press.

Swartley, Willard M.
    2003   *Homosexuality: Biblical Interpretation and
    Moral Discernment.* Scottdale: Herald Press.

Thiselton, Anthony C.
    1980   *The Two Horizons: New Testament
    Hermeneutics and Philosophical Description.* Grand
    Rapids: Eerdmans.

Thompson, Claude Holmes
    1971   "The Second Letter of Peter," in *The
    Interpreter's One-Volume Commentary on the Bible.*
    Charles Laymon, ed. Nashville: Abingdon.

Thompson, Richard H.
    1996   "Assimilation," in *Encyclopedia of Cultural
    Anthropology.* David Levinson and Melvin Ember,
    eds. New York: Henry Holt.

Turner Nigel
    1962   "Hasmoneans," in *The Interpreter's
    Dictionary of the Bible.* George Buttrick, ed.
    Nashville: Abingdon.

Tyler, Stephen A.
    1978   *The Said and the Unsaid: Mind, Meaning, and
    Culture.* New York; Academic.

Watson, Duane F.
1998 "The Second Letter of Peter," in *The New Interpreter's Bible*. Leander Keck, ed. Nashville: Abingdon.

Wendorf, Fred and Angela E. Close
1992 "Egypt, History of (Prehistory)," in *The Anchor Bible Dictionary*. David Freedmen, ed. New York: Doubleday.

Wilson, John A
1962 "Egypt," in *The Interpreter's Dictionary of the Bible*. George Buttrick, ed. Nashville, Abingdon.

Zaehner, R. C.
1988 "Zoroastrianism," in *Encyclopedia of the World's Religions*. R. C. Zaehner, ed. New York: Barnes and Noble.